The Dusk
Orphanage

For Joanne and Belinda, whose unconditional love
has made my life's journey worth every single step

The Bush Orphanage

Recollections of a British
child migrant and the
truth about Australia's
human trafficking past

JoJo

PUBLISHING

John Hawkins

The Bush Orphanage

By John Hawkins

Published by JoJo Publishing

'Yarra's Edge'
2203/80 Lorimer Street
Docklands VIC 3008
Australia

Email: jo-media@bigpond.net.au or visit www.jojopublishing.com

National Library of Australia
Cataloguing-in-Publication data
        Hawkins, John (John Patrick)
        The Bush Orphanage : Recollections of a British
        child migrant and the truth about Australia's
        human trafficking past / John Hawkins.

        9780980619317 (pbk.)

        Hawkins, John (John Patrick)
        Immigrant children--Australia--Biography.
        Immigrant children--Great Britain--Biography.
        Children--Institutional care.
        Great Britain--Emigration and immigration.
        Australia--Emigration and immigration.

        304.894041

Editor: Gill Smith
Designer / typesetter: Rob Ryan @ Z Design Media
Printed in China by Everbest Printing

CONTENTS

Preface

In 1618 one hundred homeless children were taken off the streets of London and sent to Virginia, Britain's first American colony. Over the next 350 years an estimated 150 000 children were sent to Britain's colonies to work, to populate the land and to defend their new homes. Remarkably, even into the 1940s, Britain continued to use 'abandoned' children as an arm of foreign and economic policy, responding to pleas from Australia, a faithful wartime ally, to help fill a vast continent of barely seven million people – to either 'populate or perish'. The last child migrants, supposedly orphaned or deserted by their parents – over 3000 of them – were sent to Australia after World War II.

In 1933 Canada banned child migration after years of allegations of cruelty and abuse. Ever mindful of not repeating the Canadian scandal, the British Home Office laid out specific guidelines about how these children should be raised, educated and assimilated into Australian society. However, the more child-friendly and humane model for care of children proposed by the Home Office did not exist at the time in Australia. This could have been a sticking point for the child migration scheme.

A five-page memorandum, written in 1947, from the Home Office to the Australian government, outlined principles of acceptable childcare – based on the recommendations of the 1946 Curtis Committee Report, which had condemned institutional care and promoted fostering and adoption. It was accompanied by a one-page memo from the British High Commissioner in Canberra that read, in part, 'This is a departmental view only and is not to be taken as the view of the British government', effectively allowing Australia to ignore the Home Office's standards of care. It seems likely that the hands of the British Secretary of State, who was responsible for child migrants, were all over this statement, as he fully supported Australia's ambitions for child migration.

Ideas about welfare in the two countries could not have been more different. With the passing of the 1948 Children Act (UK), Britain began formally moving away from harsh institutionalised care for apparently abandoned children, preferring to foster or adopt these children back into British society. The Act presented a much fairer social deal for the estimated 30 000 British children who, for years, had been locked away in homes and orphanages. Unfortunately some were allowed to fall through the legal cracks left open by the Act and the Secretary of State. While British social workers were removing children from institutions, private charitable and religious organisations, with approval from the Secretary of State, continued shoving them straight back into even worse institutions on the other side of the world. Australia had legislated for the care of all British children until the age of 21, but in effect this care only continued until the children were sixteen.

The Australian Immigration (Guardianship of Children) Act 1946 resulted in institutionalisation of all the British children, so preventing them from being fostered or adopted and having a normal home life. During the parliamentary debate over the Act, the member for Darwin in Tasmania, Dame Enid Lyons, warned of the possible damaging consequences and offered 5000 homes across Australia for fostering and adoptions. Arthur Calwell, the Minister for Immigration, who demanded to retain the personal power of legal guardianship for child migrants, refused, telling the Parliament, 'We certainly require more safeguards in respect of them than we do for our own children'.

During the years of postwar child migration, a frustrated Home Office frequently lectured the Australian government about the inadequacies of institutionalised care. Finally fed up, Britain was forced to ban child migration in 1956 after a withering condemnation in the Ross Report commissioned by the Home Office, citing institutionalised cruelty and abuse.

Part I of this book is the life story of a child traveller cast adrift on an ocean of uncertainties. It is my story.

Part II is a brief overview of the child migration scheme to Australia. It is a story about the complicity of governments who shirked their legal and moral responsibility for the lives of child migrants and, in doing so, negated the common misconception that the genuine but misguided authorities in Britain and Australia were driven by benevolence and goodwill to give children a 'fresh start in life'. It is also a story of the churches and secular organisations that took part in child migration, and ultimately have taken the blame for the tragedy.

Acknowledgments

I would like to acknowledge my gratitude to the Department for Communities (formerly the Department for Community Development) in Perth, Western Australia, for releasing their files. Without this assistance the second part of my book would have proved impossible to write.

I would also like to thank Dr Peter Harries for giving his time freely in the early stages helping to edit the manuscript and offering his wise guidance. And where would I be without my manuscript readers, Catherine Jennings, Salem Lizotte and John Grace, JP? Thank you for your interest and wonderful support and advice throughout the entire project, and thank you for believing in me and sticking with me. I am indebted to my editor, Gillian Smith, for her professionalism, patience and skill.

Finally I thank my beautiful family in Australia and England for your unconditional support and love. Thanks also to the Broom family in England for your enduring love.

PART
I

THE LIFE JOURNEY OF
A CHILD MIGRANT

BABY JOHN

In early 1954, when I was seven years old, Oliver Lyttelton, my legal guardian and the British Secretary of State for the Colonies, agreed with my carers, the Sisters of Nazareth, that I had no real future in England and should be sent to Australia for my own good. I was about to lose my new parents, my country and my childhood.

The Secretary of State consented to the removal of thousands of children in the years after World War II. Like his predecessors, he relied solely on the advice of those to whom he had delegated his lawful authority: the private religious and secular organisations – our 'temporary guardians' – who would gain most from child migrants, as we were officially described. Again, like his predecessors, he preferred to distance himself from any personal involvement.

An estimated 450 homes and orphanages across Britain catered to tens of thousands of 'poor and abandoned' children. Child welfare organisations were a subsidised 'growth' industry and some profited on the back of children's misery. Few organisations campaigned for social reform in the turmoil of postwar Britain, and the problem of abandoned children remained largely hidden.

The Home Office deemed that only the most socially deprived children – those with no family or family ties and of 'below-average' mental and physical development – were to be considered as child migrants. According to the 1946 Curtis Committee Report, 'children of fine physique and of good mental equipment should be kept in the United Kingdom' – one of the discriminatory recommendations adopted as British government policy at the time.

There were contrasting views on child migration within the British government. The Home Office questioned the morality of deporting children, while the Dominions Office, with a few hundred years' experience, strongly supported it. Churches supported it, yet it was generally opposed by those working in the welfare sector – the social workers and child psychologists. The British public was generally unaware of the scheme as it was out of the public eye. Those who were aware genuinely believed the spin that child migration was in a child's best interest, failing to see it as deportation masquerading as a benevolent and opportunistic way of increasing the population in a foreign country.

As a child, my life was sculpted and shaped by social engineers. My future was planned from the moment my traumatised and trusting mother thrust me into the care of the Sisters of Nazareth in the hope that I would be adopted. Like so many others, I had been promised to Australia as a child migrant and nothing could save me once I was registered at Australia House in London. I could have expected to join 50 000 children each year from all over Europe, if the Australian Minister for Immigration had his way when in the heady days of 1946 he proudly quoted the London *Daily Sketch* that Australia was soon to 'become the greatest foster-father the world has ever known'. This was certainly no claim Mother England could make, with her record of exporting children, forcing the most vulnerable children to pay a big price for being defenceless.

The Sisters had their own powerful reasons for supporting child migration. They were driven by a fervent belief in the righteousness of their cause. Getting more Catholic children to Australia to spread the faith in their new country was their objective, and God would not forget their contribution on Judgment Day. The social workers at Australia House were poised to exploit the misguided passion of these simple nuns, who blindly agreed to provide Catholic children and by 1956 had sent close to 700 boys and girls to Australia.

News of my impending deportation to Australia in early 1953 came as a complete shock. Being a frightened, insecure child with no home or family, the fear of losing my orphanage home and my country of birth shattered my young mind. I became seriously ill and was hospitalised for many weeks. I had just experienced my first physical and mental breakdown. Because of my illness, another boy from the orphanage took my place on the passenger ship.

For more than a year I was spared further trauma until suddenly, without warning, I was put aboard a ship at Southampton docks and sent to Australia, swallowed up, like thousands of others, by Australia's insatiable demand for British children.

Delivered to an orphanage near the Swan River in Perth, on the other side of the world, I served out the remainder of my childhood in Australian institutions. Left behind was a shattered foster family, who had rescued me when I had been ill the year before. This caring family were excited about the prospect of becoming my new parents. They had taken me into their home on a part-time basis and made me one of their own. For nearly a year the Sisters had assured them that their application to adopt me had been approved. Crushed and haunted by my sudden disappearance, they would spend the rest of their lives searching the world for their seven-year-old orphan boy. I missed the love and protection of this family and Roy, the only real father I ever had, never saw me again.

I was born in England on 13 March 1947, out of wedlock. Society was hypocritical and harsh, and many godly people in control of abandoned children in that era regarded my mother and others like her as wayward, loose women unsuited to motherhood. Abortion was illegal, although the business in perilous backyard abortions flourished. For a lot of young women it was easier to go through with the pregnancy and give up the baby. If a Catholic mother had the right connections, the process of abandoning a baby or child was quick, relatively painless – except for the child and often the mother – and permanent. A few mothers took advantage of this culture and gave up their children for no other reason than inconvenience; yet for most, like my mother, it was devastating.

My mother named me 'John Patrick' after her father, even though he was unpopular and was often drunk. My mother, like most members of the family, had tasted his violence. Her naturally rebellious nature and her dreams of a better life encouraged her to leave the family home when she was very young to study as a nurse.

My grandfather worked as a clerk in the coal industry, writing letters for the illiterate to earn extra money. He died at 52 of an illness related to coal mining and is buried somewhere in the Midlands – the exact place is unknown as, apart from my mother's husband, no-one went to his funeral. His grandfather owned a little steamer, transporting coal backwards and forwards from France. Quite a few of the Hawkins forebears were shipowners and sea captains. We are related to the Irish offshoot of the Hawkins family, who settled in and around Wexford in the late 1500s after leaving Devon to take up a land grant made by Queen Elizabeth I to John Hawkins as reward for defeating, along with his cousin Sir Francis Drake, the Spanish Armada and returning a good part of the plunder to the English crown.[1] Sir John Hawkins's descendants have lived there ever since.

My mother never believed that we were Irish and, after moving to England in the late 1930s, she had always felt at home there. Despite 300 years in Ireland, we were still English: 'Hawkins' is an English name.

My natural father's identity remains little more than family rumour and speculation, a fleeting ghost crossing the family canvas, best laid to rest. A few in the family were in the know yet took the secret to the grave, including my mother. The discretion of the Catholic Church could be relied upon in the case that a child survived life in an orphanage and came back later to ask questions.

My mother met my father in 1946, when they both worked at St Bernard's Hospital in Middlesex, London. She was a pretty 24-year-old nurse and he was a young Irish doctor from a well-known medical family. They had fallen in love and planned to marry. My mother fell pregnant so the marriage had to take place as quickly as possible to avoid family shame. The church, guests and celebrations had all been decided when suddenly my father fled back to Dublin. Before he left, he offered my mother a 'legal' abortion at the hospital.

My mother was from a strong, proud Irish Catholic family with traditions and values typical of the times. To escape family pressures, and to give herself space to think, she fled south alone, where she gave birth to me in 1947 at Grayshott in Alton, a small southern English village. Several days later, Father O'Riordan baptised me and suggested she accompany him to his presbytery on the Isle of Wight to think things through in a quiet place while working as his housekeeper. We stayed on the island for six months while she hoped against hope that her love might return. Father O'Riordan suggested that she have me adopted, advising her to try the Sisters of Nazareth who ran a home nearby on the mainland in Romsey. She handed me over to the Sisters, devastated she was about to lose the baby she had breastfed and loved.

Without support from her family, and frightened that she would be permanently ostracised, she begged the Mother Superior to have me adopted into a good English family, readily believing the nun who said she could adopt me out that very day, as young couples who couldn't have children were regular visitors to the home. Soon after my mother signed the official release papers, the Mother Superior pointed to a young couple leaving the home with me in a pram and said to my mother, 'There goes John. A good Catholic couple has just adopted him'. Shattered though she was by our separation, she was gladdened by the thought I would be loved and cared for. However, this was a cruel performance put on for my mother's benefit, and soon after she left, the couple wheeled me back to the orphanage. This ruse was frequently used by the Sisters of Nazareth to prevent mothers changing their minds and coming back the next day for their child.

The mainly Irish Sisters of Nazareth reared me from the age of six months in an efficient and mostly loveless Catholic home in England that cared for 20 to 30 boys about the same age. The Sisters of Nazareth, known for their poor record-keeping, took a narrow line, demanding little information from the parent (usually the mother) parting with the child. The book entry describing my circumstances reads, in just a few words:

> *Admitted to Nazareth house 26 Sep. 1947. His mother was housekeeper*
> *to Reverend Father O'Riordan, Shanklin, when he was admitted and by*
> *whom he was recommended. Since then she has deserted the child.*[2]

These few words were the only written proof of my existence.

Relinquishing mothers were frequently teenagers – just children themselves – who were too stressed and immature to know their own minds and were glad of the 'few questions asked' opportunity offered by the nuns. However, many mothers, like mine, felt differently and given the opportunity would have chosen to have a say in the future of their babies.

Taking in children like me was a typical charitable response by the Sisters at the time. They had a long, proud history of helping the poor, the sick and the needy. Originally a French order, they had arrived in England in the mid 1800s and set up their mission on 10 acres of vegetable gardens in Hammersmith, then located on the outskirts of London.[3] The Sisters ran homes all over Britain. In most of the homes there were children being raised until they were five or six years old when they would be sent to Australia. My time with the Sisters started badly – I imagine myself red-faced, fists clenched, defiant and demanding. I presume that I screamed constantly for the comfort of my mother's smell and her breast milk, along with dozens of other babies who were also desperately missing their mothers, until, exhausted, we would fall asleep. My mother's face strangely remains embedded in my memory.

I'm sure there were pleasant moments, but my mind remembers mainly the negative times. I recall as a three or four year old standing up in a high-railed cot looking across a dormitory nursery, watching nuns in long dark habits and black-and-white hoods, which covered everything except their faces, seemingly glide across the polished wooden floor as though on a cushion of air. Busily coming and going, they carried sheets, nappies, pots and pans. Some sang quietly to themselves while others shouted orders.

Young girls were helping too, shushing crying children to calm them for sleep or simply yelling at them to shut up. The girls were ex-orphanage recruits who had failed to adjust to life outside the home. We were probably raised as much by these girls as by the nuns. It was the usual practice for one of the girls to gather us around in a tight circle on the floor while she read us a story. In the evening, the girls bathed us two at a time. We wore linen modesty slips around our waists and they finished our bath by ducking our heads under the soapy bathwater, which caused a stinging sensation when it got into my nose and ruined what was always a lovely bath.

Life at the orphanage was strict and spartan. There were few privileges. Food was basic and there was barely enough, so we were often hungry. When some of the children were reunited as adults with their siblings, they discovered that the lack of good nutrition in childhood had made them physically much smaller than their siblings who had grown up outside.

Quite a few of the Irish nuns seemed unhappy, including the Mother Superior, which didn't help the general atmosphere in the home. Religious orders sometimes placed 'difficult' members in orphanages and homes, as they couldn't afford the cost of care for these people. It was also common for the least qualified in their ranks to work in orphanages. One nun – a tall, thin stern-looking Irishwoman called Sister Dominic – was regularly aggressive and often frightened the children with her swishing strap and constant yelling. Her behaviour towards us may have been affected by her attitude towards the English.

Birthdays were never celebrated, coming and going without our knowledge as no-one knew their date of birth. When I was five years old, I experienced my first normal Christmas. A British military helicopter carrying Father Christmas landed on our field with bags of toys, probably donated. I remember many excited children and strange adults being there. I received a toy double-decker bus and a conductor's hat. We played with our toys for a couple of hours until all the visiting dignitaries and well-wishers had left. I proudly showed off my gift to one of the nuns, who appeared more interested in the box in which the toy came. 'Where's the box? Don't damage that box!' she shouted, as the nuns gathered up the toys and put them back into their boxes. We never saw the toys again and they were probably sold or donated to another charity. Despite this loss, no child cried or became upset, so thoroughly ignorant were we of gifts and the meaning of giving and receiving, or indeed, of ownership. It was the first time we had ever received a present or heard of reindeers landing on rooftops and Father Christmas making his way down the chimney.

The strangers who visited us that day had us enthralled with this story, and we were both excited and confused. All we had known about Christmas before this was what the nuns had told us about its religious significance as the time our saviour Jesus Christ was born. The nuns did go to a special effort to give us a nice meal and put up streamers, balloons and a colourful Christmas tree at the front of the dining room. Carols were played and sung – the hymn 'Silent Night' was easily our favourite.

The early years of my childhood were tragic – as was the childhood of many children in similar circumstances. I'd like to think there were kind nuns who cared for me before I was old enough to remember. One kind person I do remember was a young, pretty Irish nun who named me 'Baby John'. Kind and happy, she provided the only music in the home with her beautiful singing voice. I remember the day we were told we would get pillows to sleep on and we could tuck our neatly folded pyjamas under the pillow just like the older children. We had ceased being infants and were now considered to be boys. The nuns stopped calling me Baby John and I became just John.

1   John Hawkins, Drake's cousin and partner, earned notoriety for developing the slave trade, shipping human cargo from Africa to the Americas. To maximise the commercial potential, Elizabeth gave Hawkins two Royal Navy warships and, again, the Crown shared in the profits of the slave trade.

2   The comment 'mother deserted child' appeared on many children's files. This categorisation was important to the social workers at Australia House who conducted the interview of prospective child migrants because it made the child an automatic candidate for migration.

3   The Sisters of Nazareth continue their work from their headquarters in Hammersmith, caring for the elderly. Today, their 10 acres is one of the most beautiful private gardens in London.

2
LEAVING HOME

The Sisters in my orphanage at Romsey had created in my mind a powerful negative image of the Christian Brothers in Australia. Whenever they violently chastised a child using a strap or their hands they would often yell, 'If you think this hurts, wait until the Christian Brothers in Australia get hold of you'.

The Sisters had a long tradition of association with the Christian Brothers in Ireland. Young boys were expected to attend Christian Brothers secondary schools after their primary education with the nuns. It was expected, therefore, that the male British orphans would go to Christian Brothers orphanages and girls to the Sisters of Nazareth orphanages in Australia.

Most of us desperately did not want to go to Australia, despite the rosy picture the nuns painted of sunshine and fruit trees. In my eyes they had successfully demonised the Christian Brothers there. Yet the nuns' own punishments were often brutal enough. They could whip a child's legs red raw with a long leather strap that hung down the side of their habit.

When my time came to be deported, I planned to hide among trees in a wood nearby. My plan came unstuck, however, when panic broke out among the nuns one day. They gathered all of us inside and told us there was a murderer – worse, a child murderer – on the loose and hiding in the wood. I peered through the window with the other children and saw the police take away a bald-headed man whose arms were handcuffed behind his back. Whether he was a murderer or not, the incident forever ended my hope of hiding in the wood.

At Romsey I was often ill and bedridden. Lack of decent protein didn't help my frail body. A man who was employed by the convent befriended me and sometimes brought sweets to the dormitory. One day he took out his penis and forced me to stroke it with my hands. He then threatened to kill me if I told anyone. I was too young to understand what he was doing, but I understood clearly what the death threat meant. I became withdrawn and very frightened. The nuns suspected something was wrong and moved me into a small room with a bed and locked the door. I was told to knock on the door if I needed to go to the toilet. I was belted one day with a leather strap for peeing in the corner after my knocking failed to bring a response. I learned to climb out the large window in the room, stand on the windowsill and pee a long way into the courtyard, never daring to look down.

Over time, I observed small groups of children, many crying, leave the orphanage. I knew my time would be coming soon. One black West Indian child cried as he couldn't go due to his colour – he was lonely and sad because all his friends had been sent away.

Some of the children had spoken about Australia, passing on stories other children had told them, building images of monsters worse than any storybook. It was where orphans disappeared across a vast sea, never to return. I was never ready or willing for this journey.

On the 2 May 1953, at the age of six, I underwent my first medical examination at Australia House in London for the Department of Immigration. This was the day I had feared most as it signalled that it would be only a few weeks before I was forced to leave. I was consumed with fear and, after the examination, I cried, fretted and stopped eating, breaking down mentally and physically. Seriously ill, I was hospitalised for many weeks.

I do not know what illness I suffered. I had been walking around the statue in the courtyard with the other children, saying prayers. I was limping very badly and one of the nuns took me out of the group to investigate and found an enormous lump in my groin. I was rushed to hospital almost immediately. I recall only the kidney-shaped hospital tray with the big needle that was injected into my bottom twice a day, which hurt so much that I cried every time I saw the nurses coming. My illness meant that I literally missed the boat and the nuns found another boy to take my place on the passenger ship.

Shortly after I came out of hospital I was transferred to Nazareth House in Hill Lane, Southampton, one of many orphanages the Sisters ran in England. By now I understood without doubt that I was an orphan, that my parents were dead and that my life depended on the charity of the Sisters, who had cared for me in hospital.

Pressure from children's officers from the local authority forced the nuns to open their doors to the public for the first time, and soon after my arrival at Nazareth House, they placed advertisements in the local daily newspapers seeking families to visit children on the weekends. Local authorities were suspicious of the secretive nature of church institutions and, since the passing of the new Children Act in 1948, the role of the local children's officers was to place the thousands of children back with their families, into foster care or have them adopted. In reality, a disproportionate number of children from orphanages run by nuns ended up as child migrants.

I first met the Broom family soon after my arrival in Southampton. They were fishmongers, who followed the Church of England and had a house in Bugle Street, about 100 metres from St Josephs Catholic Primary School, which I was now attending. The Mother Superior allowed the family to take me home on weekends, an unusual privilege as I recall no other child being given a similar opportunity. It may have been because of my poor condition after my lengthy illness but the visits by children's officers were undoubtedly having an effect on the nuns' behaviour.

Joy Broom was a tall, young, attractive and strong woman who, with husband Roy, soon made me part of the family. After the birth of her daughter she had been unable to have other children. Her daughter, Wendy, a year younger than me, was excited to have a new brother and I had my own bedroom and toys. Mrs Broom read me stories at night until I fell asleep curled up on her lap.

At first I was shy and withdrawn, not used to all the love and affection. Yet, they were happy days as I adjusted to life outside the orphanage. Mrs Broom was very protective and held my hand every time I left the family home to stop me running onto the street. Everything was new and different, and the street was dangerous. There was much to learn about life on the other side of the orphanage wall. We travelled together on a double-decker bus and I ran upstairs, with Wendy in hot pursuit, to get to the front for the best view of the street. Mrs Broom taught me how to behave, how to share and how to love. She asked me one day if I would like her to be my mother. I had begun calling Joy and

Roy 'mummy and daddy', which seemed perfectly natural as Joy had made formal approaches to the Mother Superior to officially adopt me.

Every school day I crossed the road, had lunch with Joy and Wendy and played until it was time to go back to class. I spent weekends and holidays with the family. I met other members of their family, who were curious to meet Joy and Roy's new boy. All the children played hopscotch on the footpath in front of the fish shop in downtown Southampton. For the first time, I felt love and security, and looked forward to the day when I would finally be released from the orphanage and move in permanently with my new family with whom life was pleasant and idyllic – it was a place where I was learning about birthdays, Christmas, toys and love. I was also learning rapidly how to read and write thanks to Joy's private lessons for Wendy and me.

Mother Superior told the family she had no objections to adoption, but that the paperwork would take time and the family would need to be patient. At first, relations between the family and Mother Superior were cordial, but over the last months they deteriorated and became strained. Often while I was waiting in the parlour for Mrs Broom, the Mother Superior would come in and say, 'That stout woman is here to fetch you!' and then abruptly walk out. If I was returned a little late to the orphanage, I was taken by the hand by one of the nuns and yanked without ceremony back inside.

The nuns began sending small groups of children to the local cinema during the week and we sat on the floor jostling, with our hands in the air, to be chosen. I was always overlooked and was too young to realise that I was being punished in a custody battle turning nastier by the week. I now know that my hospital treatment, opening the orphanage to the public and sending children to the local cinema and outside schools was a radical departure from the usual harshness of orphanage life. These privileges had come about as a result of a recent overhaul of British child welfare. At the time, though, I had no idea that I had become the object of an increasingly ugly tug of war between the Brooms and the nuns. Frustrated by delays and failed commitments, Joy and Roy had demanded of Mother Superior the right to adopt me. I was supposedly an orphan and, for my foster family, it was a simple case of need, love and humanity.

They had cared for me for just over a year when, on 6 March 1954, I was made to undergo another medical examination by staff from Australia House. This time the process was supposed to be different. Official criteria stipulated that any child presented a second time for migration should be most carefully assessed, especially if there had been a medical or psychological problem.

My heart sank. Again I was overcome by fear of the Australians. Surely it was a mistake. My tearful protestations during my examination the year before had cut no ice, especially with the female social worker with the strange accent who aggressively asked questions and put 'yes' and 'no' answers in my mouth. She had almost ordered me, 'You are going to like Australia!', while the Mother Superior enthusiastically nodded in agreement.

I was sure it would be different now that I had an English family – as my mother had wished. My future was no longer bleak and insecure. They couldn't possibly send me away. I pleaded with the Australian social worker and the Mother Superior. This time, they assured me it was just a routine medical. They didn't even mention Australia and my mind was put at ease. The social worker asked 'You're a clever boy, John. Would you like to write your name here?', tricking me into signing a medical report that failed to include details about my hospital treatment, doctors' reports or medical history.[1] The nuns and the social workers at Australia House had conveniently forgotten about my illness the year before and what had caused it. I was not represented by an independent social worker, a requirement under the Children Act that was supposed to give orphans protection.[2]

I continued my life with the Brooms for the next three months, giving no further thought to the interview, medical or the documents prepared by Australian immigration officials.

In June 1954, at the age of seven years and three months, I weighed just 19 kilograms and stood 104 centimetres, as recorded on my travel documents. My weedy below-average frame was the result of years of inadequate nutrition. The nuns had not conducted an IQ test, another requirement of the Act, so I have no record of my intellectual status, though I was able to read and write a bit. I had now met the three main criteria for child migration: I was small in stature, of below-average intelligence and had no family links.

Suddenly my life was turned upside down. Strange children began arriving at the home, and we were put into a room together. I was given a small case with new clothes, shoes and socks. The next day we were bussed to the wharf and put aboard the P&O passenger ship *Strathmore*. The Sisters told me bluntly at the wharf that the Broom family didn't want to see me anymore. A couple of the ships' officers ushered our little group up the gangway and onto the ship while a brass band played 'Auld Lang Syne'.

Disoriented, tears streaming down my face, I searched intently through the bottom rails of the fence on the ship's deck to see if the Brooms had at least come to see me off. I desperately needed them.

On the dock three nuns stood motionless, with arms folded inside their sleeves, like black-and-white statues, in contrast to the movement and colour of people laughing and crying, the balloons, streamers and noise. People packed the ship's rails, pushing, waving and yelling. Bewildered, I watched the ship slowly pull away from the wharf, stretching hundreds of colourful streamers that I hoped might hold the ship from leaving.

One, then another, then all the streamers broke and drifted down into the murky water below. My heart floated down with the streamers, stretched and torn apart. The blackest cloud of grief, helplessness and irretrievable loss descended. Weeping inconsolably, I left my little suitcase by the rails and wandered off to find a place where I could be alone. All the orphanage children's stories came flooding back – the ship, the vast ocean, the fear – but worse, I had lost my family.

A day later, Joy and Roy were happier than usual as they drove to the orphanage to fetch me for the weekend. During the week, Roy had purchased two new bikes: a blue one for Wendy and a red one for me. They had kept the secret from us both and they knew my eyes would fairly pop when I saw my new three-wheeler. Mother Superior coldly delivered the news that I had been sent away. The Sisters had raised me from the age of six months, yet few tears were shed when they sent their children off. They were deeply religious yet had little humanity. Joy was rocked to the point of collapse and wept bitter tears. Mother Superior refused to provide any further information and shut the orphanage door on the family.

A few years later, a kindly nun told Mrs Broom that I had been sent to Australia, although she couldn't say where. Joy continued to mourn her loss, worrying about what had become of her little boy, and began a lifetime's search with Roy for me, the child they loved. They kept the drawings I had made of them all sitting by the fire.

From the deck, I watched England grow smaller and smaller until the last vestige of land became a mist-shrouded speck then disappeared. Only seagulls followed, swooping and diving along the ship's wake. A long white river was carrying me away from my world. My mind shut down, collapsing inwards. Realising that I may never again see my home or the only people who really loved me numbed my emotions. Little registered with me except the pain in the pit of my stomach, which wouldn't go away.

The thought of climbing the ship's rails and falling into the sea had already entered my head. I was sitting, weeping quietly when I heard children's voices: 'We've found him. He's here! He's here!'

A ship's officer was carrying my suitcase and he grabbed my hand and dragged me like a rag doll to a cabin deep in the bowels of the ship, a space I would share with five other children I barely knew for the six-week voyage to Australia. I climbed into a top bunk and cried myself to sleep.

1   Part II, pages 272–275, describes how the protocol at Australia House was often ignored so as to increase the numbers of child migrants being sent to Australia and extract children's consent under false pretences.

2   Part II, page 258–259, describes the promise by the Home Office that independent social workers, who were supposed to know the children being prepared for migration, would be involved in any interviews to protect the rights of the orphans.

GREAT OCEAN ADVENTURE

Early next morning, peering over the ship's rails, I could see only misty sky and grey rolling ocean. Even the ship seemed lonely and abandoned in this great wilderness of water. The day before, I had watched the seagulls swooping and diving on graceful wings and screeching baleful goodbyes. I envied them as they had long since flown home to England.

Most of the children and many of the other passengers were seasick during the night and few were around to face the early morning. I wasn't so affected and began to wander the decks, climbing stairs and investigating corridors until I became lost. A steward recognised me as one of the orphans and he and a couple of others took me to their quarters and asked where I was going. In tears I told them I wanted to go home. I was given a bag of sweets, a few hugs and then led back to my cabin.

After that, our group received special treatment from the ship's passengers and crew. I soon discovered the great advantages of shipboard life. Everything was exciting and luxurious, brightening the mood of even the most sorrowful and grieving among us. Not only was the food unlike any we had before, but amid the ship's many nooks and crannies lay freedom. There were no threats of dire punishment or nuns with swishing habits and lethal straps; here were kind, generous passengers and crew who spoiled the little orphans on board. Stewards brought biscuits, cakes, sweets and anything else we asked for.

Appointed by the nuns, our two minders, young Catholic women, one of whom appeared to be involved in a shipboard romance, struggled to keep order among our excitable group. It was their job each morning to get us up, washed and then fed in the huge dining room, a job complicated by the menu with its vast range of choices.

After breakfast, came shipboard 'school work', games, lunch, a nap, more school and then competitions on the deck with prizes. We played games such as quoits and competed in egg-and-spoon and sack races. After dinner, we might have story time before bed. I won the ship's souvenir teaspoon with 'Strathmore' emblazoned on the handle.

We had been given a little pocket money, a suitcase with a change of clothing and shoes and socks, and some toiletries, so when our minders accepted an invitation to dine at the captain's table, we looked proper little gentlemen. This jovial man laughed and said his name was Captain Cook and that he had been given the job of getting us to Australia. Despite the heady shipboard life, I continued to feel a deep sense of foreboding as, day after day, the distance between me and my loved ones in England increased.

When the ship crossed the equator there was great jubilation and we were allowed to join the passengers and crew, who had dressed up to celebrate the event. That evening we mingled with King Neptune, Cleopatra, Julius Caesar, the devil, pirates, painted ladies and gentleman in top hats. For children who had never experienced anything like the colour and the music, it was pure excitement. As I moved through the crowd, one of the passengers, who I was soon to meet in less festive circumstances, patted my head and gave me a shilling. There were certain advantages in being small and cute, but there was a major disadvantage and I would soon find out what it was.

The day we crossed the equator the crew put on a spectacular poolside performance, swinging off ropes tied to temporary rigging, and falling and diving into the pool from a great height while the band played 'What Shall We Do With the Drunken Sailor?' The playful sailors threw some of the children in my group into the water. I managed to keep my distance, as I was very frightened of water.

That night, nine-year-old John M. woke me and asked me to follow him to the ship's pool, now in semi-darkness, as he wanted to show me something. He stole around to the deep end, pointed into the water, crying 'Look!' As I peered down, I felt a violent push to my back. I screamed as I fell in, thrashing hard to stay afloat. I couldn't swim and the more I flailed about, the further away from the edge of the pool I moved. Soon I gave up the struggle and sank to the bottom.

Everything was fading into an incredibly painful blackness when I felt someone pull me out. A smiling man in a crumpled wet cocktail suit carried me gasping uncontrollably to the ship's infirmary. Yelling for help, he rushed me to a room where medical staff pumped water from my lungs. Their quick action saved my life.

Fortunately my rescuer had seen part of the incident from a deck above the pool where a late party was still in progress. In the dim light he could make out the motionless body of a child under water and had run down several flights of steps and dived in to rescue me. Meanwhile, John had fled to his cabin. Nothing was said of the incident and I never complained to our minders. They assumed that we were playing and I had just fallen in. Terrified of John, I avoided him from then on.

A few days later, my rescuer appeared at our dining table to see how I was getting on. Again, he patted my head and gave me a shilling. Little did I know this was fuelling John's hatred and envy, putting my life at risk.[1]

We sailed through the Suez Canal, stopping at the port of Aden, where locals surrounded the ship in an assortment of small boats and canoes filled with goods. Business between passengers and the traders was conducted using ropes and baskets. Some locals were allowed aboard to entertain us by making day-old chicks and coins appear and disappear. The coins seemed to come out of their ears. We were completely in awe, believing these men were wizards or magicians.

Our journey finally ended when the ship entered Fremantle Harbour in Western Australia on a wintry June day in 1954. We would miss the beautiful, white streamlined *Strathmore*[2] and her crew, who had given our group such care and attention.

Accompanied by our minders, of whom we had become quite fond, we boarded a bus bound for Castledare to what felt like the most remote place on earth they could send us.

Having seen us to our destination, our minders headed back to Fremantle to rejoin the ship, now headed for Sydney.

1   Forty years later, in 1998, John phoned me at my farm. I had not seen him since he was about fifteen. He told me of his life after the orphanage and asked me if I remembered the incident at the ship's pool. 'Yes I do, and I nearly drowned,' I said. 'I'm phoning to apologise,' he said. 'I did it deliberately; I wanted to kill you.' He went on to explain how jealous he had become. 'There were two cute-looking boys in our group. You were one and I was the other. When I realised the passengers were giving you more money than me I admit I lost the plot!' I told John he shouldn't feel bad and jokingly added that, as a farmer, I knew how hard it was to kill weeds. He was relieved. I felt sad that he had carried this awful burden throughout his life. He was only nine at the time and, like the rest of us, was 'damaged goods' to some extent.

2   The P&O *Strathmore*, which had a top speed of 20 knots and accommodation for 445 first-class and 665 tourist-class passengers, continued to bring new settlers to Australia until she was sold to Greek shipowner, John S. Latsis, in 1963. Her name was changed to *Marianna Latsis*. Built in 1935, the third of five 'Straths' in the P&O line, she and her four sisters were involved in the 1942 landings in North Africa, where her sister ship *Strathallan* was torpedoed on 21 December. She spent her final days transporting pilgrims to Jeddah, and in 1969 was sold to ship breakers at Spezia.

CASTLEDARE

All the buildings at Castledare were simple single-storey, red brick and tile, some with steel roofs painted red – not like the grand three- and four-storey mansions in England that we had been brought up in, with their splendid entry gates and courtyards surrounded by manicured lawns and gardens. Here, a single giant pine tree, known as the 'piece tree'[1], where all the children gathered underneath in summer between morning and afternoon school sessions, dominated what served as the courtyard.

Situated well east of the mouth of the Swan River, Castledare was bordered on one side by a small river, a tributary of the Canning River. To the east of the property was swamp and what looked like a small dairy farm. Thick pine forest encircled the rest of the property. This was indeed a strange land.

We found ourselves completely surrounded by English children aged between six and ten, who were curious about and even envious of the new arrivals. Most of the children were thin and dressed in ill-fitting, tatty clothing: cotton khaki shorts that ended below the knee, making the children's legs look even skinnier, and plain cotton shirts of different colours and sizes half hanging out of their trousers, and an assortment of jumpers and cardigans.

None of the children had footwear and most had dirty feet, some with small festering sores on their arms and legs, the combined result of mosquito bites and poor nutrition. By comparison, we looked like the little plump princes from the kingdom of plenty, thanks to six weeks of shipboard food. We were smartly dressed in our new English woollen trousers, shirts and jackets, with shiny shoes and socks. Each of us carried a small case filled with clothing and knick-knacks from the ship.

By the stare on the unsmiling faces of children, this looked an unhappy place to be. Len B., the oldest in our group, had seen enough and, like the rest of us, had sensed the gloom and depression that hung like a fog on a dull morning.

'I'm not staying here,' he declared. 'Have a look on your suitcases, lads. It reads Fremantle, Port of Fremantle. This dump is miles away from Fremantle.'

A confrontation between us and the tough Christian Brothers was inevitable, as Len demanded we be returned to Fremantle. The principal, Brother Patrick O'Doherty, was having none of it. Dissent of any kind was quickly nipped in the bud. Brother O'Doherty, then 29 years old, was easily just under 2 metres tall, the biggest man I had ever seen. Covered in a tent-like black habit and white collar, he looked twice as big again.

He marched us off into a room where we were stripped of our fine English clothes, footwear and cases, and dressed as 'proper' orphans in clean, ill-fitting, well-worn clothing, which had our allocated number discreetly written on it. We were then marched in bare feet into Brother Murphy's classroom and lined up in front of the blackboard before his class of around 40 highly amused children whose envy had dissipated somewhat now that we were dressed like them.

All of us were in a state of shock, hardly believing what was happening. This was to be a passage from disbelief to despair. I stood nearest Brother Murphy, a man as tall as O'Doherty but thinner, with a lean and creased face, who towered over me while still sitting in his chair.

'So what do we have here?' he said. 'A bunch of spoilt brats demanding to be taken to Fremantle. Indeed!'

A muted nervous laugh came from some of the class. He took the cane he kept near his chair, rose to his full height, and began to thrash it against the side of his habit, making a thwacking sound. His message about what would happen to us should we try to escape or 'do a bunk', as it was commonly called, was clear and unambiguous.

'We don't like children who run away. We have to report missing children to the police. It is very inconvenient. But good boys we reward,' he said, as he sank back into his chair.

'You like lollies, son?' He turned to me, at the same time unwrapping a small toffee that he popped in his mouth.

'No,' I said.

I had never heard of lollies as we had called them sweets in England.

'We have a cheeky one here,' he cried, 'he doesn't like lollies!', while grabbing and twisting my ear at the same time. The class laughed.

My ear had never been twisted this savagely before, not even by the nuns in England. I struggled to free myself and before I knew it, I was caned on the hand. Brother Murphy had risen to his full height, and gave me one stroke of the thin cane on the palm of my hand.

Most of the new children were crying. Brother Murphy proceeded to lay down the rules, regulations and punishments, swishing his cane for emphasis. He taunted us for being 'sissies' and 'sooks' and encouraged the other children to laugh at our despair, which most did, following his lead.

One thing became clear – we were going to have to toughen up and get used to being beaten. Corporal punishment, combined with an inculcated fear of authority, was used to control children here. Instead of being raised by women, who had mostly sheltered us from men until now, we were cast into a sea of tough men and older boys. Despite their hard edge, the nuns had definitely been softer. This was like stepping out of kindergarten into a military camp and Murphy was the brutal sergeant major – yet this was where the nuns, who we once thought had genuinely cared about us, had sent us. The shock was instant and great. Our sense of bewilderment, abandonment and betrayal was overwhelming.

The magic cocktail of 100 small children, often out of control, and ineffectual management, meant that Castledare had descended into a 'time of trouble'[2] in the early 1950s under the administration of Brother McDonnell, a deeply religious man who lacked teaching and organisational skills. Professional qualifications among the Brothers were rare, as they were considered expensive and unnecessary, and outside advice was unwelcome.

The visitation reports of the time give an impression of what happened during the 'child uprising' of 1951. Children absconded en masse, swimming the river fully clothed to escape. There was general disorder in the classrooms with boys jumping out of windows, calling the Brothers names and throwing stones. The house annalist at the time wrote,

> *Young as they were, these boys were accustomed to test in diverse ways the powers of endurance and disciplinary strength of the newcomers on the staff. He added, the milder methods – detentions, withdrawal of privileges etc. – having failed to restore order and discipline, the Brother Superior was compelled to allow the use of more drastic punishments as necessary to bring about the desired effect.[3]*

These punishments proved effective. To regain control, the 'ringleaders', a handful of nine- and ten-year-old children, were sent away to Bindoon, another institution.[4] Order was restored.

Brother McDonnell had resigned as director in late 1952 and was replaced by Brother O'Doherty, a charismatic no-nonsense young superior who set about restoring order. The regime at Castledare when I arrived in 1954 was likely an overreaction to the earlier breakdown of order, and drastic punishments had become more or less a permanent feature, especially for runaways. Corporal punishment was often used to dominate and control children.

Running away was a real option for the residents and they often talked about it. The Brothers had a hard time preventing it. In Britain, and especially in the United States of America, homes where children were regularly running away were often investigated by the authorities, who took this as an indication that something was wrong and checked for evidence of malpractice. In Western Australia, runaways were investigated by the police and then returned to the homes and flogged, a brutal practice that was known about by the government authorities. Unhappiness was never accepted as a legitimate reason to run away. Official paranoia in the early days about runaway children roaming wild in the streets of Perth reached absurd levels. Children were often fingerprinted like common criminals – more than 150 boys and girls aged five to thirteen were fingerprinted on their arrival at Fremantle so that the authorities could keep track of them.[5]

Castledare during the O'Doherty years apparently entered a golden age and there were glowing reports of vast improvements and an air of progress and contentment. However, the children would not have endorsed these reports. They were never asked their opinion – the administration did not bother to ask if they liked their new homes or even the country.

Typical thinking in Australian institutions at this time was that if you improved facilities, building new classrooms, new toilet blocks, new chapels and so on, everything else would fall into place. Even in medical examinations the focus was on the physical – as long as a child was physically healthy, it didn't matter if they were an emotional and psychological wreck. No-one made the link between the severe depression suffered by abandoned British children who had been uprooted from their country and sent away against their will to their antisocial behaviour. The 'child uprising' of the early 1950s was the direct result of dislocation, betrayal and plain misery. But their behaviour was to be 'cured' with religion and more violence.

The administration at Castledare was ignorant that, after the passing of the Children Act 1948, Britain was moving away from institutional care. It took until 1956, when the Ross Report was published, savagely criticising Australian institutions as unfit places to raise children, before child migration to Castledare was stopped.[6]

By now there was no chance of returning home to my family. Section C of my immigration documents demanded repayment of my free passage from my sponsoring organisation in case of repatriation, so this ruled out any possibility of return. I had no choice but to accept being banished from the country of my birth and loved ones. This period proved to be the very lowest point in my life.

I was never able to settle at Castledare, fervently believing that the authorities had made a big mistake and that once they realised it they would send me home. I missed my country and my loved ones with whom I had experienced my first sense of joy and belonging. All my pathetic history was bound up in England. Emotionally I resembled a Russian doll, layered shell on shell and only emptiness within.

Soon after arriving at Castledare, I suffered my second breakdown. I began having 'falling' dreams in the middle of the night. I woke up just before hitting the ground and realised I was sitting up in bed screaming.

Other times I was awakened because another child was having a nightmare. Often I could hear children quietly sobbing or calling for their 'mummy'. The large main dormitory, one of two in which more than 70 children slept, was noisy at night. I spent countless hours lying awake, feeling miserable just thinking about England.

I had no idea how far away I was from my homeland or, if I ran away, how long it would take to be back in the comforting arms of the Brooms. I no longer believed that they hadn't wanted to see me because I knew Joy loved me too much. I began asking myself why and searching for answers other than what was preached to us day in and day out: have faith, trust in God; this is his plan. I seriously doubted this was God's plan as even Jesus had a loving family. The Sisters and Brothers, too, must have families and loved ones. I concluded that most of the adults around me made wrong decisions believing they knew best and called it God's work. This way it was nobody's fault – God worked in mysterious ways through religious adults who prayed often for God's guidance.

The pine forests that surrounded the orphanage suited the dark mood into which I had been plunged. For the first few months I withdrew deeply into myself, seeking neither solace nor friendship from other children, and keeping a low profile and trying to be invisible. We were jailed in a foreign country and someone had thrown away the keys. We were told escape was impossible – and we knew it.

I began having powerfully lucid dreaming experiences. I discovered I could leave my body almost at will and see it lying in bed in the middle of the night, while I flew back to Southampton to visit everyone. I could speak to the family but no-one could hear me. I could see Joy and Roy sitting by the fire and little Wendy showing off her latest drawing. My bedroom was empty and some of my toys were scattered on the floor. My bright-eyed teddy bear was propped up against a pillow, as though beckoning me to bed. I could wander through all the rooms and see that they were just as I had left them. The dreams were incredibly real and lasted for several months. They were my refuge and the only thing I lived for. Then they suddenly ended and I was never able to get them back. While they lasted, they were of great comfort.

Castledare in 1954 was overcrowded, a foreign place in a strange country with poor facilities and too many children being cared for by too few people. It was staffed by people with an abysmally poor understanding of the needs of disoriented and disturbed children.

The Brothers, who I constantly feared, carried short, thick leather straps and gave usually one or two painful whacks on the palm of the hand, often for the most innocuous offences such as talking during mealtimes or getting a sum wrong in class. Corporal punishment was excessive and was delivered on a daily basis. The wail of yet another child echoing throughout the buildings achieved the desired result.

On the weekends we all gathered in a small theatre. The names of troublemakers or runaways were read out and they were punished on the stage, caned or strapped on bare buttocks. Thomas T., one of the altar boys, was gruesomely beaten after he broke into the sacristy in the chapel and got drunk on altar wine. Runaways, troublemakers and children having difficulty at school were generally earmarked to go to Bindoon.

The starting point to 'bunk', or run away, was the laneway to the left of the entrance near the ghost tree (a giant Moreton Bay fig tree said to be haunted). As most of the running away occurred during daylight, children seen crossing the paddock were reported and often a Brother would be waiting at the other end to bring them back. One of the children became a hero after he managed to get all the way into the city of Perth by conning several bus drivers into believing he had lost his money. His extraordinary achievement in our eyes was the equivalent of manned flight to the moon. Wandering the city, he was picked up by police and promptly returned, being given the obligatory hiding.

Bullying among the children was rife. Older children snatched biscuits or bread and jam from the hands of smaller children during the morning and afternoon breaks. Brother Murphy's pet was a big ten-year-old boy who was a renowned bully. The other children warned us from the beginning to do his bidding. Some of the smaller children had become almost like slaves to this bully, handing over their 'piece'. I watched the greedy boy act out his fantasy as youngsters pulled him through the pine forest by rope on a sled made out of corrugated iron, while he whipped them with an imaginary whip.

Food was a big issue with all the children. Twice a week the truck travelled to the Perth fruit and vegetable market to pick up spoilt produce for the pigs. The better quality food ended up in the kitchen. Sometimes the quality was excellent – it was either feast or famine, depending on the season. When the van arrived from the Clontarf bakery with freshly baked bread and currant buns, the delicious smell lured hordes of children and we surrounded the van until the food was safely delivered to the kitchen.

I used to think the whole world was short of food and, because we were orphaned, naturally we were at the end of the queue. Poor Rosie, the Aboriginal cook, often had to scream at children to get away from the slop bucket outside the kitchen door where they were fighting over food scraps from the dining room of the Brothers and staff. I know this because I was one of these children.

The staff at the time consisted of five Christian Brothers, Rosie and her two helpers, and Jim, the dairy and pig man, and his offsider, usually an 'old boy' from Clontarf or Bindoon. Other helpers included three refugee nuns from a Hungarian order who lived and worked on the property, a resident priest and an auxiliary women's group, who, with the nuns, were mainly responsible for washing, stitching and patching our clothes and dispensing medical treatment. We never had real contact with these women – the Brothers looked after us.

We comprised more than 130 boys aged between six and ten, and had four classrooms for classes between first to fourth grade. Two main dormitories served as sleeping quarters: one for the children who wet the beds and the other for the 'dries'. Kapok mattresses, packed hard over time, were covered with a thick piece of rubber. Sheets, blankets and pillows were ex-military issue and the woollen blankets were especially thin. Porcelain cups and plates in the dining room were also from the military.

Life at Castledare was strict and regimented – each day a humiliating carbon copy of the day before. Up in the morning, make your bed and stand next to it for inspection. After inspection, join the line of children waiting for bread and porridge. After breakfast, do your 'charge', the cleaning job you were allocated by the Brothers, like sweeping the dormitories or mopping the bathroom floors. After charges, join the lines being readied for the march into the classrooms. After morning class, join the line for the march into the dining room for lunch – and so it went, day after day, like an endless military parade. Not even birthdays interrupted the routine – they were recognised but without fanfare.

After school the routine varied little. We either did sport or played on the oval, or did work such as weeding the gardens, scraping up pine needles in the pine forest or collecting dried cow manure patties for the flowerbeds. At 5 pm, we were herded, 40 or 50 at a time, into an open shower block for a shower. The taps were operated by one of the Brothers. The first time we were all terribly embarrassed and tried to cover ourselves with our hands, but we soon learnt that at Castledare there was no room for modesty and personal dignity. Being inspected by a Brother sitting in a chair after the shower was humiliating. After Brother Marques arrived it became worse, as he sometimes sent us back in for another shower. As he looked down at our pivate parts he would say, 'Go and clean your dirty feet this time'.

The Castledare Fair was held once a year. It was a charity event from which all proceeds went to the home. We looked forward to it with great excitement – the fair, and the concerts given by the choir, were the only events to interrupt the drudgery of our lives at Castledare. Overnight a little tent city emerged on the property and sellers sold trinkets, toys, sweets, jams and homemade cakes. Each child was given 10 shillings to spend and within half an hour at best, most had spent all their money.

The mix of children from all over the British Isles gave the Brothers a unique pool of talent of budding singers and actors. Castledare had a brilliant boys' choir and competed well against other schools in the annual Eisteddfod. At Clontarf, our brother orphanage, the singers were considered by some to be second only to the Vienna Boys' Choir. Much time and effort went into preparing the choirs for the Eisteddfods, along with the annual concerts, which always played to packed houses. The Brothers were keen on the musical classics of great modern composers such as Rodgers and Hammerstein and Gilbert and Sullivan. Thus we learnt the songs from *HMS Pinafore*, *The Pirates of Penzance*, *The Mikado* and *Oklahoma*, and others. In 1956 I took the role of Princess Chrysanthemum playing to a packed house at His Majesty's Theatre. Concert night was always exciting. An army of women appeared to dress us in splendid costumes and paint our faces. Then we put on the performance, always greatly appreciated by the people invited to attend.

Unlike St Josephs Primary School in England, there was little by way of normal primary school activity, especially for the very young like me. There were no nursery rhymes, story readings, colouring-in books, plasticine, building blocks or toys. On the blackboard, written in large capital letters, was 'All My Work Done for God', followed by 'AMDG', the compulsory signature we wrote at the start of each page of our school exercise book. Our education seemed directed at turning young children as quickly as possible into pious and obedient little adults. There were activities for the older children, such as playing on the very large swing and monkey bar, rolling large truck tyres around the field, and playing with a football that was the wrong shape and bounced awkwardly on the handball courts.

Almost immediately I had difficulty in school and had to start again in grade one. I had lost most of the reading and writing skills I had learnt in England. I had been capable of writing simple messages to the Brooms on the drawings I made, but here I could not resurrect even those skills. I slowly relearned and progressed more or less normally, although I would always be two years behind my age group throughout the rest of my primary education.

The regular morning class march always included a number call and response, so that missing children could be readily identified. When we had first arrived, we were given a number. Mine was '113'. It appeared on all my clothing and even my wooden toothbrush. At roll calls our numbers were called out. We were expected to respond by calling out our surnames, military-style. Whenever my number was called, I simply responded 'Hawkins'. The rest of the time my number substituted for my name. This process, combined with the other invasions of orphanage life, stripped away what little identity I had. I was reduced to a number at roll call. I succumbed to a robot-like obedience and only physical pain could make me cry.

We were forced to walk on sharp gravel stones in our soft bare feet, eat appalling meals and suffer the bites of the mosquitoes that invaded the dormitories every night. The only mosquito control involved burning dried cow-dung. The smoke from the smouldering manure was said to drive out mosquitoes. We spent long periods on our knees praying – especially for our benefactors and for more donations. This was the land the Sisters of Nazareth in England described to us as being made of fruit trees and milk and honey.

Religious teaching was regarded as more important than anything else and the best cure for disturbed minds. We recited the Catechism over and over, and learnt hymns in English and Latin. Many of the children became altar boys and joined the roster for regular masses and benediction in the chapel. We had a very good choir and could sing different Latin masses right through in Gregorian chant. We found most of the Latin hymns boring, with their repetitive themes, and we didn't understand what they were about. I had first heard 'Amazing Grace' on holidays and wondered why we couldn't sing such a song in our chapel. It seemed wonderfully melodic and the lyrics spiritual and beautiful. Later I realised it was written by a Protestant. The stirring 'Faith of our Fathers', which we sang constantly, was essentially our Catholic equivalent.

The principal, Brother O'Doherty, was a deeply religious man and like the majority of Catholic Brothers fervently believed we were, in the main, true orphans in need of Christian charity. He was privy to the only information about us in existence – our names, birthdays and certificates of baptism supplied by the nuns – although often even this information was wrong. He and his colleagues were aware that some children had foster families in England who had wanted to adopt them, although I never told O'Doherty about my English family, so withdrawn had I become. He often praised the good Sisters of Nazareth for their deep charity and compassion and this boxed me into a terrible dilemma about what to believe.

O'Doherty believed that if you prayed for something, you would receive it. Mesmerised by his faith, at times during prayers he appeared lost in a world of his own. He ruled that pride, confidence and self-esteem were sins, while humility, chastity and poverty were godly and holy.

He recited *ad infinitum* his favourite mantra 'children should be seen and not heard', regarding us as too immature and unsophisticated to deserve privacy, an opinion or any credibility. Like many Christian Brothers inspired by his teachers towards a spiritual vocation, he joined the order at fourteen and went to study at a house of formation known as 'The Juniorate', an Irish Catholic version of an English public boarding school. Undoubtedly it was his experience there that formed his ideas on childcare.

A popular notion was that the Catholic orphanage system would produce new recruits for religious organisations, as well as produce large numbers of solid Catholic citizens who would marry and reproduce an army of like-minded Christians. This gave the Brothers a rare opportunity to try to shape the hearts and minds of the young Christian soldiers raised in a military-style 'monastery'. The ritual of Holy Mass in the morning, catechism and religious instruction during the day, followed by rosary and benediction at night should have produced a legion of dedicated followers. The children, however, found few role models among their teachers, who appeared to live their religion only in church. The loving Jesus we knew in our simple understanding would have reached out and comforted a runaway child. This contradiction turned a small army of children away from the church before they had even reached adulthood.

Outwardly O'Doherty had a happy, carefree disposition and, while we generally liked and respected him, especially for his awe-inspiring religious convictions, we feared him in equal measure. He effectively shut down any meaningful communication he might have had with us. By putting children down, amid the laughter of the other children, he discouraged us from speaking out or 'showing off'. He demanded absolute respect for himself and for the other Brothers, who he said had given their lives to the service of God. When necessary, he enforced this respect with corporal punishment.

O'Doherty taught religion with a fire and passion. A simple man, but one with enormous belief, he taught about the god of love, but also about the god of fear, and he could terrify us with his sermons. God divided the world into two groups of people. On one hand were the Catholics who were extremely lucky to have inherited the one true religion through baptism and thus earn the right to eternal salvation. The rest were tagged 'non-Catholics'. The worst of the 'non-Catholics' were the Protestants. God was particularly annoyed with them. They had turned their back on Him when they split away from the mother church. Whenever the subject was broached, O'Doherty scattered like confetti angry-sounding words like 'Lucifer', 'Luther', 'Hell', 'heretic' and 'excommunication'.

He warned us many times not to die in mortal sin as we would spend all eternity in Hell. Eternity was described as a beach where each grain of sand represented one year. When all the grains of sand had been picked up from all beaches of the world, this represented a single day in eternity. Hell, he described as burning hotter than the sun but without having the power to consume the flesh of the damned sinners, who would wail, gnash their teeth and beg for water for all eternity.

The two most common mortal sins appeared to be the sin of impurity and that of deliberately missing mass on Sundays. O'Doherty told us the story of the Protestant and Catholic boys who went fishing together one Sunday morning. The Catholic boy had told his mother he was going to mass when in fact he was sitting in a boat on a lake with his Protestant friend. The boat overturned and both boys drowned: 'We only hope that God in his infinite wisdom and mercy had pity on the poor Catholic boy's soul.' The very best he could expect was a long stretch in Purgatory, which we were told was also a place of fire where those who died having committed venial sin would languish until their sins had been atoned.

I could only take an educated guess about the fate of the Protestant boy. It didn't really bear thinking about. He couldn't go to the first-class Heaven, because he wasn't a baptised Catholic. Also, it would appear that he was directly involved in keeping a Catholic boy away from holy mass, and worse. If it were true that in the eyes of God a good Protestant was equal to a bad Catholic, he really didn't have a feather to fly with and God was bound to throw the book at him.

Seeing that we all had committed venial sin (mere misdemeanours when compared to the mortal variety), as well as being born in original sin, it was extremely likely that we all faced some time in Purgatory. But the question of how much time had everyone stumped. The thinking was that because eternity was so infinitely huge, a few thousand years in Purgatory was a mere drop in the bucket. But a few thousand years of cleansing fire was something none of us looked forward to.

Babies who died before they could be baptised went to Limbo – an in-between place, neither Hell nor Heaven – for all eternity. This was the place I wanted to go to most. I didn't like the devil and I didn't like God – both were cruel and sadistic.

Irish Catholic theology about Purgatory and Hell was very popular at the time. Fire-and-brimstone sermons were particularly damaging to already frightened and insecure children. We were encouraged to make friends with only Catholic boys during the holidays, as Protestant boys were likely to lead us astray. We were also to remember that when we grew up we should never marry a Protestant, especially as there were so many good Catholic girls available.

To me the story of the Catholic and Protestant boy seemed a contradiction as we had been taught in the scriptures that the way humans treated others was more important than the way humans treated God: 'love one another' was constantly drilled into us. I presumed it meant the whole human race, so I had to conclude that the God of fear was indeed illogical and vindictive.

As I believed almost everything that I was told, I was fearful and worried about the awful punishment that surely awaited me when I died. It was possible to avoid Hell and Purgatory if you confessed your sins to a Catholic priest, but timing was important. If you confessed your sins to a priest on your deathbed and at the same time received the sacrament of extreme unction and had no evil thoughts, your chances of immediate salvation were very good. By comparison, Purgatory was the long way round and could take thousands of years, though it could be avoided if you managed to die in time before committing another sin.

The God of love was an entirely different matter, always portrayed as Jesus in the pictures we were shown. A beautiful man, often surrounded by children, he loved the downtrodden, the marginalised, the sick and poor, but especially the children. And he threatened those who might harm them: 'Better to tie a millstone around their necks and cast them into the sea, than harm any one of these my little ones.'

So it seemed clear that Jesus was on our side. Yet I couldn't understand why O'Doherty was passionate about building a new chapel at a cost of thousands of pounds. Castledare couldn't have been poorer, and neither could we. Why would Jesus want this money spent on a grand building to himself? Surely he would want the money spent on the children, putting flywire on the dormitory windows and doors to stop the mosquitoes biting us, or seats on the often-freezing porcelain toilet bowls. Wouldn't he want the children to have footwear and underwear, like we had when we arrived, or to eat properly as the staff and the Brothers did?

The difference in quality between what we ate and what everyone else ate was immense. While the new chapel was being built the food became even more unpalatable and sometimes made me physically sick. Apart from drinking the nightly cocoa beverage, I often went to bed with an empty stomach as I could barely eat the bread puddings, lumpy rice puddings or sago, rhubarb and custard. To force the children to eat this unpalatable stodge, we were forbidden to leave the dining room until all the food had gone. I got around this by rolling what I couldn't swallow into the bottom of my shirt, tucking it into my trousers and disposing of it as soon as I left the dining room, a trick learned from others. Sometimes we stole potatoes from the piggery and cooked them on a fire of pine needles in the forest. The half-burnt offerings were far more palatable then some of the food coming out of the kitchen.

In 1956, two years after my arrival, a new monk arrived to manage the small farm with Jim and his helper. Brother Marques's duties included night-watch in one of the dormitories. He began to interfere with some of the children, sexually abusing the more gullible. He would put chocolates or lollies under his pillow and invite individual children to his bedroom to keep his bed warmed until he returned. On several occasions Marques tried to seduce me. I was terrified of him and avoided any eye contact.

Marques attacked me one evening while the rest of the children were at the pictures. I was ill in bed. He approached me in the main dormitory and asked me to go to his room where I would find chocolates under his pillow. The temptation of the chocolates was too much, so I retrieved the goodies from under his pillow, ate them and went back to my bed. I feigned sleep as he pushed and shoved to wake me. At one point he tried to lift me from my bed. I held grimly to the mattress, fortunately making me too heavy for him to lift. He stopped, to my great relief, as the children spilled in from the picture theatre. I never really trusted a man for the remainder of my childhood.

Brother O'Doherty, who often preached about the evils of impurity, remained ignorant of what was happening because children wouldn't risk telling him or seeking his protection. After all, who would he believe –

the accused Brother who had given his life to the service of God, or the child who should be seen and not heard? Worse, if O'Doherty revealed the name of the accuser to Marques, what future would the child have? This man, cleared of any wrongdoing, could kill a child with fear.

Another 'benefactor' and frequent visitor was Leo, who worked at His Majesty's Theatre and had a small flat near nearby. He took many photographs of the children and sexually fondled some of us. On some Sundays he was allowed to take children who were not visiting with a holiday family back to his flat. I was among this group and we travelled on the back of his little green utility to spend a day with him. He fed us well and was generally very kind, and although I saw him abuse some children, he never touched me.

In my first few months at Castledare, I had watched excited boys leave for the city every third Sunday of the month on the back of a truck to visit their holiday families. Soon it would be my turn to meet an Australian family.

1   'Piece' was a snack, usually bread and jam, eaten by the children during the morning and afternoon school breaks.

2   Barry M. Coldrey, 'Trouble at Castledare', *The Scheme: The Christian Brothers and Childcare in Western Australia*, Argyle Pacific, 1993, p. 357. Dr Coldrey is a Christian Brother.

3   Barry M. Coldrey, *The Scheme*, 1993, p. 357.

4   Barry M. Coldrey, *The Scheme*, 1993, p. 357.

5   In 1947, the Undersecretary for Lands and Immigration, with permission from the Minister – the legal guardian of the child migrants – wrote to the Police Commissioner that a police officer was to meet the children arriving on the *Asturias* and fingerprint them so that 'the Department will, in future, be able to identify each individual child'. At this time, the rights of child migrants in Australia were ignored. In 1948, 150 children from Bindoon and other institutions had their tonsils forcibly removed – not at the Children's Hospital, but at the Clontarf orphanage under the supervision of a nursing sister. News of this kind of treatment would have caused outrage in Britain.

6   The Ross Report of 1956 effectively brought child migration to an end, although it did continue on a smaller scale with some secular organisations into the 1960s. Read more about the impact of the Ross Report, and the Australian government inquiry set up in response, in Part II, pages 281–282.

5
MY AUSTRALIAN FAMILY

Brother O'Doherty was keen for the children to experience family life and arranged for Catholic families in Perth to take children into their homes. I found it bizarre that they had removed me from my English family a few months before but now they wanted to put me with an Australian one. I loved and missed my English family so much that I only thought about being returned to their love and protection.

On visiting day, we were taken by truck to a location in St Georges Terrace in Perth, just outside the Christian Brothers College, where we were met by our host families and taken home for the day. We would be returned to the same spot to be taken back to Castledare. The truck, an 8-ton Ford fitted with stock sides, had 'Castledare Orphanage' emblazoned on each door. Curious onlookers stopped and stared as we travelled through the city, the truck filled with standing children all dressed the same in their best clothes in what was almost certainly a way of drawing a charitable response from the public. I loathed this scrutiny and felt both shamed and humiliated. I avoided eye contact with people and tried to be as inconspicuous as I could, hiding behind the throng of children standing on the back of the truck.

Most of the children visited families, although perhaps 20 to 30 children, probably those regarded as dysfunctional or problem children, remained behind at Castledare. Most if not all of the 'problem' children were serious bed-wetters.

The families gave the children a great day out, and we often arrived back at the truck carrying bags of goodies including fruit, cake, biscuits and lollies. These had to be handed in to be shared with the children who missed out. The thought of going back to the orphanage upset some children so much that they refused to climb on the truck and had to be physically lifted up. Crying children could be heard up and down St Georges Terrace. This miserable scenario was repeated at 4.30 pm every third Sunday.

About four months after my arrival in Australia I was introduced to my holiday family who lived at the city end of Charles Street, North Perth, in an area commonly known as Little Italy. The Harringtons were a good family who genuinely cared about me, especially Meg, who took to me as if she was my real mother. Her husband Bernie, however, was an argumentative, volatile character who could explode at any moment. The tension caused by Bernie's mood swings could dominate life in the house. Sometimes they argued in front of the children, and though I'd never seen adults argue before, I would come to learn that for them this was normal behaviour.

The first time I went to their home, Robert, their son, collected me at the Terrace and took me by bus all the way to Charles Street. I was impressed with his navigational and logistical skills – knowing which bus to catch and how much change to give the bus driver for the two of us. Considering he was nine at the time, this was indeed an impressive feat.

I arrived at their neat little brick-and-tile house amid great fanfare. Bernie, Meg and daughter Margaret made a great fuss of me and before long I was eating a slice of cake and drinking Coca-Cola from a tall glass. I had not experienced such luxury since the *Strathmore* days.

Mr and Mrs Shaw from next door were invited in to meet the little English orphan, complete with his English accent. By now Bernie was cleverly mimicking my accent and roaring with laughter. We were joined later by Sam and Mary and their daughter Christine who lived a few doors up. Sam was a Greek body-builder with enormous muscles. His wife Mary was Bernie's niece.

Christine, the same age as Margaret and me, was excited at the prospect of having a new friend to play with. Mrs Nicholi from across the street arrived with daughters Paula and Roberta and gave me the biggest hug. A short but large woman with enormous breasts and a deep, rich baritone voice, she cried 'Johnny! Johnny!', taking my head in her hands and plunging my face into her enormous cleavage. For a moment the light went out and I stopped breathing. Suddenly being a celebrity and a curiosity to all manner of strangers was daunting but the children seemed to genuinely like me and allowed me to play with their toys.

Mr Shaw was a gifted silversmith who earned his living by selling religious trinkets and artefacts from his home. Sam was a trucking contractor who owned several trucks. Mr Nicholi had a shoe-repair shop with a house at the rear where he lived with his family. He kept a 78 rpm record player in the shop and often accompanied the 'Great Caruso', his voice carrying up and down Charles Street as if the two were singing to an adoring and admiring Italian audience at La Scala. Bernie worked at the PMG (Postmaster-General's Department) in the building and maintenance division.

Later I met the Wittington and Mulligan families who lived just up the road. The Mulligans were a typical large Irish Catholic family and their sons, like Robert Harrington, attended the Christian Brothers College in Leederville.

This new family experience stirred up memories of happier times in England, and made me long for the Brooms. I missed the smell of fresh fruit and fish wafting up and down the street in Southampton. The pleasant neighbourhood aromas in North Perth, both similar and familiar, kept reminding me and I still wept for my family back home.

After the day with the Harringtons, Castledare was even more intolerable and it would be a month before I would see the family again. But I was happy again in the knowledge that, like in England, there were good, loving people in Australia. Again, as in England, I began living in two different worlds. Life outside the orphanage was utopia: different and pleasant but completely unattainable. It was an illusion, but one that gave me hope. My life became one of despair punctuated by love and hope, and the contrast between my life at Castledare and my life outside with the Harringtons couldn't have been greater.

I was becoming more and more preoccupied with the Harrington family, and luckily I received a letter from Meg saying that they would love to have me for the Christmas holidays. This was just the best possible news, and I counted the days and hours until the start of the holidays. This time I took my suitcase and I was met again by Robert and taken back to Charles Street for six weeks of bliss with a caring family. It was my link to the outside world where people were kind, loving and generous, and again I was perfectly happy. It wasn't long before I made firm friends with the family pets: Lassie, a handsome Border Collie and Tiger, one of Lassie's offspring. Margaret became my constant companion and she and I and the dogs wandered Hyde Park and nearby parks and gardens with no agenda other than to play and have fun, only going home in time for meals or when we were hungry. The dogs were quite protective of us and often would growl at an approaching stranger.

I got to know the shopkeeper at the delicatessen on the corner. Without me needing to ask he would smile and hold out Meg's Turf cork-tipped cigarettes. I just handed him the money. Meg sometimes sent me alone with the dogs to the butcher's shop to buy pigs' trotters or a rabbit and bones for the dogs.

Bernie kept chickens in the backyard and it became my job to feed them and collect the eggs. There were always a few clucky hens sitting on eggs that were about to hatch. Whenever this happened I ran into the house and pleaded with Mrs Harrington to come see the new brood and she always appeared just as excited as me.

We spent countless hours at Christine's house, innocently playing doctors and nurses, or mothers and fathers. Christine made a solemn promise that she would marry me one day and we could have our own children. Christine's mother, Mary, had recently given birth to a little girl and I asked her one day where babies came from. She just smiled and said, 'You can find them under a rose bush'.

'How do they get under a rose bush?' I asked.

'Oh the angels leave them there.'

'Any rose bush?'

'Usually outside the hospital,' she replied. 'That's why people go to the hospital to get their babies.'

Even more confused, I asked, 'Do the babies that people don't want go to the orphanage?'

She paused. 'Sometimes.'

So now I knew – there was something wrong with me. But that didn't make sense either. The Brothers and Sisters had always told us that we were orphans and that both our parents were dead: 'May Almighty God have mercy on their immortal souls,' I often parroted. I began to suspect the truth was that my parents weren't dead and that there was nothing wrong with me.

On Sunday mornings we walked up to the North Perth Benediction Monastery for mass. Mrs Harrington gave me a silver threepence to drop into the collection plate on its way around the congregation. This was the first time that I had been given money to give to someone else and I was very reluctant. With a stern look and wagging finger, she motioned to me to drop the money into the plate.

One Sunday, after mass, we visited a grand Federation-style house in Vincent Street where Bernie's mother, old Mrs Harrington, lay bedridden and close to death. We were met by Bernie's sister, Dorothy, who was caring for their mother. A few minutes later the priest arrived with his chalice to administer Holy Communion. We all knelt down and said the rosary and a few other prayers. The old lady showed a lot of interest in me and beckoned me to come close. Surprisingly strong given her frail condition, she reached out, took my wrist and pulled me forward. In a croaky voice she asked if I liked it at Clontarf (another Christian Brothers orphanage in Perth).

'No,' I said. 'I'm at Castledare.'

Ignoring this, she said, 'You are lucky to have the Brothers. The Brothers are very good to you poor children.'

As everybody told me this, including Bernie and Meg, I thought I was supposed to be grateful too.

Meg told me on the way home that the old lady was in her late 90s and didn't have long to live. She explained how fortunate the family was that Dorothy was looking after her mother and, to do so, had sacrificed a promising career in opera. She had even sung in London. Every Sunday after mass for the six weeks of the Christmas holidays I visited the old lady with the family to say prayers, stare at the walls and fidget until it was time to go home.

Christmas morning was the most exciting time I could remember. Father Christmas had come to the house during the night and left presents under the tree. Some of the parcels were addressed to me and I couldn't wait to open them. I was given games, colouring-in books, pencils and paints, storybooks, rubber balls and lots of clothing – shirts, pants, footwear and swimwear – and a beach towel. Mrs Harrington kept the clothing at home in Charles Street where I could wear it during the holidays. I was never allowed to take clothes back to Castledare for fear they might be confiscated or lost.

One day I met Dorothy's son Tex, who had inherited his mother's musical ability and become a country and western singer. He had a hit song 'On Our Selection' playing on a number of Perth's radio stations. Tex had a big Chrysler car with 'Tex Croft, country and western singer' painted on the side panels. For his hit the 'Chicken Yodel', which he wrote himself, he became the first West Australian to be awarded a record contract. His girlfriend, Mary, who he later married, was a vocalist at a dance-band nightclub. The pair met through the Dawn Lake and Bobby Limb 'Find a Star' competition.

I met Tex at his sister Mary's place, a few doors from where we lived in Charles Street. He was washing his Chrysler and asked me if I would help. As payment, he said he would give me every penny he had in his pocket. Unbeknown to me, he had changed some silver into pennies and, after the car was cleaned, gave me more money than I had ever seen before. It didn't matter that the coins were pennies – there were so many, I felt rich. I often washed his car after that – it was his way of giving me pocket money for the holidays. I spent a weekend with Tex and Mary at the family house near Little Trigg Beach. I was still extremely frightened of water, especially after my near drowning on the *Strathmore*, yet with Tex I felt safe. He taught me to swim and body surf.

One day just before the end of holidays, I spilt some oil while Sam was servicing his truck. He angrily gave me a backhander and I fled back to the Harrington's crying. Bernie demanded to know what happened. He stormed out of the house and returned a little later with his shirt torn to shreds. He was no match for Sam, but he was very protective and would not allow anyone to hurt his children.

All too soon the Christmas holidays ended and I was back at Castledare more miserable than before. Mrs Harrington wrote to say the old lady had died and that, as she had been so impressed with me, she left in her will 100 pounds, an enormous sum for those days – to Clontarf. How she expected this to benefit me was a mystery. I was disappointed – not a single shilling for me. I later discovered that the old lady was very wealthy, with property up and down Charles Street, houses in Bayswater and a big tract of land at Trigg, most of it right on the coast.

That March, for my eighth birthday, I received my first birthday card ever. As was customary, it had been opened and inspected.[1] It was signed 'With love from Mum and Dad and Robert and Margaret', with kisses and a lick each from Lassie and Tiger. I was promised a birthday present when I arrived home in May. I felt an overpowering surge of joy at being loved and wanted again.

Life at Castledare continued until the May holidays when I went back with the Harringtons. By now I had been encouraged to call them 'mum' and 'dad' and I was firmly part of the family, yet I began to feel slightly uneasy with Robert. He appeared not to like me anymore and no longer invited me to play with his mates or take me to their houses, ignoring me most of the time. He made fun of my English accent. For the first time I heard Bernie threaten his son Robert to improve his behaviour or else: 'If you're not careful I'll send you to Castledare where the Brothers will straighten you out,' he once said.

This threat was used nearly every holidays although Bernie never seriously considered it.

Margaret continued to be my constant friend and companion. We were inseparable. I met more of Margaret's friends and we played at their houses. Meg was an usherette at His Majesty's Theatre and was able to acquire free passes for pantomimes, movies and plays, so Margaret and I often went to the theatre.

I missed the following Christmas holidays in 1955 with the Harringtons. Meg's sister and her husband, who was stationed in New Guinea, were coming to stay with the family over Christmas. I was very disappointed but the Brothers found another place for me.

The O'Brien family owned and ran the Court Hotel in Northbridge. Mrs O'Brien drove down to St Georges Terrace in a big Mercedes to pick me up at the truck stop. She was heavily pregnant. We walked to her big car parked off the street and, after she opened the door, she began to cry almost hysterically, holding my head tightly against her swollen stomach. This made me feel strange and uncomfortable – I'd never seen an adult cry before.

The following day, after inspecting the meagre contents of my suitcase, she took me to Aherns department store in the city and bought me several outfits, sandals, shoes and socks. I was the smartest dressed child in Perth with new colourful Hawaiian shirts.

The O'Briens had two children: a boy and girl, both older than me. I don't recall having much to do with them. With typical sibling rivalry they seemed to argue a lot. We enjoyed sneaking out of our bedrooms on the weekend nights to watch, through the rails at the top of the stairs, people dance to the live jazz band in the beer garden.

In the morning the beer garden would be awash with empty beer jugs and broken glasses scattered around the messy tables. If I came downstairs early in the morning, there was a treasure trove of coins left on the ground. The yard man, a foreigner who spoke poor English, smiled and encouraged me to look for the coins. I didn't realise then that this was his territory and his money to find.

The Court Hotel's main lounge contained a grand piano, and I spent countless hours tinkling when the room was empty, learning some basic chords and coming to love the piano. I had free access to the bar, and the staff were always ready to pour me a squash or some other drink I fancied.

Many of the male patrons were missing arms and legs. I was unaware that they were victims of the Great War and the more recent World War II, and that drinking was how they dealt with their memories. I felt scared and uncomfortable and avoided talking to these laughing larrikins who spent the day drunk and loud. I saw the police take some of them away, still protesting, for being drunk and disorderly.

Across from the pub was the Perth Museum. It was free to enter and whenever I was bored I wandered up and down the stairs checking out the amazing stuffed animals, birds and insects. The great blue whale skeleton was my favourite exhibit. In awe at its size, I could imagine Jonah making his home in the whale's belly. Sometimes I was completely alone in the museum and one of the attendants I got to know would say, 'I'll take you to the big cats, John, and we can talk about them today'. I learned more staying at the pub for the holidays than I did during that entire year at school.

About a week before Christmas, Mrs O'Brien took me to the toy section at Boans department store, where I sat on Father Christmas's knee for the first time. Whispering in my ear, he asked what I would like for Christmas. I whispered back, pointing to what was probably one of the most expensive and popular items in the store – a bright red scooter – not thinking for a moment that he would take it seriously. To my surprise, on Christmas morning under the tree was an expensive bright red scooter, the one I had pointed out in the toy department. I was thrilled and had no reason whatsoever after that to doubt the existence of Father Christmas here in Australia. There was magic, after all – you just had to believe in it. Father Christmas existed and, like the story said, arrived on time in every place across the nation to bring toys, gifts, happiness and goodwill to all the boys and girls.

I wasn't convinced about the tooth fairy though. I had proved for a fact during the previous August that the tooth fairy never went to Castledare. But during the May holidays in 1955, some of my baby teeth at the front had come out. Mrs Harrington had put the teeth in a glass of water and sat it on top of the cupboard. She said the tooth fairy would come at night and give me sixpence for each tooth. She was right – it happened in Charles Street. When I tried it later at Castledare, the tooth was still in the glass and there was no money. I desperately wanted to believe in the tooth fairy, but I was now nine years old and doubts were beginning to trouble me. Other children in the orphanage were telling me it was all a load of rubbish, but whenever I asked Mrs Harrington, she hugged me and said that I must continue believing.

With my new red scooter I was now quite mobile and could go anywhere I liked. I discovered Charles Street was quite near to the pub so I regularly scootered across to the Harringtons to play with Margaret, Lassie and Tiger, who were always excited to see me.

The O'Briens had a big car and we all travelled to Bunbury for a few days. I became terribly carsick during the journey and we had to stop a few times to let me out. This was the first time I had seen the Australian countryside and the size of the country was daunting. We spent our time mainly swimming and visiting friends of the family.

One day some friends of the O'Briens visited the pub. A youngish couple, they took me out for the day and we went to a fair where I won some toys and then to the movies. The next day the young woman asked if I would like to be adopted by her and her husband. I had talked to Mrs O'Brien about my family in Southampton and how much I missed England and how I hated Castledare and Australia. The couple said I would need to spend the next holidays with them so we could get to know each other. This thought distressed me greatly and the next day I spent the whole day with the Harringtons, who I loved. The thought of losing them was unbearable. When I got back to the pub I told Mrs O'Brien a lie that I hoped would come true: the Harringtons were going to adopt me. I never saw the young couple again.

The O'Brien children told me about a rude painting hanging in their father's office, which was completely out of bounds and always locked. One day, I noticed the door slightly ajar so I quietly entered and saw a red satin curtain covering a painting behind his desk. I drew the curtain and there was a portrait of a beautiful naked girl, the first I had ever seen. I bolted at once from his office and ran to my room thinking I had just committed a mortal sin.

All too soon my Christmas holiday with the O'Brien family at the Court Hotel came to an end. Mrs O'Brien insisted that she drive me and my red scooter to Castledare with my case packed with new clothes. The next day my scooter disappeared, stolen I was told by a boy seen riding away. And none of my bright-coloured shirts made it out of the laundry. Still I had wonderful memories of the O'Brien family, although I never saw them again.

In 1957 a great change happened at Castledare. A warm-hearted Irish woman and a qualified nurse, Matron Kelly, was appointed, probably in response to the Home Office Ross Report of the previous year that had criticised Castledare for having too few female carers. Her motherly nature attracted children to her like bees to a flower. She gave her love and compassion freely and, for the first time, we had someone in the orphanage as close to a mother as we would ever have. We could relate to her, talk to her, be hugged by her and be believed by her. She took particular interest in those children who had no holiday family and no love in their lives.

Before long there was a noticeable change in the quality and variety of food: it became a little more nutritious and palatable. The corporal punishment was less harsh and the strap was used less often. Matron Kelly was having an influence in other areas too. Flyspray was being used to control the mosquito population, wooden seats were installed on the porcelain toilet bowls in the new toilet block and our general health was improving. It was obvious she was having an effect and that the administration was taking note of her recommendations.

In mid 1957, I began wondering where they might send me after Castledare. I was ten, had almost completed grade four and was nearing my time to move on. Some of the children were being sent to Clontarf, which had a fearsome reputation as being much tougher than Castledare. Clontarf's principal was a man nicknamed 'Killer Doyle' by the children. It was said that some of the other Brothers were just as bad. Other children would be sent to Tardun, an orphanage 480 kilometres north of Perth, so remote that we knew nothing about it.

Yet others would be sent to Bindoon, even tougher than Clontarf, and once used as a part-time correctional facility for 'juvenile delinquents'. We knew some children there from Castledare and once a year saw them on an annual picnic where they told horrific stories about the treatment they received and pleaded with us not to be sent there – as though we had a choice.

I had seen the enormous, intimidating buildings at Bindoon that some children claimed they helped build from local stone. Neither friendly nor homely, they seemed built to terrify children rather than to house them. In my young mind I imagined the witch's oven from Hansel and Gretel hidden somewhere beneath Bindoon's cold concrete floors. These massive buildings, built with stone the same colour as the earth, seemed to be a testament to the stories of beatings and cruelty, sombre stories about the owners of the little hands that had placed the stones in the wall.

I began to fret about my future and was again filled with fear and loathing. As in England, I lost my appetite and could hardly eat anything. Though I hated Castledare at least I knew its limits and boundaries. I worried about the beatings the boys so often spoke about in the other institutions.

Midway through 1957, Brother Thomas from Tardun arrived at Castledare. He only stayed a couple of days, but in that time we learnt enough about Tardun to make us all want to go there. The Tardun that Brother Thomas described was a vast farm with sheep, cattle, pigs, horses, kangaroos, rabbits and birds of all descriptions. Unlike so many of the Brothers, he didn't talk down to us. He was a tall, handsome man with a dark complexion. Gentle, humble, always laughing and smiling, he genuinely seemed to like us. He took us swimming in the river and invented games for us to play. He was different from any other Brother and he allowed us to act and play like children. We all felt safe with him. During his short stay, we followed him around as if he was the

Pied Piper of Hamlin. He was the first deeply religious person I had met who also had strong human virtues.

Christmas with the Harringtons in 1957 was memorable for many reasons. Mrs Harrington had written to say that Tiger had given birth to six pups and I couldn't wait to see them. Margaret and I spent many hours each day playing with the six-week-old puppies until Meg found a home for them.

Later Meg brought me a new beach towel and bathers and I spent a few days of the holiday with the Nicholi family at Scarborough Beach in a rented house close to the water where we went swimming and surfing every day. Their son Victor, who was around seventeen, was in charge of Paula, Roberta and me, especially when we went swimming. He seemed to know a lot of girls on the beach. Big, strong and good-looking, he attracted the girls and spent a lot of time kissing them. At first I thought he had many good-looking girlfriends who were really pleased to see him each time, but with all that kissing I figured there was probably another agenda, though what exactly I couldn't be sure.

During one of his beach-towel kissing sessions I was caught in a rip and was swept out to sea. I yelled as loudly as I could and one of his sisters sounded the alert. Victor, who was also a strong swimmer, sprinted along the beach, dived into the water and rescued me before I became too distressed. He was now my new hero.

He took me, and his girlfriends, to the 'Snake Pit', a venue for the latest craze, rock'n'roll. I watched Bodgies and their Widgie girlfriends jiving to Elvis Presley's 'Hound Dog' and other numbers. Victor pointed out the 'Galaxy Boys' (plain-clothes policemen) driving around in their Ford Galaxy cars, keeping order. Despite warnings from Castledare that we should avoid this new evil, I found the occasion exhilarating. I'd never seen people having so much fun and my only regret was being too young and small to take part.

Unfortunately, the last part of the holiday was memorable for all the wrong reasons. Margaret had become friendly with the milkman, who drove a horse and cart and made daily deliveries in the neighbourhood. Like Margaret, I too had gone for many short rides on his cart down Charles Street. One day Margaret came running home distressed and crying. The milkman had assaulted her. Bernie flew into a rage yelling, 'The bastard! I'll kill the bastard!'

Bernie never had a car but he knew the route the milkman took and ran down the road after his cart. What took place after Bernie caught up with the cart I don't know, but he came back with a satisfied look on his face and said, 'I fixed the bastard, Meg. I fixed the bastard.' I never saw the man drive the cart again.

I returned from the Christmas holidays full of trepidation about my fate: Bindoon, Clontarf or Tardun? I feared them all, as I'd come to realise that the welfare of a child meant little to some of the people who had been entrusted to care for us and that the only person I could really rely on was myself.

As I approached the eleventh year of my life, my four years at Castledare seemed to have absorbed the entire time I'd been alive. Virtually forgotten were the happy times in England, and the brief shipboard life on the *Strathmore*, which seemed more than a lifetime ago. The first seven years of my life were like a blurred figment of my imagination. Those years in England were lived by a boy who had become a stranger. I was no longer thinking like a child and, in fact, I had virtually ceased acting like one soon after I left the protection of the Broom family. I was neither adult nor child, growing up too fast in my head, with my thoughts focused mainly on survival. Instead of a family upbringing and cowboys and Indians, I was getting savvier at surviving by the year. I knew that I would need to continue to be patient, play the game by the Brothers' rules, avoid trouble and, where possible, learn new skills from the children who coped the best. With any luck, by my sixteenth birthday when the Brothers couldn't keep me any longer, I would be able to face life on my own in the world – along with the help of the Harringtons.

Two days after we arrived back at Castledare at the end of the holidays, Brother O'Doherty asked us to sit at our old desks in the classroom. Unbeknown to us, the desks had been divided into three sections at the beginning of the year. With a thrust of his hand he pointed to each, saying: 'Clontarf, Bindoon, Tardun'. Just like that, our collective fates were sealed. It took a moment to sink in. I was in the Tardun group with eleven others, while 24 children were going to either Clontarf or Bindoon. We had been divided up in equal proportion like a chocolate cake and each orphanage was to get a share.

The room went eerily quiet, as everyone tried to absorb and make sense of the news. Some children put their heads down on the desk and began to weep; others just stared at the blackboard in front. I began to feel elated, almost as though I had won a prize. I knew Brother Thomas was at Tardun and that was some consolation. I couldn't imagine him beating a child, certainly not in the way I'd seen it happen at Castledare. I cast my eyes over the group with whom I would spend the rest of my childhood and couldn't see any friends.

At least I would be spared the trauma of Bindoon. In five years I would be sixteen and would be free of institution life. I dreamed I could fly like a bird to some distant shore where there was no authority, where I could live my life in dignity as an equal and accepted person, and my sad, humiliating past could be forgotten.

1   Censuring and destroying incoming mail was a common measure used by the Catholic Church to guard against family members or loved ones outside the orphanage system claiming back their children. Once in the system, a child tended to stay there – the government subsidies given to the church for care of orphans were a financial incentive to keep as many children in care as possible.

6

OTHER LOST SOULS

The boys who would come with me to Tardun had their own stories about their roots and the circumstances that had led them to Castledare, but we didn't really talk about our pasts, partly because none of us knew much about what had happened to us, but mainly because we were all in the same situation, focused on our own survival and suffering. Yet common threads linked many of these stories, as I was to find out as an adult.

In 1958 Peter was sent with me to Tardun, where we soon became good friends. I later found out his background from his file, one of a handful that had remained intact and included photos. Most of the others' files had either been destroyed or were non-existent. Peter's mother was a pretty 20-year-old waitress. She married a Canadian soldier, although she was pregnant to another man at the time. Her new husband didn't want the baby to be part of their family. Under Canadian law, Peter's mother could not be granted Canadian citizenship until Peter had been adopted into an English family, so preventing him from ending up as a child migrant.[1]

To expedite Peter's mother's immigration plans, the Canadian government accepted a written legal undertaking by Father Hudson's Society in Birmingham to care for Peter until he was adopted. The contract stipulated that the home would be responsible for Peter's maintenance and education, 'Until such time as he is legally adopted, becomes self-supporting or chargeable to the Local Authority'. An original copy of the document was sent to the Canadian Commissioner in London for safekeeping.

Now under the protection of the Canadian government, Peter was registered for adoption by the society. His mother visited him at the home for the next thirteen months and desperately wanted to take him to Canada with her. She wrote dozens of short letters to the administrator, asking to see her child: 'Dear Father Flint, could I have your kind permission to see my baby? I would be so very grateful if you would allow me this privilege.'

Eventually Peter was fostered into a loving family, the Wedgburys, who wanted to adopt him. Everything appeared to be going to plan. Unbeknown to his new family, Father Flint, breaking the agreement with the Canadian government, had registered Peter for child migration at Australia House when he was three years old. When he was five, Mrs Wedgbury became ill and returned Peter to the home until she recovered. She wrote to Father Flint: 'I do hope by now Peter is settling down with you once more. It was a great wrench to part with him, he is such a winsome little fellow and oh how we miss him.'

She would never see him again. Peter was sent to Australia when he was six while his foster mother was still recovering from illness. For the next five years she sent letters, presents and cards, but heard nothing. Peter had been swallowed up into a vast black hole.

She also wrote many letters to Father Flint demanding information about her boy. Father Flint was forced to write to Catholic authorities in Western Australia but his letters too were ignored. Mrs Wedgbury then launched a prodigious letter-writing campaign in search of the truth and asked that Peter be returned to her family forthwith. While she pleaded for his return, his orphanage in Australia was pleading for more children. In 1957, a frustrated Father Flint received a letter from Brother O'Doherty. Pressure from Catholic Immigration in Perth had forced his hand. O'Doherty began the letter: 'I have to state that he is here with us and doing very well at school. We will tell the lad to write a letter for Mrs Wedgbury, but you know what lads are at writing letters.' Peter did not receive a single letter or card of the many that Mrs Wedgbury had sent since Peter had arrived in Australia. He presumed that the family had abandoned him in 1952 and that was why they sent him away.

O'Doherty mentioned that his priority was building a new chapel, which he said was badly needed, although he didn't say why. He finished by reminding Father Flint of the main goal: 'Once again I would bring under your notice the fact that we have not nearly enough lads and would welcome another 30 or more.'

Even at Tardun, Mrs Wedgbury's mail was returned to England with 'address unknown' scrawled across the envelope. She suddenly stopped writing in 1966.

Jack was another friend at Castledare. His mother had placed him in the Father Hudson's Society home when he was one, as a temporary measure, until she could re-establish herself. She agreed to pay the home a weekly amount for the duration.[2] She kept her part of the agreement for a year and then the payments stopped. Later when she went back to fetch Jack, who was by now three years old, she was told that as she had stopped paying and as they hadn't heard from her for a year they assumed she had abandoned him so putting her son up for adoption. They reassured her that he was now with a good English family. As Father Hudson's Society was a registered adoption agency, Jack's mother did not think to question the outcome. However, Jack was still behind the walls of the orphanage, having been signed up to go to Australia.

Another of my mates, Des, was cast adrift because he became 'inconvenient'. His mother started an affair when he was four years old. She dropped him off with the Sisters of Nazareth in Belfast and he was put aboard the first available ship to Australia. Des, an only child, tracked down his elderly mother in 2002 and discovered that she was quite wealthy and owned two farming properties in Northern Ireland. His angry mother demanded he tell no-one in the village. A shattered Des got drunk that night and told everyone in the bar.

Jim, Des and Frank, also at Tardun, spent most of their lifetimes never knowing their family in Northern Ireland. Their mother had died, leaving eight children – four boys and four girls – in their father's care. As it was almost impossible for him to care for the children, the parish priest insisted that they be placed in the care of the Sisters of Nazareth in Belfast, who decided the boys, aged between six and fourteen, should go to Australia in 1957. The eldest boy ran away, staying behind with his four sisters. Their father had not given consent, a requirement at the time under British law, and no-one was concerned about the fact that the family had been broken up.

Don, another Belfast boy, was born out of wedlock and taken to a Sisters of Nazareth home. His parents soon married and began a family while he was still at the home. They had five more children. No attempt was made by anyone to return the boy to his family and he remained at the orphanage until he was old enough to be sent to Australia.

Tom, an orphan at Clontarf who I met later, told me he went looking for his family after he left the orphanage. He discovered that his younger brother had been at Clontarf at the same time as him, but his brother had a different surname so they did not make the connection. There are other stories of siblings growing up in the same institution but not being aware of it at the time. Mick had an older brother at Castledare with the same surname yet he was unaware of it until his brother was sent away.

Another mystery was Paddy, who was born in southern Ireland and raised in an orphanage outside Dublin until he was eight. He was smuggled across the border and placed with the nuns in Belfast before being put aboard a ship to Australia. Paddy was an Irish citizen and child migration was illegal in that country. All records of Paddy's stay in the Dublin orphanage have disappeared and he has no birth certificate. Paddy believes that his father was probably a Catholic priest: 'Why else would they break Irish law to get rid of me? I was illegally removed from Ireland.' The demolition of Paddy's past was so thorough that today he still doesn't know who he is or where he came from.

A young single mother agreed to temporarily give up her child to the care of the Sisters of Nazareth. As she was a nurse, she sought employment at the home so she could be close to her child. The Sisters employed her at a home over 30 kilometres away. Her father became seriously ill so she left the home to look after him until he died. Three months later the nuns told her that, as she had abandoned her child, they had no alternative but to keep him and to send him to Australia. In spite of the best efforts of a lawyer, she was unable to get her child back from Australia. She married and raised a family but was unable to forget her son and sank into deep depression. Thirty years later, she met her son, who forgave her after examining records showing how hard she had tried to keep him.

There are many stories, all of them different, and not all of them sad. I recall when I was a young adult meeting one of the nuns who had known me in England. She was pleased to see me and said in her Irish brogue, 'Isn't it grand to see you doing so well, John. Aren't you glad we sent you to Australia?' I just smiled and nodded in agreement. How could I know if I would have prospered had I stayed in England. Yet some child migrants do not doubt that the nuns gave them a new chance in life. Bill C. insists that the nuns in Britain made the best decision when they sent him and his brother to Australia. Bill became a very successful farmer and appreciates that he was given a start in life in a new country. Bill's story is not an exception – there are other child migrants who feel the same way.

However, many children who 'consented' to come to Australia were manipulated by the Sisters or Brothers into believing that Australia would be a land of milk and honey and fruit trees. They often discovered that reality did not live up to the promises. Bill Keith, sent to Tardun in 1939, tells his story:

> One day Brother Crean, a Christian Brother from Australia, came to Nazareth House and was showing us films and slides about Australia and then asked us kids who would like to go to Australia. We all simultaneously put our hands up. But they only chose a few of us, especially those who had brothers, so we could have someone close to us while in Australia. My brother Alec and I and four other boys were chosen.

> We arrived at Fremantle on the 21st March and they taxied us to Clontarf on the Canning River. We couldn't wait to get into that river. Imagine us with our lily white skin and the hot March Australian sun. We finished up with blisters as big as saucers. After three weeks at Clontarf we were taken to a place called Tardun, 300 miles north of Perth. This trip was made by train and all we saw was bush, bush and more bush. And gum trees.[3]

When it was our turn some 20 years later to go to Tardun we also discovered miles and miles of unchanging bush – just endless gum trees and scrub – punctuated only by the occasional tin shed. Fortunately the main buildings had all been constructed and Tardun was now a different place.

1   Canada banned child migration in 1933 after years of serious abuse of abandoned English children and was still smarting from the aftermath. Henceforth, Canada tried to protect children with connections to Canada, such as Peter had through his mother, from being part of any child migration scheme.

2   It was not unknown for voluntary organisations to 'double dip', asking sole parents to pay for their child's upkeep, while also taking government subsidies for the same child.

3   Bill Keith in David Plowman (ed.), *Our Home in the Bush: Tales of Tardun*, Tardun Old Boys Association, 1994, p. 21.

THE BUSH ORPHANAGE

We arrived at Tardun in mid February in 1958 on a hot dry morning. The train journey from Perth had taken fourteen hours, and it seemed that we had stopped at every grain storage shed along the railway line. When there was a pub nearby many travellers got off the train for a quick drink and returned with cartons of beer. We travelled all night and into the next day. The only drink for thirsty children was rainwater from the 50-litre canvas bag that hung and swayed between two carriages.

We were met in the morning at the Tardun railway siding by Brother Thomas in his red International 8-ton truck. He was dressed in navy blue overalls and looked very different from when we had met him the year before dressed in his black clerical outfit. We climbed aboard the back of the 'Red Inter', as the truck was called, and headed off to the orphanage, about 15 kilometres down the track. The drive from the Tardun siding to the orphanage along rough, dusty corrugated roads added another half an hour or so to our journey.

Before long, we could see the main building in the distance. It was enormous, like a brilliant creamy-white Taj Mahal in the middle of a sea of dark green scrub. It seemed a complete oddity, absurdly out of place in the featureless bush of the Australian landscape. Massive concrete pillars supported the top floor of the two-storey structure and the intimidating tower at the top.

I wondered what kind of authoritarian regime awaited me here. Brother Thomas ushered us into the dining room, where we were given a meal and something to drink. History repeated itself. In a moment we were surrounded by curious onlookers, big and small, some of whom I recognised as having been sent from Castledare the year before. They were all dressed differently in a variety of coloured shirts and not in the same drab clothing that was the uniform of orphans. Most of the children had no footwear. The clothing was not marked with degrading personal numbers, as it had been at Castledare, and, as I was to find out, the shower cubicles had curtains. In time, my sense of privacy and dignity would be restored.

Some of the big children looked pretty tough – just how tough, I would find out soon enough. The younger children we already knew from Castledare began giving us the 'need-to-know' information to help us survive: who were the good and bad Brothers, who were the bullies to avoid, what we could get away with if we were careful, how we could avoid work or getting caught having fun where we shouldn't be.

Many of the children liked it at Tardun, preferring it to other places they had been sent. There were, of course, a few boys who hated the place – along with hating the British for abandoning and betraying them, the nuns who raised them and the Brothers who would keep them to their sixteenth birthday. These boys fought every inch of the way, but most us were more ambivalent, preferring to stay the distance, to survive the experience and then to reinvent ourselves after we left.

Tardun's large estate had been given by the state government to the Christian Brothers in 1928. It was nothing but scrub, low trees and shrubs, and was divided up into 4000 and 5000 acre blocks, each named after a Christian Brother who had been involved in the early days of the scheme: Mulquiney, Heffernan, Kent, Geoghegan and even Castledare (the profits from this block financed its namesake in Perth). The rest of the blocks were named after previous owners who had gone bankrupt in earlier years, or after a physical attribute, hence Red Shed or White Hill.

The Tardun orphanage was known officially as St Mary's Tardun Farm School and locally as 'the school'. An isolated outpost in 1928, by 1958 new settlers were busily carving out farms on all sides of the school's 65 000 acres. Its location, 480 kilometres north of Perth, 140 kilometres directly east of Geraldton and 40 kilometres east of Mullewa, put the farm in an extremely marginal part of the Western Australian wheat belt, tucked away in the north-eastern corner. The buildings and infrastructure were still being developed, while the fencing, water drilling and land clearing were fully underway. There were approximately 70 to 80 boys, mainly British and Maltese[1], plus a handful of Australian children, when I arrived at Tardun in 1958.

Brother Thomas conducted primary school in one classroom, catering for grades four to seven. Brother Ackary taught high school in another room, catering for grades eight, nine and ten, and ran woodwork classes after school. Brother Synan (nicknamed 'Tiny') was responsible for ten or so working boys who lived in a separate wing of the main building. They were approaching sixteen and had either finished their education or, more likely, were unable to finish it and were passing their remaining time working on the school farm.

Another of Tiny's responsibilities was to fit children with footwear. He kept an old tea-chest full of second-hand shoes of different brands, types and sizes and none of them matched. The only concession was that they were black and had black laces. But we could only wear the shoes on special occasions – mostly we went barefoot.

The farm boys were six or so 'old boys' from Tardun, now young men in their early twenties. They lived in a hostel west of the main building. They were starting their own farms with help from the Brothers.

Tardun was a hive of activity the day we arrived. Working boys rode stockhorses through the school grounds on their way for a day of droving sheep. Utility vehicles came and went with rifles and ammunition casually scattered on the ledge behind the seat. The sheepdogs barked at the surly kangaroo dogs, or 'roo dogs' as they were known, who kept an eye on the yapping sheepdogs – both packs spoiling for the first chance at a fight. Noisy tractors fired up and wiry men in shorts wearing large hats and carrying canvas waterbags, which always needed topping up, passed through. There were men everywhere, young and old: everyone sweating, talking, yelling and in a hurry. It could have been a scene out of a western movie.

There were nine Christian Brothers: three were teachers and six were lay Brothers who ran the farm. The principal, Brother Quirke, was nicknamed 'Goozey' by the children. He earned this unsavoury epithet from his habit of noisily regurgitating phlegm in his throat at irregular intervals either to swallow it or spit it onto the ground. He was a large, quick-tempered and unpopular Irishman. His job was to run the piggery. Gruff and impatient, Brother Quirke regarded troublesome English children as beneath contempt – and the feeling was mutual. He didn't endear himself to us by angrily bellowing now and then: 'You should all be grateful! If it wasn't for the Brothers you'd still be naked in the gutter where we found you.' Most of the Brothers had nicknames, and the more obnoxious the Brother, the worse the nickname. Brother Ackary was simply known as 'Acky'. Brother Kelly was named 'Ned' – obviously. Brother Thomas, who had gained the respect of most of the children, was known as 'Tommy' or, on occasion, 'Rubberneck', probably because of his ability to catch us out.

There were three Presentation Sisters, two in the kitchen and one in the laundry. Mother Superior Lawrence was in charge of the convent and also attended to minor medical problems. Sister Aidan ran the kitchen with the help of Joe, a recently returned 'old boy', who, at seventeen, had come back after struggling with life outside the institution.

Sister Bridget was in charge of the laundry and lollies on Sunday mornings if anyone had any money. The only pocket money we could get reasonably easily was from killing 'vermin'. The state government paid a bounty of four shillings a head on emus, ten shillings for foxes, one shilling for wild goats and even more for dingoes (wild native dogs).

Within days after arrival, I found myself aboard the back of another 'Inter', this time a grey 3-ton truck driven by Brother Wright, on a goat-hunting expedition with some of the bigger children. We headed for Rowley's, a semi-developed property whose previous owners had gone broke long before. The Brothers had bought the land back from the bank at the cost of the debt Mr Rowley owed.

A big bushfire had swept across the property a few years before, leaving a vast plain of low-lying regenerating plants and shrubs, punctuated by long black sticks – what remained of the higher and thicker vegetation. The low scrub dotted with hundreds of brown metre-high white ants' nests did not provide much cover for wild goats and it wasn't long before an excited cry of 'Goats!' rang out.

I could see a small mob of 20 to 30, a mixture of 'nanny' and 'billy' goats, moving at a leisurely pace about half a kilometre away. Barefooted boys sprang off at once and bounded through the scrub, one eye on the goats, the other on the ground to avoid stepping on the many menacing spiky black sticks.

With their bellies full and bloated, the goats were on their way back from drinking at the sheep trough and could barely raise a trot. In no time at all we were among them, pushing, shoving, half riding them back towards the truck and steering them by their horns.

I managed to catch up with a couple of big children who were struggling with the biggest, meanest billygoat. It had a beard that fell almost to the ground. Long, lethal horns emerged at right angles from the skull and twisted to short, sharp sword-points. This fierce creature was foul-smelling and had angry eyes. It was going nowhere, digging in with its front feet and violently shoving its head from side to side in an attempt to jag some human flesh.

The boy sitting on its back calmly took a large knife from his leather sheath, said 'Bugger Goozey and his pigs!', and pulling back on the animal's chin, in a quick flourish of hand and steel slit the goat's throat, severing the jugular vein and bringing forth a crimson stream of blood, so much and so deep in colour that the entire ground soon appeared red.

I had never seen anything killed before nor had I heard an animal howl or bellow so like a human. I was petrified and instinctively thought it murder. Worse was the callous way the killer sawed off the tail with his knife and then cleaned the blade, casually wiping the blood on the dead goat's fur – as if he had done this kind of wanton killing many times before. Still somewhat in shock, I watched as the legs of all the captured goats were tied and they were hauled aboard the back of the truck.

'What happens now?' I asked the group at the front.

'We keep the tails. They're worth a shillin',' said Tony, a tall boy with thatched, wheat-blonde hair and a strong cockney accent.

'The pigs get the rest,' he laughed. 'We do a lot of killin' for a shillin'.'

About a dozen goats were caught that day and taken back alive to the piggery. I watched with morbid fascination as they were unceremoniously slaughtered, bellies slit open, tails cut off and carcasses fed to dozens of large, hairy multicoloured pigs, who squealed with delight at the fresh bloody feast of guts, flesh and bone.

Goozey relied to a large extent on a regular supply of goat, kangaroo and emu meat to supplement the 'slops', the leftovers and kitchen scraps, he fed to the pigs every day. Often a dozen dead emus arrived on the back of a local farmer's ute and were dumped in a heap on the ground. Petrol was poured over them and the birds set alight to burn off the feathers before being eaten by the pigs.

The pigs devoured all but hooves, pieces of horn and big bones. The bare stony ground in each pig yard was littered with bones bleached white by the burning sun. The dead trees surrounding the piggery stood like sentinels, their thin, naked limbs festooned with hundreds of noisy crows, gleaming like black opals in the sun. Evil open-mouthed birds panting with their wings half outstretched as though they were shedding heat waited patiently for the pigs to eat their fill and waddle off to sleep in the shade. The crows descended and gorged in a squabbling frenzy, feasting first on the eyes and then whatever fresh or rotting meat the pigs had left them. The image of the killing grounds, on a stony ridge of blood and bones, and the awful smell of decaying flesh, is imprinted in my memory.

Tardun was self-sufficient. Killing and butchering were just a part of life and, in time, I would learn how to kill and carve sheep, pigs, cattle, chickens and even wild rabbit. There were no supermarkets: our finest cuts of meat came from living breathing animals grazing in the paddock. I would come to view growing animals for human consumption as being little different to growing fruit or vegetables and, within a year at Tardun, I had become quite desensitised to watching the slaughter of animals.

I was now in trouble as I had gone on the goat hunt without Tommy's permission. It was customary for him to keep the new Castledare children together for at least their first six months at Tardun to protect us against all dangers until we found our feet. He strictly supervised our activities and kept an eye on us 24 hours a day.

We were all expected to work after school and religion still played a big part in our daily routine. There were prayers before school and meals. After morning mass, followed a breakfast of porridge and milk, bread and tea, then charges followed by class at 9 am sharp. The Tardun bell tolled loudly, so a child could never use the excuse 'I didn't hear the bell, sir' in his defence. At midday a bell was rung for the Angelus and everyone dropped to their knees to genuflect and pray. The day ended with Benediction and Rosary before sleep.

We addressed the Brothers as 'Sir' or 'Brother', while they used our surnames, although Tommy preferred to use our Christian names. After school we were divided into working parties. Some headed to the dairy to hand milk 30 shorthorn cows and separate the cream from the milk using a manual separator. Some picked rocks and stumps off the paddocks and put them into heaps. Others worked in Brother Kelly's vegetable garden, while the youngest stayed with Tommy, who kept them occupied with small tasks.

Tommy had installed a powerful loudspeaker system and his voice boomed across the school grounds. My first experience of this was one Saturday morning when he summoned us to gather in his classroom to organise working parties for the day. His address was followed by a short, sharp, cheeky announcement, 'Forkie! Firkie! Renie! Laundry!'

'Who are those kids?' I asked, puzzled at the way Tommy had made the announcement.

'They're the three rebels, always in strife,' replied one of the children. 'We had a Dorkie too, but he was sent back to the government.'

'Why?' I asked.

'He smashed a big rock on a Brother's leg and broke it.'

'Why?' I reiterated.

'Dunno, probably because of the hiding,' the child replied.

Forkie, or Patrick Faulkner, was an incarnation of Oliver Twist's 'artful dodger'. Nicknamed 'Percy' by Brother Howe, who ran the stock, by the age of twelve he was a natural-born scammer, schemer and rorter. With an instinctive gift for survival, he knew every trick in the book and invented a few more. With Firkie and Renie, he was 'doing time' in the laundry every Saturday.

Percy had a small gang of children he could rely on and vice versa. There were useful advantages in becoming a member of his gang. Ill-gotten gains such as stolen food from Sister Aidan's kitchen or Ned's garden would be shared out. Members took equal ownership of trapped birds – parrots, cockatoos and pigeons – kept in the gang's birdcage. The gang also shared ownership of the Alston camp (named after a make of windmill) 7 kilometres east of the school and one of the most popular playgrounds at the school. Beside the mill was a small, square concrete tank, which held nearly 23 000 litres of water. After we removed the odd dead crow or galah from the water, this became our swimming pool for the day. The gang gave its members protection against bullies and could provide alibis when required.

Two other children from Castledare and I joined Percy's gang. Loyalty was the only criteria for membership. Occasionally there were skirmishes if members of a rival gang muscled in on a bird-trapping territory or stole baby parrots or cockatoos from a hollow in a clearly marked York gum tree. Different gangs and individuals marked trees with a tomahawk, cutting a number or initial into the bark. It was important to protect the territory as hand-reared and trapped birds were a useful source of pocket money and could be readily sold to visitors. Of course, not every child joined a gang preferring to remain uncommitted. There were very few fights at Tardun and even fewer bullies, which was a great relief as this had concerned me greatly when I left Castledare.

Tommy encouraged 'bird nesting', especially for the little children who had difficulty finding the elusive nests. Success required knowledge of the bush, which had to be learnt. He often dropped off groups of children at likely nesting sites after school, telling us to be home by 5 pm. It was common to walk up to 10 kilometres back to the school.

Brother Quirke, who believed we should be working after school, sometimes followed the Red Inter at a discreet distance in his car, picking children up and taking them back to work at the piggery. Whenever we saw Quirke's car, we dived for cover among trees and bushes, watching as he slowly drove past, scanning the scrub for signs of us. He caught us completely off guard one day and drove six of us back to the piggery. Along the way he stopped near a newly constructed fence and asked if anyone knew the way through the bush to the new water tank and sheep trough. One of the boys said he knew so we all followed him on foot with Quirke at the rear. Suddenly, as one, we bolted, running away as fast as we could. We could hear Quirke in the distance cursing and yelling and promising a fate worse than death when we got back to the school. We split our sides laughing, imitating Quirke's threats, not realising just how much trouble we were in. We got the strap hard on each hand, delivered with relish and power by an angry Quirke, and were then made to miss the pictures.

On one occasion Quirke had wanted to give us the strap but couldn't. A small group of us were hiding in the boiler-room, smoking cane from an old chair. The heavy door had to be pulled up from the bottom with the help of heavy counterweights attached to steel ropes that came down from the ceiling. In his haste to spring us, the strong Irishman's hands became jammed between the handle and concrete surround at the top. We fled the room as he yelled in pain for someone to free his hands. We passed Joe, the kitchen hand, who was running in the opposite direction to help Quirke. That night we were summoned to his office. His strap was on the table. After a solid telling-off, he reached for his strap and then put it down gently. His swollen, heavily bandaged hands were too sore. He yelled for us to get out of his office, but he wasn't about to let us off. A couple of days later he made three of us walk behind the 200-litre slop bucket as he towed it up the hill with a tractor. We were destined for some hard labour at the piggery. Peter Scott, Paul Price and I dragged our feet as we reluctantly followed.

Quirke bellowed to keep up and I commented to the other boys, 'Quirke cares more about his pigs then he does for the kids.'

'Who said that?' he yelled as he stopped the tractor.

Astonishingly he had heard my comment above the noise of the engine. The three of us froze, as he unleashed a verbal cyclone. That night I was called to his office and he gave me two painful whacks with the strap on each hand, which made me cry in pain. All I knew was that some Brothers loved the power the strap had over the boys.

Each Brother at Tardun had a discrete area of responsibility and often more than one. Brother 'Ned' Kelly was the water driller: it was his job to find water, then to drill a bore and equip it with a windmill, pipes and pump. He had an ancient, towering percussion-drilling machine, 10 metres tall, with its own diesel engine mounted on a purpose-built chassis with four large rubber tyres. He pulled the massive machine around the farm with his tiny 30-horsepower Massey Ferguson tractor.

In 1958, the school was desperately short of water and we showered only once a week or when there was sufficient water in the tanks. The rest of the time we cleaned our hands and feet in a washbasin. To save water, only one of our bedsheets, as well as our trousers and shirts, could be washed on a weekly basis. Ned, who fancied himself an expert water diviner, was under the hammer to find more water since the main source at Tom's Well was insufficient to keep up with demand.

One Saturday afternoon he discovered a large supply close to his vegetable garden. He was ecstatic, as few people really believed in the power of water divining, decrying it as mumbo jumbo. I was fascinated. I could see the forked twig of the jam-tree sapling twist and turn down in the palm of his rough hands as he slowly crossed a water stream nearly 20 metres below the ground. When I tried, it worked for me too, although it didn't for everyone. Slowly walking through the bush with the forked sapling, he found another stream that intersected with the first a little higher up. He marked the exact spot with a rock and later drilled a bore, which yielded 27 000 litres a day. Ned found more water at Heffernan's block and, later, another stream near Tom's Well. Within a couple of months the school had enough water and there were no more restrictions. Ned found all our water this way, not only on the school property but also on neighbouring properties. He became famous locally for his water divining skills and rarely drilled a dry hole. When he did, it was usually because he had hit solid granite, which he refused to drill through, claiming it damaged the tip of his drill bits.

Ned was a jovial, sandal-wearing Friar Tuck type, with a shock of white hair, broad-rimmed glasses and a potbelly. When he laughed or sneezed, he thundered. He suffered from asthma so the Christian Brothers hierarchy in eastern Australia had sent him to the west where the dry air was good for his health. Ned's other responsibilities included making bread and pies in the bakery, looking after 300 or so laying hens and growing and supplying the entire school with a year-round supply of fresh vegetables.

He was also well known for his hunting skills and bushcraft. He had two large 'roo dogs', Teena and Sunta, that looked like greyhounds, which he took with us hunting on Sundays to catch a kangaroo to put in a stew for dinner. He called all of us 'little man', no matter what our size, and preferred using this to our names.

Ned was also responsible for overseeing the afternoon milking shift. Some 30 shorthorn dairy cows had to be milked, morning and evening, seven days a week. Each of us had to milk by hand at least one cow. At about 4.30 pm, we would all gather at the main gate and, on a signal, race through the gate to the dairy yelling out the name of a cow as we passed the post at breakneck speed. This system prevented us from physically fighting over the cows but led to the big boys milking the easiest cows. The most sought-after cow was quiet, never kicked, took little time to get into the pen and lock its head into the steel trap of the feeding trough and gave little milk. The little boys like me ended up struggling with a bad-tempered first-time mother whose calf had just been weaned and who was in no mood to be milked by a child. We used chains and leg ropes to prevent the cow from kicking us to kingdom come.

While the milking was taking place, a group of children in the separator room would remove the cream from the milk, using a hand-driven separator device. A small quantity of full-cream milk was kept for the Brothers, nuns and staff. The cream was made into butter for the staff, and we boys got the skim milk for our wheat porridge in the morning.

Brother Sullivan, nicknamed the 'Old Man', ran the main farm, seeding, fallowing and harvesting the land. Most of his equipment was antiquated, especially the AL and GL Harvesters, which were designed to be pulled by a team of horses or a tractor. About five of these machines were the mainstay of the harvesting equipment. Their tiny grain boxes held seven bags of wheat, which had to be physically emptied into sacks and lined four abreast in rows of more than 100 metres. It was backbreaking work, as the 90 kilogram wheat bags had to be loaded from the ground into a steel bin on the back of a truck.

The seeding equipment was hardly better, most of it having been designed and built just before and after the war. The diesel International Super Six and AW7 tractors were reasonably modern and five of these, along with two D4 caterpillar tractors, did the bulk of the work.

Though he was still relatively young, Brother Sullivan's weathered face looked old from years of working outside. He ran a team of working boys who drove the tractors, while he fixed the breakdowns. Quiet and introspective, he had little to do with us, although he liked watching us play competitive football against outside teams. Like some of the other Brothers he was deeply religious and kept to himself after work.

Brother Howe was stock manager and was responsible for the dairy and care of the horses, cattle and sheep, the slaughtering and butchering of cows and sheep for local consumption and the fencing. For some strange reason, Ned took care of killing the pigs. Brother Howe's flock of 6000 Bungaree Merino sheep was the mainstay of our wool operation. He also took charge of football and cricket, coaching and organising games between us and other schools. Though a little eccentric, Brother Howe probably had the most even temperament of all the monks. Forever wearing a slightly silly grin, he couldn't be moved any faster than the pace he chose. He wore a black hat and dustcoat and his mannerisms led us to believe that he was older then he really was. Nicknamed 'Goofy', he was popular with the children, as was his working party after school and on Saturdays when he taught horse-riding, droving skills, sheep husbandry, fencing and aspects of shearing, crutching[2] and maintenance in the shearing shed.

Brother Howe had two sheep dogs, Shadow and Tip, short for Tiparosa. Unlike the other Brothers, who lived upstairs in special quarters, he lived alone in a two-room cement-brick building near the workshops.

He had a permanent staff of two young monks – Brother Wright and Brother Campbell – and two or three working boys. He drove an early 1950s Dodge ute at a leisurely pace around the farm. He referred to us as 'boy': 'Boy, pick that up' or 'Boy, fill the waterbag.'

Once he asked a couple of older boys to show him their teeth. He was recruiting for lamb marking, which involved removing the lambs' testicles. A small incision was made at the top of the scrotum and the testicles were drawn out by the teeth. This process was common in Australia in those days as it was said to be the most hygienic method and so reduced the losses of lambs.[3]

The only time I saw Howe lose his legendary cool was over cruelty to horses. Horses had to be washed, groomed and fed after a day's work droving sheep. They weren't allowed to be galloped home after a hard day, and there were no exceptions to this. Horses had to be walked over rocky paddocks: no trotting, no cantering, no excuse. If we were caught breaking any of these rules we could expect the strap, although he never lost his temper dishing it out. As well, he gave us a choice: the strap on the hands or miss the pictures. Most opted for the strap – he didn't hit too hard. Brother Howe kept the saddles locked away and we could only use them when droving, so most of us became efficient bareback riders. Some of the children developed amazing skills.

The horses at the school were much-loved members of the family and all the children had their favourites. Of the ponies, easily everyone's favourite was a creamy white mare named Spot. She was willing and speedy and didn't have a bad bone in her body. She loved to gallop and race against the other ponies. Baya, a pretty bay mare, was slightly faster than Spot, and was reasonably friendly but had a nasty streak. On a bad day she would race under the limb of a tree to dislodge her rider. Nugget, once black but now a grey mare, was plain lazy and had little ability to gallop. She was so quiet that three boys could ride her at once, slide down her backside and safely walk in, around and under her legs without being kicked. Mousey, the smallest, was far and away the worst of the ponies. She kicked, bucked, bit and had a very bad attitude. Only the more experienced riders took her out. I once saw Mousey literally climb over the rails of the horse yard to escape. I also saw her roll over to dislodge her rider.

Among the stockhorses was Smoky, a large ageing gelding who was extremely quiet, cunning and hard to convince to trot let alone canter or gallop. He hung around the horse yards, waiting for someone to ride him down to the paddock to bring in the dairy herd twice a day, after which he would get half a bucket of oats for his trouble. Smoky was an old hand with the dairy herd and had been droving the cows for years. We took it in turns to ride him to bring in the herd. It wasn't always necessary to use a bridle and often two or three of us climbed aboard bareback, hanging on to Smoky's mane and each other. It didn't matter as he would stop if anyone fell off. Sometimes he would lunge at a troublesome young heifer without warning and bite her on the backside. This was enough to dislodge inexperienced bareback riders. He did all the thinking and all the droving until the cows were in. Then he would canter or gallop back to the yards, his mind firmly focused on oats. He took us for a ride and never the other way around.

Ranger, Brumby, Fairy and old Baldy were typical Australian stockhorses and did the bulk of sheep work around the farm. Princess, a jet-black thoroughbred, was considered dangerous and no-one could ride her. She was allowed to remain just for her size, strength and beauty.

During an incident at the horse yards I first met John L., a local shearer, who often gave his time on weekends to shear stragglers for Brother Howe or to teach bigger children to slaughter and butcher sheep. He was officially registered in Australia as John Leslie Sullivan but it turned out that his real name was actually John Patrick Francis O'Sullivan.[4] In later years, he would use this to his advantage. Brother Howe nicknamed him 'John L.' after the famous Irish boxer and the name stuck. I had noticed some of the bigger children run down to the horse yards during morning and afternoon 'piece' breaks to get in a quick ride before school resumed. Spot was always available and easy to catch, so I made my move. Not finding a bridle, I quickly fashioned a halter of sorts from twine, threw it over her head and took off like the wind straight down the fence line. I could see the dust from Quirke's car as it came toward me along the main road. He stopped the car, climbed through the fence, took his hat off and held it out in his hand to stop us. But there was no chance – Spot, in a particularly frisky mood, bolted. Quirke dived back through the fence to save himself as the horse thundered passed. I could hear the curses and threats as I hung on to

Spot's generous mane until she pulled up at the back fence. I knew I was in deep trouble and I was trembling as I walked Spot back to the horse yards, where Quirke was waiting with a bridle swinging in his hands. Menacingly, he walked towards me and said 'So this is what you couldn't find'.

Suddenly John L. appeared from out of nowhere. He had seen everything. Stuttering badly as he always did when excited, he said, 'B-b-brother, w-wait, it's not his fault. It's the b-b-big kids, they h-hide the bridles'. Quirke liked John L. so he just turned to me and yelled, 'Get the hell out of here before I give you a hiding!' I sprinted like a startled rabbit back to Tommy's classroom where I got two solid whacks with the strap on the hands for being 20 minutes late. But John L. had saved me from being whipped by a bridle by arriving in the nick of time.

John L. grew up at Clontarf and it was likely that there he had developed his bad stutter. He said Clontarf had been pretty bad, but he never talked about it in detail. He spent his last couple of years at Tardun and after he left, he joined the army for a couple of years and then worked in abattoirs in Queensland. He came back west, learned to shear sheep and worked in sheds all around Mullewa. By the age of 20, he was pretty much the larrikin, often in trouble with police. He was liked and disliked in equal measure, depending on who you talked to and whether they had been a victim of his acid tongue. With enormous irreverence for authority of all kinds, John L. poked fun at what he saw was the hypocrisy in church and government, and at farmers he thought were too big for their boots. A cynic through and through, he was nonetheless genuinely liked by fellow eccentric Brother Howe and they got along well. John L. was also good friends with Brother Campbell, and the pair were often seen together telling jokes and carrying on. The other Brothers he tolerated and those he considered bullies towards the children, he disliked intensely.

Despite his stutter, John L.'s wit was sharp and legendary. It just didn't pay to be at the end of one of his deadly cruel, incredibly funny one-liners, which were quoted, complete with stutter, to howls of laughter inside and outside shearing sheds all over the district. Of a well-known and highly respected farmer who often visited the school, he said, 'His head is that far up his arse he's going to have to l-l-l-loosen his tie!'

For us, John L. was a link to the outside world and he would often sneak in contraband such as magazines, smokes and beer. Quirke forbade alcohol, although some of the Brothers enjoyed a drink. There was great commotion one night after Tommy had shut down the generators. From the dormitory window we could hear Quirke shouting at the top of his voice, while holding a torch, 'Hold it! Hold it there!'

Silhouetted in the half light below stood John L. with a large bottle of beer in one hand. Dangling on a string was another bottle, shining like a brown crystal in the torchlight, being hauled up by Brother Campbell. Quirke was roaring like an angry bull while John L. panicked, stuttering and stumbling over words searching for an excuse: 'B-b-b-Brother the k-k-kids h-hid some beer upstairs and we w-w-were getting rid of it.'

Quirke yelled even more loudly, 'You weren't letting it down, you were hauling it up!'

Hearing John L.'s pitiful excuse from our dormitory, we fell over ourselves laughing, while Tommy was running around trying to get us all back into bed. The story of the dangling beer bottle was embellished and spread far and wide. John L. laughed the loudest, helping the yarn grow arms and legs.

Quirke had his quarters in the tower above the main building, where he enjoyed 360-degree views of the vast property. In 1957 someone had broken in to his quarters and stolen his cigars. The usual suspects – Ferkie, Forkie, Rennie and Dorkie, plus a couple of others – were summoned for interrogation. Dire threats of the severest punishment could never dislodge the truth from this tough bunch. But this time they were innocent except for one, so Quirke devised a new strategy. Sitting the boys on a bench outside his office, he lit a cigar in front of them. Drawing back on his smoke he offered the cigar to the first boy and asked his opinion. Puzzled by Quirke's bizarre behaviour, the first boy coughed in disgust at the repugnant smell. 'Hand it on to the next boy,' Quirke said. He keenly watched each boy's reaction. Finally it got to Dorkie, who inhaled like a true professional, clearly enjoying the sweet aroma of the cigar. 'A beautiful cigar, Brother,' he said as he inhaled for the second time. Quirke knew he had his man. This was the first warning story I had been told when I arrived at Tardun.

Clearly visible from the main building, about 13 kilometres directly south of the school, was our immediate neighbour, the Pallottine

Mission. This was run by a German Catholic missionary organisation, caring for around 80 to 90 mainly half-caste Aboriginal boys and girls who had been removed from their families by the government. They were housed in ex-army barracks made of weatherboard and asbestos sheet with a corrugated steel roof. One of the German priests drove over to Tardun to say mass every morning at the school.

The mission had a large farm of some 16 000 acres and, like Tardun, was busy fencing and clearing, struggling to make a farm out of the Australian bush. Ironically, the Aboriginal children, who would become known as the 'Stolen Generation', and us, the 'Lost Children of the Empire', were separated by a boundary fence of just six plain wires with one barbed wire on top.

It was common knowledge that the mission had once owned Ned's dogs, Teena and Sunta, but they were biting children and had to be got rid of, so Ned got hold of them. Teena had a vicious streak – snappy and cantankerous, she often bit us as well.

An Aboriginal camp existed nearby on the outskirts of the Mullewa township. I first saw it from the back of Tommy's Inter in early 1958. Houses were made from pieces of tin sheet hammered or wired together against twisted wooden frames. Old wheat bags fluttering in the breeze covered doors and windows. There was no running water or decent ablution facilities. It was a pitiful tin-and-bag village of despair. The residents waved or mostly stared with empty eyes when they saw us pass by. I was aware of the unhappy comparison: where we had hope, they had none. The sight of such human misery made it easy to stop feeling sorry for myself. Compared to this, our little village at the Alston camp was luxury living. These people had lost their land, their children, their rights and their dignity. They had been herded off their land into an abysmal reserve to exist in embarrassing squalor by the side of the main road where all could see. It was impossible not to be moved by this every time we drove past.

1   The Catholic Church began recruiting Maltese boys and some girls in 1950, but by 1959 the numbers had reduced to a trickle. In 1959, a proposal to recruit Italian children had been approved by the Commonwealth and the Western Australian government. In response to inquiries from the Catholic Church in Perth, Italian Catholic authorities were willing to make the first 100 children available. There was no mention about how these children, who could not speak or write English, might be raised and educated. The authorities in Perth decided 30 would go to Clontarf and 70 to Bindoon. Unlike the British government, however, the Italian government was reluctant to provide a subsidy for the care of its children. The state government used this as an opportunity to temporarily withdraw its subsidy for British children, claiming it had borne an unfair burden over many years. It threatened that unless the Commonwealth increase its payments to the state, it would not support Italian immigration. The stand-off between the Commonwealth and state government brought Italian child migration to a halt. Without financial support from Italy or Western Australia, the proposal ultimately failed and no children were sent from Italy.

2   Crutching involves removing wool from the sheep's genital region to keep the area free from blowfly strike. Blowflies 'strike' the sheep, laying their eggs, which hatch into maggots, the secretions from which can eventually kill the animal if left untreated.

3   This practice continued until the more humane elastrator ring, a small rubber ring placed over the testicles cutting off the blood supply, was developed. In a few weeks the dried-up organ falls to the ground leaving the lamb totally unaffected.

4   Records of children's names, ages and birthdays were often wrong. It seemed that some Catholic organisations were determined to erase a child's personal history, often preventing them from finding their parents and siblings.

8
TOMMY'S CLASS

There were approximately 40 children ranging in age from ten to fourteen years in fourth grade to seventh grade in Tommy's primary classroom in 1958. I was put in grade five and was seated near a big fourteen-year-old Maltese boy who was having difficulty with English. It became my job to help him with his reading. The standard text for reading was the Dick and Dora book series.

While Tommy read aloud, I would point out each word and the Maltese boy then repeated it. Sometimes he became frustrated and bad-tempered, refusing to cooperate and deliberately saying 'cat' when I pointed to a picture of a dog. When he was in this mood I rarely disagreed and said 'Correct!'

Twelve months after I arrived at Tardun, the Child Welfare Department conducted an IQ test at random on approximately half the children. Of the 29 Tardun boys surveyed, none were described as bright, one was above-average, seven were average, nine below-average and twelve described as dull. The results from other institutions ranged from Fairbridge Farm School at Pinjarra, easily the best, to Bindoon, easily the worst.[1] The IQ tests were conducted as part of an examination as to why a disproportionate number of Bindoon boys were appearing before the Children's Court.[2]

Sometimes when a boy got out of hand in Tommy's classroom he would use the threat of Bindoon: 'Want to go to Bindoon, sonny?' None of us relished the prospect of a stretch in Catholic 'Siberia' and the threat was enough to concentrate the mind. Tommy must have known that by using this threat, he was also admitting that there was something very wrong at Bindoon.

Occasionally, if a child was playing up badly, Tommy strapped him on the backside through his cotton trousers. To avoid humiliating a boy in front of his classmates, he took him to the metalwork room, where two or three appointed witnesses observed the punishment. Even with the door closed, we could still hear the student wailing.

In early May 1958 I suffered a shoulder injury after falling from the back of a truck and was taken to St John of God Hospital in Geraldton. Brother Quirke drove me to Mullewa and Reverend Dean Lynch, the local Catholic parish priest, drove me the rest of the way. Father Lynch was a popular character in the town. He ran the annual Mullewa Cup, the biggest day of the year, in which quite a few of the local farmers entered their racehorses. Mullewa in those days was on the main racing carnival circuit that included towns like Mount Magnet, Cue, Meekatharra and Yalgoo. Reverend Lynch loved a drink and sipped on a bottle of wine hidden in a woollen sock all the way to the hospital and, ten days later, all the way back.

The first couple of days in hospital were rather lonely until one of the cleaning ladies heard about the Tardun boy and came to visit. She was a Maltese woman and her sons, David and Jim, were also at Tardun. She came every day, bringing comics books, biscuits and homemade cake. She made such a fuss of me that I didn't want to leave.

After a couple of months at Tardun, I had become a little less frightened of authority and often wandered off alone through the bush to admire the abundant wildflowers and shrubs. I came to love the bush and it was becoming my refuge: no-one could find me or threaten me there. The freedom I craved I partly found among the birds and animals.

Compared to what I'd been used to, there was enormous liberty at Tardun and this was helping me change the way I thought about myself. A lot of the boys simply laughed and made light of their situation and this attitude was infectious. Displaying outright defiance and little fear, some of the boys took 'six of the best' on their hands, showing no emotion or pain. This infuriated the Brother dishing out the punishment, but witnessing this courage and defiance was having a positive effect on me.

The cut and thrust of life in Tommy's classroom was also having a good influence. He was an unorthodox teacher who allowed students to engage him in debate and dispute his point of view. This was a radical departure from the classroom at Castledare where talking back to the teacher was regarded as seriously disrespectful and punishment was swift and painful. Here Tommy encouraged it, deliberately drawing out a response from even the most frightened and timid child. This was his way of reaching out to these children. He seemed to know what the children were going through and in this way drew some venom from their wounds.

Tommy was a brilliant orator. He often spoke about the persecution of religion in Communist countries – his pet hate was communism and all its evils. America was the 'good guy', the knight in shining armour in the front line of our defence, and Tommy spoke admiringly of President Eisenhower, believing the future of the free world was in his hands. He demonised the Russian premiers Khrushchev and Stalin before him. He talked so enthusiastically that we would sometimes miss an entire maths session, which was just fine as few of us enjoyed the subject. He also talked just as passionately about new advances in science, once predicting that science would find a cure for cancer in ten years.

Aside from teaching, Tommy had numerous other responsibilities. His day began in the engine room before 6 am, starting one of the two International diesel generators, which he also serviced and maintained, that had been donated by the Lotteries Commission. After starting the generator, he went back to the dormitories to get children up and ready for mass. He then supervised breakfast and our charges. After morning school he supervised lunch and, after school, various working parties, then showers, dinner and night study in both classrooms.

Tommy never slept in his bed, preferring instead to nod off in a cane chair he claimed was better for his back. He slept barely three hours a day and was a workaholic. When not sleeping or otherwise occupied, he could be found in the metalwork room, designing new models to teach or rewiring a faulty power line, or praying in the chapel.

The Brothers at Tardun, as elsewhere in the institutions, were not trained in childcare and some, like Quirke, were unsuited to caring for disturbed children, often doing more harm than good. Quirke was a fine teacher and a brilliant administrator. He too believed that the children in his care were genuine orphans in need of Christian charity. However, too many years with 'defiant' children had hardened his heart and he rarely experienced gratitude from us. Quirke's remarks often inflamed the feelings of children who already felt that the lottery of life had delivered a very dodgy deal. Joe G. recalled the day he left the school in 1956, crying and in a state of despair. Quirke, who had found some *Pix* magazines under Joe's mattress, yelled in a booming voice from the balcony 'Good riddance to bad rubbish!' as the truck carried Joe away from his childhood friends for the last time.

One day Quirke gathered us all into Brother Thomas's classroom to sing for Irish visitors, a couple of whom were his relatives. The Tardun Boys' Choir was well known – with Tommy as choirmaster we had come second in Perth's annual Eisteddfod. Tommy was absent that day, so Quirke was taking a serious risk as we had little respect for him. Looking positively benign, he walked into the classroom with arms outstretched and wearing a broad smile. He said, 'Now I want you all to sing that lovely Irish melody, in your best singing voices please, for our very good friends here, "When Irish Eyes are Smiling". One, two, three!'

The choir murdered the song. Humiliated, Quirke stormed out of the classroom with his visitors amid howls of laughter and hoots and whistles. Moments later he re-entered the room in a rage, took from his pocket a ten pound note and waved it around, thundering 'Today I was going to spend this on you. Now you'll get nothing but work. We should have left you where we found you – in the gutter!'

A lot of the choir were still angry with Quirke because, the year before, he had shot their pet donkey. Many of the children had pet birds or animals – white cockatoos, galahs, joey kangaroos, rabbits and goats – but the donkey had been hard won, and there was still a lot of bad blood towards Quirke over its death. Tommy had taken the children out on the Red Inter on a goat hunt beyond Rowley's to Fitzgerald's, known as 'Fitzies', another property the Brothers bought from the bank by paying off the debt. The children spotted a wild donkey moving through the bush and gave chase. The property was surrounded by an unusually high-quality boundary fence, trapping the donkey in a 600 acre paddock of low scrub and half-burnt sticks.

The chase lasted till sundown until, finally exhausted, the children gave up and went home. They had learnt that a donkey could keep up its annoying gait all day and, when cornered, it could sprint past the fastest child, with its ears flat and kicking and bucking as it sped away. The following day, on a Sunday morning, the children begged Tommy for another go at the donkey. He obliged but this time made them work in relays as he figured they would need to run the animal hard to the point of exhaustion to catch it.

Beginning early, they ran the donkey in a canter round and round the paddock. Finally, the beleaguered beast gave up. The children were all over it, bringing it down amid calls of distress, bites and kicks. They tied its legs with rope, covered its head with their shirts, hauled it onto the back of the Red Inter and set off home, everyone a hero.

The young female donkey soon settled into her new home and became very tame, allowing the children to ride on her back. Several months later, for some inexplicable reason, Quirke shot the donkey and fed her carcass to the pigs. The children declared war on Quirke – he later 'lost' a couple of his best pigs down the bottom of a disused well. The choir's humiliation of him was more payback.

Quirke's attempt to get rid of the cat was viewed with similar dismay. Skinny White, as the cat was known, was a refugee from Geraldton, having climbed onto the chassis of the Red Inter and clung there for the entire journey back to Tardun. Its amazing survival feat, clinging to a narrow piece of steel over two hours of rough road, won the respect and admiration of the boys. Quirke viewed cats as destructive pests and so caught the cat one evening and gave it to a visitor at the pictures. The cat found its way back to the school several days later. In the second attempt he put the cat in a bag with some house bricks, tied the top and tossed the lot into the swimming pool. A couple of children had followed Quirke in the dark and retrieved the cat from the bottom of the pool. The superstitious Irishman never tried it again, perhaps a little spooked when he spotted the cat as large as life the next day.

The children had built tiny dwellings on a salt lake near the Alston windmill. It was a little tin village built in the middle of scalded white salt plains. The houses were laid out in neat rows, the quality of each depending on the building skills of the owners – usually three or four children or more. The Maltese boys generally were better builders than the English boys. Their camps were often constructed with proper gabled roofs, ceilings, glass windows, lockable doors and homemade furniture and fittings, often made from materials 'borrowed' from the school's building depot. One even had a homemade windmill driving a bicycle dynamo for lighting when the wind blew.

Tommy loved the camps as much as us and transported building materials on the back of the Red Inter. He ran competitions on construction, neatness and good behaviour. This approach was unusual among the Brothers – using both a carrot and a stick – and he rewarded good behaviour and excellent work with a jar of honey.

He ran a game known as 'British bulldog', in which two sides competed until only one boy was left standing. He told outrageous stories and had us in fits of laughter. He described how before he had become a Brother he had been a great white hunter from Africa, saving village after village from voracious man-eating lions and tigers that he shot with his Lee Enfield .909 rifle, supposedly three times bigger and more powerful than the Lee Enfield .303 issued to British and Australian troops in World War II.

Tommy was also a benevolent opportunist. Whenever the Brother Superior was away, he opened up the tuckshop and handed out ice-cream and soft drink, often for no particular reason. During the evening meal he liked to read aloud serious or funny stories from the *West Australian* newspaper. One day he read out the headline 'Baby drowns in washing machine' and we all erupted in laughter. He angrily threw the paper down and lamented that we were all sick to laugh at such a tragedy. He condemned our collective lack of sensitivity – it didn't pay to snigger when he was in this mood.

Third Creek was a favourite picnic spot and we often went there on the back of the truck. One hot day our little gang wandered off to explore the bush and got lost. After several hours of aimless wandering, we spied a house in the distance and made our way to the backyard where a single giant orange tree was loaded with ripe fruit. We quietly climbed through the fence, grabbed an orange each and hid behind a small shed to feast. We were taking a few for the road when an old man came out of the house and roared at us. We dropped the oranges and fled but could hear him yelling, 'You won't get into trouble for stealing my oranges!' We stopped running. He said, 'Come back and pick the oranges off the ground. You can take them with you.' He asked us who we were, assuming we were from Tardun. He also guessed we were lost: 'Jump on the ute, boys, and I'll run you back to the truck.'

We arrived on the back of old Sam Eakin's ute to find Tommy sitting in the truck reading a book. To our great relief Sam said, 'The boys got a bit lost, Brother, and I gave them some oranges'. We would have copped it if Tommy had found out that we had stolen the oranges. In later years Sam could still recall the names of the boys who stole his fruit.

Third Creek was the only place where I saw the English and Maltese boys fight. It started with a game of cowboys and Indians and got serious when prisoners were taken. Fighting with sticks, throwing rocks or using 'gings', or catapults, was not uncommon. A visiting Brother, who had little control over us, stood between the warring parties and was nearly knocked out by a flying rock to his head. He fell to the ground bleeding and the fighting stopped as he appeared to be badly injured. He recovered sufficiently to drive us all home. Once home, he forgave us and everything returned to normal.

Joe, a tough Maltese boy, ran away from Tardun a dozen times. No matter how brutal his punishment, he continued to try to escape until he eventually settled down. On one occasion he stowed away on a train that took him to Perth. He was met at the station by two burly representatives of the Child Welfare Department, who escorted him 480 kilometres back on the next train. Joe absorbed little education. One day one of the Brothers gave him ten simple mathematical sums and threatened the strap for each one that he got wrong. Joe strode to the front of the class and demanded five of the best on each hand. Joe regarded Tommy, who eventually took over his education, as the best teacher who ever lived.

It was much harder to run away from Tardun because of its remoteness, and few made the attempt, although we knew the rumour about two Maltese boys who, a few years before, went missing for several weeks. They wandered into a farm over 30 kilometres away and offered to work for money. The farmer put them to work clearing paddocks of rocks and stumps. Meanwhile everyone was searching for the boys. After two weeks they demanded their pay and the farmer refused. They took off up the road a little way, waiting for the farmer to leave his house and then burnt it to the ground. They walked back to the school, saying nothing about the farmer or his house. The farmer also kept quiet because he would have been in serious trouble for harbouring runaways. Once Tommy had been appointed deputy principal, there were only a few attempts at absconding. I can recall none while I was there except for Jimmy G.'s great escape – he hid for many hours in the washing machine in the laundry while everyone went searching.

It was traditional for the school to put on a free concert – a mixture of excerpts from plays, songs from musicals, gymnastics and harmonica playing – for the people of Mullewa once a year. Tommy had inherited part of the Castledare choir. Dolores, a local farmer's daughter who had learnt music at Stella Maris College in Geraldton, was our pianist. Working prodigiously as usual, Tommy cleverly created backdrops and scenery and organised children for the various parts.

Ned contributed by teaching another group of children how to play the harmonica, and young Brother Brown had a group of gymnasts ready to perform. Perfectionist Tommy took a professional approach and demanded our absolute best. To avoid any surprises we practised in the Mullewa town hall.

On the big night, Tommy frantically conducted and directed from the side of the stage. I was the admiral Sir Joseph Porter and Frank played the captain in *HMS Pinafore*. The concert went exactly to script, until disaster struck. Shading his eyes with his hand, the boson, with a '28' parrot[3] on his shoulder, looked across the bay to his right. Pointing, he said in a loud voice, 'I see Sir Joseph's barge!' The captain, shading his eyes, turned in the opposite direction and said, 'Aye, you're right!', as the baby parrot squawked '28' then fluttered to the floor. It brought the house down.

The Julius Caesar skit went little better, because Mark playing a dead Julius Caesar couldn't stop giggling and shaking under the body sheet just as Mark Antony began his famous 'Friends, Romans, countrymen, lend me your ears' speech. Our two-hour concert was given a standing ovation by the appreciative audience. Two weeks later we were on the truck again bound for Geraldton to give a concert at Nazareth House.

The Sisters of Nazareth had established a home for girls just north of the Chapman River. Typically grandiose, the large two-storey brick-and-tile building, complete with courtyard statue and lawn, was home for approximately 70 girls. With river and ocean frontage, the school was in those days just far enough out of town to be out of the reach of prowling young men. We sang a few numbers for the girls, who in turn sang some songs from their concert.

After lunch we went outside to play on the netball courts, boys versus girls in a game of 'keepy-off' with a basketball. Being bigger and stronger, the boys became bored with dominating possession of the ball and began deliberately throwing it to the girls so they could wrest it back. Brother Thomas and the nuns, who were watching closely, reacted like lightning when they saw a boy and girl rolling on the ground as others, laughing hysterically, followed suit. 'Keepy-off' is usually a non-contact sport, so Tommy was absolutely furious and the nuns flew into the melee to break it up.

Tardun boys and Nazzy girls, as they were known, got along well. There was a natural affinity. We saw the girls two or three times a year. The girls were far too young and naive to face the world on their own when they left the home at sixteen. The nuns found them domestic or factory jobs or jobs anywhere that accepted workers with minimal education. Some girls became cooks in shearing sheds or house cleaners on farms, often being abused by owners. Their naiveté meant they could be easily exploited.[4]

The early days at Tardun had been a steep learning curve: I was learning more each day about the pitfalls, traps, rules and regulations and, importantly, the boundaries. I was feeling better about myself and growing in confidence.

Soon I was riding on the back of Tommy's truck with a large group of children, heading for Perth to spend a fortnight's holiday with the Harringtons. The Aboriginal camp near Mullewa had clearly shown me that there were people and children infinitely worse off than us, and a whole new perspective was developing in my mind. As well I could feel a sense of camaraderie among us: we are all in this together and we will all survive it together. On the trips to Perth, we would break the boredom of the long road trip by singing, especially our anthem, which we sang nearly every time we travelled by bus or truck. It was a simple tune with simple words:

The Tardun boys are happy
The Tardun boys are free
The Tardun boys are jolly good boys
And jolly good boys are we.
We never fight or quarrel
We never disagree
The Tardun boys are jolly good boys
And jolly good boys are we.
Chorus: Banana banana, banana is good enough for me.

I loved being with the Harringtons and, as usual, the two weeks went by far too quickly. Bernie was intrigued with Tardun and wanted to know everything about the place. I told him I was much happier there and that some of the Brothers were good to us, mentioning Brothers Thomas and Howe and some of the younger ones. Bernie said he would be travelling to Mullewa soon on business and would call in to Tardun to see me. Sure enough, a few months later, he arrived in his official PMG car with bags of goodies for me. Quirke got me out of Tommy's class and told me to show Bernie around. After about an hour, Bernie got back into his car and drove away seething with rage, as I would discover the next Christmas holidays when I saw him again: 'I drove all that way to see you and the Brothers couldn't even offer me a cup of tea,' he fumed. He never let me forget it.

At Christmas time, as usual, the Harringtons went out of their way to give me the best holiday possible. Margaret and I were still inseparable, exploring the local parks and gardens with Lassie and Tiger. I helped Bernie to kill and dress a couple of his roosters for Christmas dinner and looked after his chickens during the holidays.

However, things with Robert and I were different. For the first time, he started challenging me to wrestling matches on the back lawn. He was much bigger than me and it didn't matter that I declined; he threw me to the ground anyway and corked my arms and legs with his fists. Bernie thought we were playing a regular game and laughed at his two boys roughing it up on the back lawn, but I knew otherwise. Bruises appeared on my arms and legs. These so-called games continued until the day our relationship abruptly came to an end.

This time after the holidays we travelled back to Tardun in an old Bedford bus the Brothers had bought and painted green and gold (the school colours), still with the home's name, 'St Mary's Tardun', emblazoned on the sides. This was a great improvement. I had hated the embarrassment caused by travelling on the back of the old truck, which to me was akin to tattooing the words 'destitute orphan' on my forehead, advertising the fact to the rest of the world.

1   Information about the results of the IQ tests conducted in the Christian Brothers' homes came from Department of Community Development files.

2   In February 1959 the Child Welfare Department received instructions from the Supreme Court in Sydney to conduct a survey on antisocial behaviour among migrant children compared to the rest of society. It also asked the Department to comment. The Department furnished the Supreme Court with a comprehensive breakdown of IQ tests carried out in all institutions. In addition it revealed that of all the 278 appearances for that year in the Children's Court, 66 were from Bindoon. It said these numbers would be much higher when appearances in the other courts were tallied with the figures from the Children's Court. Young adults often had to face a magistrate without backup or support. It was clear in the remarks from the Child Welfare Department that they regarded institutionalisation as little more than forced incarceration that created uneducated, angry and aggressive young adults and then unleashed them on society. But, in those days, courts rarely considered the mitigating circumstances that might have led to antisocial behaviour. Following the Bindoon disclosures, the federal government now at least had proof that institutionalisation was detrimental both to society and to the children it was meant to serve. The reports were buried, and nothing was done to rescue the children from a childhood of misery.

3   The '28', or Australian Ringneck parrot, is so called in Western Australia because of its distinctive call.

4   Catholic authorities in England were reluctant to send orphaned girls to Australia and had to be reassured by the Catholic authorities in Australia that the girls would receive the highest education and training available. Ironically, one communiqué from a senior official reads, 'We must prevent these poor girls becoming drudges on farms and in towns'.

HUNTING AND TRAPPING

Ned took us hunting most Sundays unless sport or some other activity intervened. His little grey Ferguson tractor, the 'Fergie', pulled a homemade trailer made from the tray of an old truck. A couple of thick planks of timber running down the middle made two rows of seats holding 40 to 50 children at a squeeze, most sitting around the edge with legs and feet dangling over the sides.

The Fergie had a top speed of less than 25 kilometres per hour. This suited Ned as he was never in a hurry to get there or back. He always carried an axe and, over the years, had built tracks through mallee scrub and York gum forest over huge areas of salt-lake country so that every part of the property was accessible to his tractor and trailer. We would visit the garden first and gather vegetables such as potatoes, onions, cabbage and cauliflower and, in summer, watermelons and rockmelons for the kitchen.

Ned's two hunting dogs stood together at the front of the trailer, keen and tense, noses in the air. At the slightest scent of a kangaroo they were off at breakneck speed through the scrub or across the lakes to bring down their quarry. The dogs worked as a team: Sunta, the heavier and slower dog, brought up the rear, while Teena, who was very fast and smart, outflanked the kangaroo and cut it off at the front. Mostly we waited on the trailer until the dogs barked, which indicated they had bailed up a kangaroo and then off we would run to find it.

Once the kangaroo had been caught, Teena seized the poor animal's throat, choking it to death, while Sunta held on to its tail. If the dogs bailed up a very large marlu or worse, a euro – the most powerful and dangerous of Australia's kangaroos – Ned called them off, because these powerful creatures could easily injure or kill a dog. A fleeing kangaroo would often head for water in a dam or a soak hole and drown the dog. Another common defence used by the kangaroos was to latch on to the dog's collar with its paws and choke the dog to death.

The best eating marlu was a young 'blue flier' – a half-grown buck or doe. They were very fast and also very tasty. Animals too big or too old had tough gamey meat, so Ned would add more curry to cover the gamey taste and boil the stew longer to make the meat more tender. Ned believed that the kangaroo was a valuable resource and once the dogs had caught one or two that was enough. If we had enough to eat, and the dogs had meat for a couple of days, he was happy.

Sometimes the dogs wouldn't bark and 20 or so minutes later would return to the trailer, puffing, heaving and dripping heavily with saliva. Ned had a way of determining whether the dogs had caught a kangaroo, even when there appeared to be no sign of blood or hair on their bodies. We then had to rely on Ned's tracking skills. Ned had inherited one of Brother Howe's old sheepdogs, Pooch. He had trained Pooch to track kangaroos and the pair worked together. When Pooch found a dead kangaroo, he howled and stayed by the carcass until we arrived.

Emus were a different matter. As they were declared vermin, the government paid four shillings for the top beak of the bird, which we regarded as a fortune. The sight of the dogs working together to kill emus was both horrible and awesome. Sunta with her long-gaited gallop drew alongside the fleeing bird, tripping it up, while Teena bit the bird's head, killing it instantly. I saw the dogs kill nine in a row in a single paddock one Sunday afternoon. These two animals were killing machines. Yet the birds could retaliate and sometimes kill a dog. The birds used their powerful feet, with claws sharp as nails as weapons. More than once, Sunta's neck was torn open, laid bare as if a surgeon had cut all the skin with a scalpel and left it hanging. Ned stitched the wound, dressed it with a blue liquid and bound it with an old wheatbag. Sunta howled in pain day and night until she recovered.

Neither Brother Howe nor Ned allowed their dogs to chase goats, for good reason. Ned's hunting dogs were killers, and if they learned to chase and kill goats, the sheep also would never be safe. Dogs that killed sheep were shot – everyone accepted that rule. But Brother Howe's sheepdogs sometimes had learned to bite, as goats, unlike sheep, were difficult to herd. The goats were often aggressive and fought the dogs.

Ned was the quintessential Australian bushman, and would set off with the tractor and trailer on his annual holiday to explore the country east of the school. Ned cut tracks through the bush or followed old tracks to the long-abandoned Mugga Mugga and Gullewa goldmines and to Barnong Station.[1]

No-one would see or hear from him for a month, and he would live off the land along with his dogs. He had a great knowledge of the bush and he could name plants, animals and insects. Anyone who was interested could learn a great deal – those who weren't were told regardless. He liked to dispute anyone with superior knowledge on any subject and would argue at length until he won.

Ned named the vast salt-lake country north-east of Rowley's block 'no man's land' and here he discovered a number of Aboriginal soak holes and granite outcrops. As well, he found a native pine forest missed by the early woodcutters, some of which the school was able to use for strainer posts in the fences. Unlike other Australian timber, native pine is impervious to white-ant attack and many a property's fence built from this wood 100 years ago still stands today – a testament to its unique properties.

Regularly joining our bush expeditions was the Catholic bishop of Geraldton. Bishop Thomas, like Ned, loved the Australian bush. One day near a soak hole in 'no man's land', while the morning billy was boiling for tea, an Irish lad named Mick found a lizard and asked Ned to identify it. We all gathered around as Ned described its features and habitat, turning it over before giving its Latin and common names. Later that afternoon, Mick lifted a rock and found another lizard, so we gathered again to hear Ned's description. After another lengthy description he gave this lizard different Latin and common names to the one Mick had found earlier. With this, Mick stood up and declared it was the same lizard. We all laughed, including Ned and the bishop, although Ned's eyes weren't laughing. He was embarrassed and furious. Mick was deep in it.

Next day Ned said to Mick, 'Little man, I've got a job for you in my garden' and set him two weeks of pulling weeds. However, so inspired was the bishop that later he too put one over Ned.

'I see a pair of yellow-throated pardalotes nesting in the tree by the hostel,' he casually declared over a cup of billy tea.

'Well, it's the time of year, Bish. They're migratory birds so we can expect them from now on,' replied Ned.

The Bishop unable to contain his laughter said, 'I just made that up. I doubt that such a bird exists.'

August was the beginning of the nesting season when the birds began laying eggs in hollows of York gums. One of our gang had spotted 'grassies' (mulga parrots) gathering on a regular basis in a thicket of scrub about 100 metres south of the explosives magazine, a reinforced concrete storage room for gelignite and other explosives, in front of the main building. We spread some grain on the ground to get the birds used to feeding, then a few days later set the trap, an old bed-frame covered with fine chicken wire, one end propped up by a stick attached to a long piece of twine.

A small group of 28s were under the snare when we pulled the string, trapping two of them. Percy held each screeching bird by its wings, one in each hand, and we headed back to our cage with our two new additions. Attracted by the noise, Quirke suddenly appeared, demanding that Percy kill the birds.

'How sir?' he asked, tears streaming down his face.

'Knock their heads against the wall,' demanded Quirke. 'Now!'

Percy's feeble attempt only angered Quirke. 'Harder! Harder!' he yelled. Soon Percy was holding two dead parrots that he would have rather set free.

Quirke's behaviour that day was hard to fathom because usually we were allowed to trap and cage birds. He saw the parrots as destructive pests while we, of course, viewed them as lovable pets. Despite this setback we later discovered more parrots' nests and hand-raised the chicks, even selling some for pocket money.

In 1959, Brother Hewat replaced Brother Quirke as Superior, and few, if any, of the children or the Brothers were sorry to see Quirke go. Quirke was a fine administrator who saved the school from financial ruin and, despite his shortcomings, made it possible to settle English, Maltese and Australian young men on their own farms. Without his financial ability, 'The Scheme', as it was called, would have floundered. In a strange way I would miss this gruff character, whose only real fault was his inability to deal with the extraordinary demands of disturbed and angry children who often stoked the fires of resistance. A tough man, he had been shaped by his era. An unintended consequence of Quirke's attitude was that we toughened up, ready for the hard life awaiting us all once we left the institution.

1   'Station' is an Australian term for a large holding of land, the minimum size of which would be around 1 million acres. In North America it would be known as a ranch.

HEWAT'S REGIME

Brother Hewat was the first Australian-born principal in the 30 years of Tardun's existence. Unlike previous Irish-born Superiors, he held no preconceived notions that most English children were bad, preferring instead to give us the benefit of the doubt.

Hewat began making changes almost from the first day. He believed that we should be playing more sport and therefore largely abolished mandatory work after school. He improved the food and bought us new clothing and sporting equipment, including footballs, cricket bats, pads and balls. He even spent time bowling to the children in the nets. He was keen to learn how we trapped birds so we showed him our snares and the techniques we used. This attitude was revolutionary to some of the older Brothers, who still believed that the best way to discipline troublesome children was prayer and a damned good hiding. Also revolutionary was the fact that he allowed the Brothers to drink alcohol in moderation.

'Old boys' were encouraged to visit their mates at the school, again causing consternation among those older Brothers who believed the old boys would bring bad ideas with them when they arrived on weekends on their Lambretta scooters or motorbikes or in their old 'bomb' cars. Hewat accommodated them all at the hostel and gave them a bed and food. The old boys brought hope to the school, telling us of life in the real world.

New young Brothers – McPherson, Thornton, Rowbottom, Gee and Thiel – arrived. McPherson was hardly older than the working boys. These young men were genuine in their determination to make a difference and improve the life of disadvantaged children. The old authoritarianism and the arrogance that went with it was not evident in the new staff as none had worked with disadvantaged children before.

This ended the damaging practice that had existed in the orphanage system for years of moving abusive and hardened Brothers from one institution to another and quickly led to a cultural change and more respect for and understanding of the needs of children.

The winter wheat-growing season in 1959 was ending as it had begun – with little rain. Though bringing much bounty the year before, the season was now turning against the farmers. By spring, tens of thousands of emus were making their way south to escape the dry conditions in the north, devastating hundreds of wheat crops along the way. It was an invasion of such magnitude that every farmer prayed that the rabbit-proof fence[1] to the north, the longest vermin fence in the world, would hold the bulk of the emus at bay. After school, Tommy had us busy fixing wire nooses to the boundary fence, the idea being that should an emu stick its neck through the noose on its way through the fence, the noose would tighten and strangle the bird. The only flaw in this plan was that if enough birds were caught at the same time – a likely scenario as they travelled about in large mobs – together they could pull the whole fence down in their struggle, allowing other birds through unimpeded. Farmers were shooting emus wholesale and ute loads of dead birds were being delivered to the piggery daily. Hewat, who had taken over running the piggery, spent afternoons driving around in the school's car shooting emus.

One Sunday afternoon in late September we were bird nesting and could hear Hewat shooting in a paddock to the east. Tommy had taken us all out on the Red Inter to a large York gum forest south of the shearing shed to collect parrot and cockatoo chicks. As usual the big children held all the likely nesting hollows, so our little gang headed off across a 400 acre paddock sown with a tall variety of wheat to the forest on the other side. We were small and only our heads were visible above the canopy of the wheat.

Hewat drove down the side of the paddock and stopped the car. He rested the .303 Lee Enfield rifle across the roof, took aim in our general direction and fired. We figured there must have been emus in the same paddock and looked around as he quickly fired off two more rounds. The fourth bullet whistled past my head. I felt the pressure as if a balloon had popped close to my ear. I yelled, 'Get down, it's us, it's us he's shooting at!'

We removed our shirts and waved them above the wheat heads. Hewat slowly eased himself back into the car and drove away. For the next few minutes as we wandered around I could hear a loud ringing in my left ear. We didn't really give the incident much more thought. We were focused on finding likely nesting hollows and hopefully some precious chicks. The shooting hadn't concerned us greatly and was quickly forgotten.

When we got back to the truck a couple of hours later, Tommy was extremely agitated: 'Brother Hewat wants to talk to you as soon as you get back.' Hewat was visibly shaken and berated us about the dangers of walking through wheat fields. As punishment he made us miss the pictures for two weeks. We thought, 'Typical! We get shot at and nearly killed, and then we're punished for it. What a joke!'[2]

In May 1960 Hewat allowed a rodeo to be held at Tardun – for the first and last time. All the cattle were brought in from the outback, and suitable steers were graded into lots. With a single piece of rope to hang onto, the big children rode the bucking shorthorn steers out of the crush and into the open paddock, while Brother Howe held the time watch. Guido, a Maltese boy, rode a mean bucking steer, to our cheers and whistles, until it stopped bucking and trotted back to the herd in the paddock. The smaller boys rode calves, and the really young children, newly arrived from Castledare, rode excitable freshly shorn wethers. Brother Wright stood by with a loaded .303 rifle in case any steer turned on its rider.

After this came the horse-riding competition, and all horses were entered except Princess, who couldn't be ridden. The rodeo finished with a greasy pig competition. A half-grown porker was smeared in animal fat and let loose in the open paddock. The little children gave chase first, followed by the rest. The panicked animal headed for the piggery. The pig was soon overtaken, slipping and sliding out of our arms, and turned back weaving and darting through arms and legs until it ran past me totally exhausted. I dived onto the poor animal, which had little grease left on it and little will to continue. I thought it might die but I held on. Brother Howe gave trophies and prizes to the winners and I received a fine bone-handled sheath knife useful for killing goats for their tails.

The latest crop of Castledare orphans arrived at the start of 1960 and I found myself among the curious onlookers checking out the new arrivals. This group of about a dozen was the last major intake of English children to come to Tardun. Later only a dozen or so Maltese children and three or four English children were to arrive. By 1962, no further children came from overseas and the school began taking boarders from local farms and towns.

The tiny island of Malta had been a colony of Britain and had served as a British naval base in World War II. The British influence meant that many Maltese children had English fathers and therefore had surnames such as Plowman, Russell, Gould, Fullbrook and Berry. We even knew a Charlie Brown, who spoke no English. Unlike the English children, the Maltese boys still kept family links, except in rare cases, as a result of the policies of a more humane Maltese Catholic Church. This showed twice a week in the dining room when Hewat distributed the now uncensored mail. Bundles of letters and good parcels arrived for the Maltese boys but little came for the English boys – it was a painful twice-weekly reminder of how much I had lost.

In addition, the Maltese Catholic Church visited the school at least once a year to check on any problems and to report back to the Maltese government.[3] One of these reports actually assisted us as well as it had criticised the fact that we had no footwear. In Malta this indicated poverty. Hewat could hardly just buy sandals just for the Maltese children, so he had to buy them for everyone. By the end of 1960, we were all wearing cheap but effective plastic sandals, giving us greater mobility around the farm and saving our feet from the freezing concrete floors in the classrooms. Before this, we had sometimes used twine to tie thin timber slats taken from the fruit and vegetable boxes to our feet. Walking as if over snow, we could negotiate the paddocks full of double gee, a prickly weed. Once we reached the bush, we could take off the slats as the prickles and thorns grew only in the paddocks.

Every Saturday morning, those who weren't rostered to work in the laundry gathered in Tommy's classroom to be split into small workgroups for the day. Laundry was the worst job at the school. About a dozen children washed and ironed the clothes and dried and folded the towels, sheets, pillowslips, handkerchiefs and underwear – never ours, as we had none – and stacked them into bundles to be delivered to their owners. It was a boring all-day affair and we were rostered there once about every four or five weeks. If you were there as a punishment it could mean six weeks in a row. Sister Bridget ran the laundry and was a hard-working no-nonsense Irishwoman who ensured that everyone worked at least as hard as she did. Any malingerers automatically got an extra roster.

Some of the workgroups would be assigned to the farmer 'old boys' who were developing their own properties with the help of the Brothers. Most of these young farmers were good to the children, never working them too hard – some even going out of their way to give us a good day out.

Farmer X. was the odd one out – he was always determined to get the maximum amount of work out of his group. One stinking hot day he lined us up against the side of a vast paddock covered in half-burnt sticks, mallee roots and rocks and instructed us to move in a line across the paddock picking up all the objects and stacking them into heaps. Someone asked if we could bring the waterbag.

Farmer X. replied, 'No, we leave it hanging on the tree and we drink when we get back.'

The paddock was nearly a kilometre wide; it could be hours before we got a drink. The morning was already hot and I could hear murmurs of discontent. I knew trouble wasn't far away. We worked our way 200 metres into the paddock and by then most of us were thirsty and needed a drink. One of the boys, John Asciak[4], told Farmer X. that he wouldn't move another metre until he got a drink. Farmer X. picked up a stick and, waving it at John, said, 'You get back to work, you cheeky little bastard!'

John picked up a long black stick with a sharp point and began approaching Farmer X. like an Aboriginal warrior about to spear his quarry. Farmer X. backed off and we all went back for a drink. After that, we took it in turns to carry the waterbag. Tommy got to hear about the incident and Farmer X. struggled to get any helpers in the future.

Hewat's sister, a registered nurse, often visited from Victoria and saw to any medical problems. One day she spotted me as I hobbled past while she and Hewat were sunning themselves on the veranda. She examined my foot and declared that I would have to go to hospital for an operation on a badly infected ingrown toenail. Hewat drove me into Mullewa and, again, Reverend Dean Lynch took me in his car to St John of God Hospital in Geraldton where I underwent surgery. Once again the Maltese woman looked after me. Dean Lynch drove me back to Mullewa early in the afternoon, sipping from his bottle of wine in a sock; however, this time, some two years after my first visit to hospital, his driving had deteriorated. He dropped me off outside the Bank of New South Wales telling me to wait as Brother Hewat would be in directly to pick me up. I waited several hours outside the bank until the manager's daughter Carol took pity on me and invited me into the house to put my foot up. She played all the latest hits on her portable record player while I sat back in a lounge chair with a nice drink, enjoying her hospitality. Hewat had forgotten about me but this suited me, as I got to have dinner with the family. Hewat later arrived, apologising for being late, while I was very sorry that he had come at all.

Total respect and obedience had been drummed into me from Castle-dare days, but I began to feel a sense of defiance and I noticed a subtle change in the other children. Some of us were fighting back.

Ned grew magnificent watermelons and rockmelons in his garden that we ate after our meal of kangaroo stews on our regular outings. He guarded his garden against theft as best he could, but such juicy temptations were hard to resist. He caught a few of us red-handed one day and ordered us to bend over the cart for a couple of strokes across the backside with a leather machine belt. Having experienced this belt before, I desperately looked around to see what I could do – our thin cotton trousers provided little protection against its stinging blows. Comics and magazines supplied by Brother Hewat were strewn all over the floor of the trailer. I managed to shove a couple of *Phantom* comics inside the back of my trousers while no-one was looking. I howled as loudly as the others, but later shared my secret with them. They didn't believe me until I showed them my pair of milky white cheeks; theirs were bright red. Ned whacked quite a few *Phantom* comics after that and never caught on. This was the first time I had ever put one over the Brothers but it wouldn't be the last.

Tommy's straps began disappearing from his desk in the classroom. Sometimes he was only out of the room for a few moments when the strap would disappear. As each went missing he was forced to make another, stitching six short strips of cow leather together into one thick band. He was determined to catch the culprit and demanded that someone own up. He called for witnesses and searched the room, believing that the straps must be hidden somewhere nearby. Few knew how the thefts happened, as it was easy for a child to dive behind his desk unseen while the rest of the class was distracted. It only took a few seconds. The concrete floor of the classroom served as the roof of a giant rainwater tank and Tommy's chair sat over a concrete manhole, covered by a small piece of carpet. It was easy to lift one end of the manhole using a steel ruler and drop the straps into the tank. Tommy never found the culprit – or his straps.

Theft of food from the kitchen or bakery, or stealing of eggs from the chicken yard, was viewed as a serious offence. Punishment was swift and painful. A lot of the older boys regarded it more as a game and were prepared to cop the punishment if caught, but the trick was not to get caught.

The prime target, the kitchen, was run by elderly Sister Aidan and eagle-eyed Joe, who was always alert and knew most of the tricks of the trade. David sneaked in one day while Joe was temporarily absent and moved quietly past the elderly nun, who was partly deaf and had poor eyesight, heading for the large fruit bin. He stole a couple of apples, thrusting them down the inside of his shirt. Sister spotted him trying to leave and demanded to know what he was doing in her kitchen. His excuse was more than plausible: 'I just came in to see if you could give me a job Sister so you might reward me with an apple.' Sister Aidan's heart melted: 'Here's an apple for you for being a good boy. I don't have a job for you today, so off you run.'

The food at Tardun was plain but better than at Castledare and there was more of it. Breakfast consisted of wheat porridge: farm-grown crushed wheat, cooked overnight over a slow coal-fired stove. This thick sticky gruel was a relic of the 1930s Depression and along with 'underground mutton' (rabbit) sustained many an Australian family through those tough years. The porridge, full of protein and fibre, was endured – it was impossible to enjoy – and remained a Tardun staple to the mid 1960s. Weeties or Cornflakes were a rare delicacy saved for special occasions such as feast days celebrating the life of a special saint, although there was one memorable exception. Early one morning just before mass, a wild cat chased by the boys darted into the kitchen and tried to escape by scaling the wall near the big stove. The panicked cat fell back into a large pot of hot porridge and, scalded, leapt out of the pot and slipped and slid its way out of the kitchen into the safety of the bush in front of the main building. We got Weeties that morning! Included with the porridge were a couple of slices of bread and tea to drink. When the chickens were laying, we had boiled or scrambled eggs. Lunch was soup or vegetables and meat – often sheep liver and kidney stew – bread and butter and tea. The evening meal was generally the best, consisting of vegetables and roast meat followed by sweets such as bread pudding, sago pudding or rhubarb and custard.

As at Castledare, talk was of the desperate need for a new chapel and steps had been taken to finance it. The farmer old boys had been donating fertiliser and seed since Brother Quirke's days, bringing their tractors and seeding equipment to sow a wheat crop. Later they brought their harvesting equipment and trucks to harvest and transport the grain to the bin. They had been doing this for a few years, building the school's financial reserves. Harvesting the 'chapel paddocks' as they became known was a social affair with fancy food prepared by the women and nuns. We looked for any excuse to be there, helping clean the dishes, folding wheat sacks – anything at all to be near the leftovers.

The old chapel was a plain cement-brick building with an elevated floor or stage at the front and was more suited to being a theatre, gym or workshop. An old-fashioned wooden altar stood at the front and timber pews filled the rest of the room. The building got hot in the summer and the double doors were left open to allow cooling breezes through.

One of Ned's clucky chickens that had been sitting on eggs in a hidden sanctuary noisily emerged from behind the altar one Sunday morning halfway through the priest's sermon. So pleased to leave her nest, her loud clucking took the congregation and the German priest by surprise. The bird was chased around the altar by one of the altar boys. Panicked, amid floating feathers and laughter, it then launched itself into the middle of the congregation causing havoc. The Brothers and nuns were not amused and neither was the new German priest from the Pallottine Mission, who had been having considerable difficulty with the English language. He was hampered by his strong German accent and few parishioners had understood a word of what he'd said. He abandoned the rest of his sermon and launched straight into the business of turning the bread and wine into the body and blood of Christ. This incident, Hewat reminded us, was one of the reasons why it was so important to build a new chapel.

The German priest was popular at the confessional, unlike the Australian priest, who wanted to know every minute detail, especially about sins of impurity, and who kept us back giving long lectures and a painful penance. The German priest by comparison would say very slowly, 'For your penance say please three Our Fathers and von Hail Mary'. No matter what you told him, he was more merciful than God himself and so it went until he finally cottoned on to English.

The Aboriginal children and their carers from the Pallottine Mission came to the school every Saturday and Sunday evening to watch the movies. One of Brother Tommy's duties was to prepare and censor the films, physically removing many metres of film to ensure that nothing untoward was seen or heard by the audience. To do this, he worked late into the night cutting, removing and gluing pieces of film. What often resulted was a movie with a plot that was almost impossible to follow. He cut all the kissing scenes, some of the romance, any plunging necklines – indeed anything he thought may have had a corrupting influence on us. He was so pedantic that at times he even annoyed the other Brothers.[5] After the pictures, it took him just as long to restore the movie to its original condition. He was so clever that the distributors at MGM, United Artists and Warner Brothers never once suspected that he had hacked their films to pieces.

The movie equipment, donated by the Lotteries Commission, was state-of-the-art and was capable of playing the latest CinemaScope releases. The movie theatre had a large outdoor screen and the audience could sit and watch from under a large overhanging roof or from their cars. We watched a lot of westerns. The Aboriginal children often screamed warnings to the cowboys or Indians if anyone was sneaking up to unexpectedly attack – an event that seemed to happen often in Tommy's heavily censored westerns.

1   Rabbits were introduced to Victoria in 1859 and they spread to the north and west of Australia, causing severe damage to the natural environment and agriculture. Between 1901 and 1907, the Western Australian government built a 1700-kilometre rabbit-proof fence from the south coast to the north-west coast of Western Australia. It was the longest unbroken stretch of fencing in the world and was maintained by eight boundary riders.

2   Years later, an elderly Hewat visited me and we discussed the incident. I asked how he could have missed four targets so close to him, especially as he was a crack shot. He said our dark heads bobbing about in the wheat looked like half-grown emus walking away. He had open sights still set on 400 to 500 yards and was in the process of readjusting, shooting just above our heads, when he saw our waving shirts. Hewat never used a gun again.

3   In contrast, British officials did not visit Tardun so no reports were ever made to the Home Office about our welfare.

4   John, considered a 'problem child', was eventually sent back to the government after he pulled a knife on a child in a fight. He was put in Fremantle jail at the age of fourteen. In time he became one of the state's most notorious criminals, serving most of his life behind bars. Yet I admired him for standing up to a grown-up bully twice his size and winning. John, like the rest of us, had a tough life. He was an Italian orphan but everyone, including himself, thought he was Maltese. No-one could understand how he became a Maltese immigrant.

5   David Plowman, in his book *Enduring Struggle: St Mary's Tardun Farm School, Perth, WA* (Scholastic Press Australia, 2003), recounts an incident in which a farmer travelled 80 kilometres to the film night as a wedding anniversary treat for his wife. When they got to Tardun, they discovered that Brother Thomas had severely censored the films and all they got for their long trip was coffee and biscuits and an apology from the Superior.

11
SOMEONE – AT LAST

By 1959 I had started to develop more confidence and, for the first time in my life, I felt that I could make it on my own. I had begun to build friendships that would prove to be lifelong. I was no longer a loner. That year was memorable for two main events: I survived an accidental shooting and Brother Howe inducted me into the Tardun under-18 Australian Rules football team.

The latter was proof, in my eyes, that others were recognising my increasing strength and maturity. In reality, the age of the team members ranged from twelve to seventeen, as the school didn't have the numbers to make up a proper under-18 team. At twelve, I was one of the youngest in the side. Our main competition was Saint Patrick's College in Geraldton. St Pats was a Christian Brothers boarding and day college for fee-paying students and they had hundreds of players to choose from. In recognition of the obvious imbalance, St Pats allowed a couple of the young Tardun Brothers to play on our side. One of the young Brothers, Don McPherson, was nearly 2 metres tall and was useful in the ruck. The other, George Thontan, from New South Wales, was shorter but powerfully built and knew nothing about Australian Rules, having only played rugby. He was useful in the backline. Whenever he got hold of the ball and began his run up the field, the St Pats players got out of his way. Despite our best efforts, we mostly lost all our games but we had fun playing. We were proud to wear the Tardun colours and I felt good being accepted as one of the team.

Whenever possible, Brother Howe arranged for games and competitions in which we were more evenly matched, yet when we competed against the Aboriginal boys at the Pallottine Mission, we played in proper studded football boots while the mission boys played barefoot on a solid gravel football field.

Brother Howe went to great lengths to write up the details of the game in a way unique to him. After one game against Morawa High School, he wrote a voluminous editorial in which he mentioned every Tardun player. He praised in glowing terms those who put in a solid effort and condemned with faint praise those who dragged the chain. This game against Morawa was memorable for another reason. Howe played me in a forward pocket, regarded as a reasonably safe place for a youngster in the rough and tumble of a vigorous game of Australian Rules. Tardun was well ahead when one of the bigger boys on the opposing side violently tumbled me over the boundary line in an act of anger and frustration. Within moments Tardun boys surrounded me and there was some pushing and shoving and the odd swing of a fist. I felt enormous pride that my teammates would come to help me.

Brother Howe was the only one at the school who bothered to check a child's background, writing to Catholic immigration authorities to ask for records. It was becoming obvious to him that the lack of information was wrong and he had unanswered questions about what had happened to us. Occasionally he would inform one of the children that his birthday was wrong and that he was older or younger than he had thought. Sometimes he even told one of us that our name was wrong.

He called me over one day: 'The boy Hawkins come here. Know what your mother's name is, boy?'

'No sir,' I replied.

'Anne Elizabeth, that's her name. Anne Elizabeth Hawkins. That's all I know, boy, off you go now.'

My head was spinning as I ran away. Anne Elizabeth, Anne Elizabeth. I had a mother. I was twelve. I was someone at last. Excited, I told Tommy what I had just learned about my mother. I had expected the next step would be to see if we could find her and was surprised when he seemed only slightly interested. He had always preached the undeniable value of mothers and families.

Brother Howe also made it his business to check up on the old boys who had left Tardun. He wrote letters and visited them to see that they were all right. Sometimes he was their only contact. The seaman's union in Darwin wrote in 1957 to tell Brother Howe that Jim, a nineteen-year-old youth from Tardun, had been killed in a freak accident and his body had been buried at sea by the union. Brother Howe was the only person they could find to notify.

The year 1960 was momentous for Tommy. A Catholic had been elected president of the United States of America and, more importantly, President Kennedy and his wife, Jackie, were devout Catholics and went to mass every Sunday. They were also glamorous, like American movie stars, and photos of the president with the Pope at mass began appearing around the classroom. We would miss more school lessons than ever, as Tommy extolled the virtues of Catholicism in America. Often when he spoke for too long, he became angry at himself, suddenly saying 'Right, turn to page 23 of your maths book!' He would scribble a sum on the blackboard, take us through the exercise and demand that we do one on our own. He would then lose patience and, thumping the blackboard with his fists, berate the class for being too slow. The chalk would snap in half as he angrily drew on the blackboard, demonstrating how easy the maths problem was to solve.

We would stop to listen to his fiery oratory on the evils of communism. One day he railed against what he believed was the communist practice of brainwashing through which ordinary Russian folk could be sucked into believing that communism was better than democracy and capitalism. Worse, the communists brainwashed the population to believe there was no God and closed all the churches, jailed the priests and nuns and persecuted the believers. As ever he was ready to field any questions. Somewhere from the back of the classroom a thin brave voice asked, 'Sir, aren't we being brainwashed too?' You could hear a pin drop. Jim, a skinny Irish boy, had just signed his death warrant and wanted to commit suicide too.

'And just how are you being brainwashed, son?'

'Religion, sir,' his voice barely a whisper.

'And just how are you being brainwashed by religion, sonny?' asked Tommy, hands clasped behind his back, scowling at the trembling student.

'Well, sir,' came the boy's voice, barely audible, 'the Catholic Church tells us we must believe in the resurrection of Jesus and the Virgin

Mary's immaculate conception, and that if we don't believe in these things then we will go to Hell.'

'Is that so?' said Tommy his face breaking into a smirk, like a cat who realises the mouse is trapped. He now had our undivided attention.

Like a prosecutor about to deliver a mortal blow to the defendant, he raised his voice, 'So you mean to tell me, and the rest of the class, that Soviet brainwashing of the Russian people is no different to the teachings of the holy Catholic Church; that the ramblings of Nikita Khrushchev and his henchmen and executioners equate with the word of God?' His clenched fist was pounding the blackboard. 'It just doesn't balance, sonny, it just doesn't balance!'

He launched into a story he had read in a religious magazine about the heroic deeds of Catholic priests who avoided capture and delivered communion in secret to Catholics in Russia, while constantly under the threat of torture and execution. Tommy's tirade was pure theatre and we were enthralled at the amazing courage of these people. We forgot that it all started from a simple question, which still hadn't been answered and was never likely to be. We had just missed another maths lesson.

Mid August was time for retreat: three days of quiet reflection, prayer and meditation. Silence was mandatory except at the evening meal. A Jesuit priest took us through each day of religious instruction and prayer, lessons and talks. As we were allowed to ask questions, one of the boys asked the priest how much money you would need to steal before you committed a mortal sin. Somewhat taken aback, the priest said that it would depend on the situation and he would need to speak to Brother Thomas and let us know tomorrow. The next day he solemnly declared that, at a place like Tardun, we would need to steal two pounds of another boy's money before we committed a mortal sin. Given that nobody had two pounds, the sin was never likely to happen. It seemed the perfect answer. For the three days of retreat we took to the bush when we could and made campfires to cook rabbit, eggs and wild mushrooms, and then return in time for each lesson.

A lot of the students in Tommy's class were quite backward in English and maths and were not making any progress. The metalwork room was adjacent to his classroom so he often had this group working for hours designing and making models out of sheet metal. This not only kept them busy but also honed their skills. Some of them were so clever that they could make anything and one of the boys was awarded the highest marks for manual arts in the state.

The Mullewa Show was held in late August and we prepared for this day for months. Tommy encouraged all the children to enter something they had made, such as paintings or drawings in crayon or metalwork objects such as dustpans, oilcans and vases. Even intricate wildflower presentations were entered. There were good prizes to be won: five shillings for first prize and two and sixpence for second prize. Brother Howe organised Baya and Spot and riders to represent the school in the equestrian events. He also entered his best wool fleece, while the farm Brothers entered oaten hay and the best examples of oats, wheat and barley plants, as well as grain.

It was a big day for us. We travelled in to Mullewa on the back of a truck. The show organisers let us in for nothing and the Brothers gave us a couple of shillings to spend. The most popular event on the day was Stewart's Boxing Troupe. Stewart thundered from the stand, challenging anyone in the crowd to last three minutes against his boys. The troupe organisers were particularly wary of the Tardun boys, who had a way of getting in without paying. Some of us would distract the attention of the tent attendants while the rest dived under the flaps.

The judging of our exhibits was a hit-and-miss affair. The judge, usually a local farmer's wife, had to decide which of 20 oilcans, vases or dustpans made from sheet metal, all looking exactly the same, deserved first prize. Often the least talented boy got first prize for his object.

Like Brother O'Doherty before him, Brother Tommy was keen for us to experience at least some family life. We were never taught social etiquette at the school and had to learn how to behave acceptably in a family environment and, later, in society mostly through trial and error. To achieve this, Tommy had approached a women's Catholic group in Geraldton with a proposal to place Tardun children in family homes during holidays. This worked well and some children, for the first time in their lives, began to experience life on the other side of the wall of an orphanage.

Tommy saw to it that everyone wrote a letter back thanking the family for the holiday. The problem was that too few of us could write the kind of letter that he had in mind, so he wrote a letter on the blackboard that we all copied word for word in our neatest handwriting. During one of their regular group meetings, one of the women excitedly pulled a letter from her handbag, proudly sharing young Billy's wonderful grasp of English. She read the letter to the women, who looked at each other in amazement – they had all received the same letter.

Learning social etiquette was beyond the reach of some of boys. One boy had refused to help with the dishes, declaring, 'I'm here for a holiday, not to wash dishes'. Percy Faulkner, an avid dog lover, had managed to fill the home where he was staying with stray dogs while the rest of the family were out shopping. Another boy, Joe, had 'borrowed' a bike and peddled down the street where he ran over a large cat sunbaking on the footpath. The poor cat had become tangled in the front spokes, tearing the front tyre to pieces with its claws. On several occasions, Tommy had to drive to Geraldton to pick up some of the badly behaved boys and bring them back to Tardun. He saved his wrath until after the holidays when he had as all gathered in the classroom and then berated them for letting the school down and failing to live up to expectations. It was hard not to laugh, but it didn't pay to when Brother Thomas was angry. We saved our laughter for later, especially when a couple of boys would mimic Tommy in a hilarious comedy routine.

Not all of the boys saw the lighter side of Tardun. The place was full of flawed characters and damaged personalities – a microcosm of the entire orphanage system. Some children were still suffering badly from their treatment and often refused to cooperate, reacting in all manner of ways when punished by the Brothers. And some of the Brothers appeared to take a deal of satisfaction when they dished out punishment. Taking revenge by damaging or stealing property was par for the course. Sometimes we all suffered together because a culprit could not be found. We were forced to stand for hours on end in the schoolyard until the culprit gave himself up. This, of course, never happened – the culprit knew he would cop it from us as well.

Midway through 1960, Hewat sacked one of the Brothers. Some boys had complained of sexual harassment by Brother McLaughlin, who had arrived from Victoria barely a year before. Brother McLaughlin was a fine carpenter and worked on the new chapel, usually with a couple of the older working boys. Fortunately he had very little to do with us, although we avoided him as news travels fast in a closed society.

I was able to compare Castledare with Tardun, which was infinitely better, and realise that my life had actually improved. I found happiness, as did many of the children, in events such as the birth of Sunta's new pups. Ned had her served by a champion 'roo dog' from a farm near Canna to breed out the greyhound features, preferring a bulkier and stronger animal. He kept two of the pups and gave the rest away. He named them Salome and Leone; the latter, he soon nicknamed 'Cheeky Face'. Within 18 months these two dogs would become as quick and efficient hunters as the older two. Cheeky Face would eventually turn out the best dog Ned ever had and, better still for us, neither of the two dogs was a 'biter'. Teena and Sunta just disappeared one day. Teena, especially, was showing early signs of arthritis and her keen eyes were a little less bright and the scars that disfigured her face and neck made her look much older then she really was.

In May 1960, I was back on holidays with the Harringtons and once again was treated like royalty. Meg had bought me a couple of new woollen windcheaters to get me through the cold Tardun winter. We were allowed to keep and wear any gifts of clothing at Tardun.

One night Bernie began talking about my future: 'Education, John, that's the key; we'll get you into the public service!' He promised to allow me to get a job the next year selling the *Daily News* for pocket money. He knew a good corner where I could sell plenty of papers. The thought of earning my own money pleased me immensely. I could be the same as all the other children selling papers on the street and no-one would know where I came from.

Halfway through the holidays, an incident occurred that changed everything. One evening, just before dark, Bernie marched into the house, grabbed my arm and began dragging me out of the house yelling at the top of his voice, 'Come and look at what you did, you little bastard!'

By the time we got to the chicken yard he had already removed his belt and began whipping me all over my body. He screamed, 'Why did you do it? Why did you do it, you little bastard?'

He continued flogging me. I went down on the ground and curled up into a ball, protecting my head with my arms. Meg became hysterical and grabbed Bernie's arm, yelling, 'Bernie stop it, stop it. Let the boy go.'

She took me back inside and held me. We were both sobbing and she asked me, 'Did you do it?' I shook my head, ' No!'

Someone had tipped out Bernie's entire supply of wheat for the chickens and spread it around the yard until grain covered the entire area, making it yellow. The big bin that had held all the grain was still sitting upside down in the middle of the yard. Suspicion fell on Robert, as he hadn't returned home yet from his friend's house. When he arrived, Bernie was ready. Robert admitted doing the deed in a defiant instant and then fled out of the house through the backyard and into the darkness of the vacant paddock at the rear with Bernie hot on his heels. Meg held me for a long while. We both knew something precious had died, and nothing could ever be the same again.

Robert saw me as the cuckoo egg in the family nest and wanted me out. In a way I could understand why he would want to protect something that belonged to him. Bernie apologised profusely and the next day brought me a fishing rod. But I remembered how childhood jealousy had resulted in my near drowning on the *Strathmore* and I didn't want to be on the receiving end of it again.

I was determined not to mention it to anyone when I got back to Tardun and, in any case, I fully expected to be blamed for what had happened. The Brothers would be angry, as good families who would take Tardun boys for holidays were hard to find and the Harrington family was held in high esteem. But Tommy, ever alert, spotted the bruises on my arms and legs and demanded to know what happened. When I told him he simply asked, 'Do you want to go back?'

'No!' I replied.

'Don't worry, we'll find another place for you.'

I loved the Harrington family and I would miss them dearly.

I spent Christmas 1960 at Tardun with about 20 other children who had nowhere else to go. Tommy was almost a different person at holiday time – gone were the demands, instructions, reprimands and discipline. He never took holidays and devoted the whole time to making our holiday as enjoyable as he could.

On Christmas Eve there was a present under the tree for each of us and he had hidden extra presents for us to find. On Christmas Day, we were all given an envelope that contained the first of a number of clues, all cleverly constructed. It usually took a couple of days to solve one clue and find another, and so on until we eventually found the hidden present that he had planted anything up to 2 kilometres away from the school.

He would ask us where we wanted to go: to the beach at Geraldton, to Third Creek or to the Alston camps. It didn't matter. We had all the time in the world and he had the Red Inter.

On a hot Sunday evening towards the end of January 1961, before all the boys had returned to the school, we were watching a movie with local farming families under the asbestos roof of the outdoor theatre when suddenly the ground shook. An enormous explosion followed. Tommy turned on the lights and we looked at each other wondering what had just happened. A few moments later, rocks and debris began falling on the roof of the outdoor theatre. The horrifying noise caused the small children to cry in terror.

Tommy shut down the film and the debris stopped falling. An eerie red dust cloud descended then just as mysteriously disappeared. Once the shock had worn off, panic erupted and a few people began running towards the main building about 100 metres away. Shards of glass were strewn throughout the classrooms and dining room. Doors were ripped off their hinges. The cause of the explosion was soon discovered. The culprit was the concrete explosives magazine in front of the main building. Boxes of gelignite stored in the reinforced concrete block had sweated through the heat and the explosive material had become unstable. Spontaneous combustion resulted, leaving nothing but a 3 metre hole in the rocky ground.

We went upstairs to our dormitories to see the damage there. Not a single piece of plate glass in the entire building remained intact. The force of the blast caused splinters of glass some 10 centimetres long to pierce mattresses, even splintering the wall on the other side of the main dormitory 25 metres away. More then 250 sheets of glass at the front of the main building had blown inwards, creating pure bedlam. I was stunned. Only half an hour later I would have been standing near the window near my bed with the other children. And if the explosion had happened a week later with everyone back from the holidays there could have been 40 casualties or more. By pure luck, a bloodbath had been avoided. The main building, which bore the brunt of the blast, had save us from being injured at the outdoor theatre.

Brother Howe was the only casualty. He had been walking up and down in front of the main building saying his rosary when he was knocked over by the blast. He was found wandering, totally incoherent. He never really recovered from the incident and lost his confidence. Soon after the explosion while out driving he lost control of his Dodge ute and tipped it over. He survived but went into semi-retirement.

I began thinking there were plenty of ways to die at Tardun. Only a few months before I had been shot at with an ex-army .303 rifle and I had escaped death or serious injury again.

I thought of the three young English boys who lay in the school's cemetery. They had not survived Tardun. Tommy never allowed us to forget the anniversary of their deaths and we would gather at the graveside and pray and say the rosary. Tommy ensured that the cemetery and the three graves were kept tidy and free of weeds and that the picket fence gleamed with white paint.

The death of Tony Gale at age twelve, a few years before I arrived at Tardun, was probably the most tragic, as his death had been avoidable. He had been complaining of pains and sickness for some time, but he was given medical treatment too late. His appendix had burst and he died of peritonitis. The first child to die at Tardun was ten-year-old Charles Brunard in October 1943. He accidentally fell under the wheel of a truck driven by Brother Thomas as the vehicle was coming to a halt in the schoolyard. He was killed more or less instantly. The third boy, Kevin Glasheen, died sleepwalking. One of the nuns found his body in the morning. He had been sleeping on the upstairs veranda and fell to his death during the night.

After the eventful Christmas at Tardun, for the holidays in 1961 I was sent to stay with the Migro family in John Street, North Fremantle. They were Tommy's friends and often took boys for the holidays. Their neat timber cottage heaved with children – there were six children already. They had a talking white cockatoo they got from Tardun that kept repeating, 'Anyone in the toilet, anyone in the toilet?'

Jacko, who lived next door, had a 5 metre clinker runabout that we took on the river to go crabbing. The shallows of the Swan River were alive with blue manna crabs and we used a Tilley lamp and a scoop net to catch food for the family in no time at all.

I had now been at Tardun for four years and was approaching fifteen years of age. I had seen a lot at the school but I was anticipating more and more the time when I would leave and start life on my own.

THE BIRD MAN

In 1962 I jumped a class and went from year six to year eight, or first year high school, and was now in Brother Ackary's class with about a dozen other new children. Brother Ackary taught years eight, nine and ten in one class and so divided the blackboard into three sections. He was a small, slightly built man with grey hair and a very studious look. He was nowhere near as strict as Tommy and sometimes had difficulty controlling us. He was patient and was determined to get as many students as possible through their Junior Certificate, which was regarded in those days as being highly educated.

Brother Ackary was a fine teacher, despite the workload of teaching three classes in all subjects in one room. I settled down fairly quickly and progressed normally through the year. I did well enough in the first year to be dux, along with Vincent Pace. Tommy bought us both a wristwatch as a reward. However, I missed Tommy's theatrical talks on communism. In our time with him, we must have exhausted every question and every angle on communism, anything we could think of to keep him going so we could avoid schoolwork. We needn't have worried – the Cuban missile crisis was soon to happen and would provide enough drama to keep the boys in his own classroom entertained for at least another year.

We gave some of the Brothers a particularly tough time – once with disastrous results. One of the most popular Brothers at the school in 1962 was Brother Wright, a tall, well-built, easygoing young man from Queensland. He worked on the stock with Brother Howe and did a lot of the fencing. He got along well with us.

He took us by bus one day to Dongara, south of Geraldton, where we swam and picnicked on the beach. On the way home, some boys began to play up, throwing wet towels around the bus, one of which struck Brother Wright on the back of the neck. After repeated warnings, his patience finally snapped. He stopped the bus about midway along the Tardun–Wongoondy Road and ordered us all out. Furious, he told us we could 'bloody well walk home'. He locked the bus then jumped into a car that had been following us along the road and got a ride into Mullewa where he went to the pub and got on the booze. We were walking along the gravel road about 50 kilometres from the school, when a farm worker on a motorbike rode down the hill from a nearby house to investigate. In pure devilry, some of the boys grabbed paddymelons that were growing wild on fallow land close by and hurled them at the worker as he rode by. He turned his bike around and, like Steve McQueen in the movie *The Great Escape*, hurled his bike back towards us. He was met again by a barrage of melons, nearly knocking him off his bike. He rode back to the house and rang Brother Hewat to complain about the unruly mob of feral boys loose on the road a long distance from anywhere. Hewat was appalled at our behaviour and sent a truck to pick us up. Brother Wright left the Brothers soon after and returned to Queensland, where he married and raised a large family. He was a good man, nowhere near as tough as some of the other Brothers, and we would miss him.

In 1962 a small group of Maltese boys, much older and bigger than the previous boys from Malta, arrived at the school. They were the last of the Maltese immigrants to Tardun. One evening, Brother Morgan was assigned dining-room duty and, as was customary, he called for silence towards the end of the meal. The new Maltese boys were sitting at a table together and continued talking. Brother Morgan removed his strap and demanded that the main offender follow him upstairs to receive six of the best. We could hear thumping coming from the ceiling above our heads and Brother Morgan emerged battered and bruised, bleeding slightly from his nose. Soon after, Hewat found a job in the city for the boy and sent him on his way.

Brother Thomas organised night studies for both classrooms. Our classroom door was kept closed, as he believed the older boys should have the self-discipline to study quietly without supervision. But he often put his ear to the door to hear us talking behind the thin timber. He would quietly and slowly turn the big round doorknob, noiselessly release the heavy latch and burst the door open, catching all the offenders in the act. Out would come his strap and the offenders would be punished on the spot.

My desk was nearest the door and it became my job to keep an eye on the doorknob in case it moved. As I couldn't study and watch it at the same time I had to find a solution to the problem. I balanced a ruler across the doorknob and placed a small piece of carpet on the concrete floor to deaden the noise of the ruler falling. For weeks whenever Tommy turned the knob, the ruler would fall silently to the floor and we would all stop talking. One day, in sheer frustration, he suddenly opened the door, jamming the ruler at the bottom. Red-faced and angry, he demanded to know who was responsible. That was the first time I got 'six of the best' from Tommy – and he hit hard. I refused to give him the satisfaction of knowing that the punishment actually hurt, despite the fact that my hands felt as though they were on fire. I was now toughened up Tardun-style and it would take more than this to upset me. Next day he approached me with a jar of honey saying, 'Don't get me wrong, sonny, you deserved to be punished. This is for the trick. It was a good trick. Well done!'

Ned inducted me into his 'Fergie' tractor-driving pool where I joined three older boys who were allowed to drive the tractor on hunting excursions. Ned preferred to sit on the trailer with his dogs and tell yarns about the bush and boast of his skills in bushcraft. He particularly liked to relate the story of how he found a downed American pilot during the war. The aircraft went down somewhere around Bindoon and teams of army and air-force searchers scoured the heavy forests, on the ground and in the air, using army jeeps and motorbikes. Ned went looking in his horse and cart and found the pilot, who, by that point, had been missing for a week.

In May 1962, Ned would have the chance to prove his skills again when one of the Maltese boys, Walter Berry, failed to return after an all-day hunting trip with him in 'no man's land'. The land to the north and east of Tardun was bush and scrub, all the way to Alice Springs. The boy was a recent arrival and everyone feared for his safety as the country was dry and he would have little chance of finding water. Unlike the rest of us he hadn't yet developed bush skills and a sense of direction.

Local search parties went out all night, lighting fires on hills, making noise and waving spotlights. The next morning, the police arrived with a couple of Aboriginal trackers and the search was now in full swing. We joined Ned's search party, trying to pick up tracks, which was difficult as all the boys on the hunting expedition the day before had worn exactly the same plastic sandals leaving the same prints all over the ground. Even the Aboriginal trackers were stumped. They complained to the police that there were too many prints on the ground and we were only adding to the confusion with our plastic sandals. This infuriated Ned, who too was wearing similar sandals, and he ignored the police sergeant's suggestion that we pack up and go home. Ned told them he knew the country better than anyone and had the best chance of finding the boy. We walked many kilometres that hot day. As we gulped down water, we thought of poor Walter, who we assumed by now was probably dying of thirst.

Towards the end of the day we all gathered along a track to discuss plans for the night and the following day. It was now too late in the day for aircraft to join the search, although they would have to be brought in if the night search failed. In the distance walking towards us along the track was a lone figure. We thought it was one of the searchers arriving back late. Suddenly we yelled almost as one, 'It's Walter, it's Walter!'

He was very thirsty and had egg yoke all over his face. He had stumbled across an emu's nest the day before and was still carrying a couple of its eggs in his shirt. The irony of it hit home: the boy had survived the bush and had found us. The Aboriginal trackers, the police and Ned couldn't stop laughing for a week.

I went to Tardie station about 145 kilometres north-east of the school for the May holidays that same year. The Seaman family, who owned the sheep station, were friends of John L. and had taken him for holidays when he had been at Clontarf. Their two youngest daughters, Judith and Jocelyn, were about the same age as me. They were typical country girls who helped their father, Reg, with the sheep work. I was fascinated with station life and joined in as much as I could. During the two-week holiday we visited two other stations – Malangata, about 50 kilometres north-east of Tardie, which was owned by Reg's brother Jim, and Bullardoo, about 80 kilometres to the west, owned by the Jensens – where I met all the other children.

The rabbit-proof fence ran close to the Tardie homestead and it was a good place to test an old Aboriginal trick Reg had told me about how to spear an emu at close range. Emus would wander up and down the fence and, being naturally curious, would investigate anything unusual. As Reg had instructed, I lay on my back with my legs in the air and began waving them about. Sure enough, a small mob of emus came out of the scrub and began walking in circles around me with their feathers ruffled. My only concern was that they might attack me with their sharp feet while I was in a vulnerable position on the ground, but it was rewarding finding that the trick had worked.

I got along extremely well with Judi and her mother, Dorothy, made her views known that the two of us would make a fine pair one day. Judi and I were both fourteen and we communicated our affection with our feet under the table at meal times. We could never be alone together as Jocelyn made it her business to follow us everywhere we went. One evening, we heard Judi calling out for a towel from the shearers' quarters about 100 metres away where she was having a shower. Mrs Seaman shoved a towel in my arms, telling me to take it to Judi. I walked towards the quarters, worried because I had never seen a naked woman before. I was extremely worried that Judi would scream in horror when I arrived at the shower door. I needn't have worried – a naked arm was all I saw as she snatched the towel from my hands from behind the door.

In the middle of the second week, the station had received enough rain to fill some of the shallow creeks near the homestead. The girls and I headed off on a warm afternoon to paddle and splash about in the muddy water. Suddenly a truck arrived and the boys on the back were laughing and hooting at the girls as they fled into the bush. It was Ned, here to pick me up. Without any warning he decided it was time to take me home. As I climbed aboard the back of the truck, I could have killed him for shortening one of the best holidays of my life. Dorothy told me later Judi cried for the rest of the holidays.

I spent the Christmas holidays of 1962 in Perth with the Seaman family at their city home in First Avenue, Mount Lawley. We went swimming in the river and going to the movies and, for the first time in my life, I went dancing, at Wrightson's dance studio. I sat in the back of Reg's car, my knees trembling and knocking uncontrollably. The girls said nothing and pretended not to notice but I could tell they were highly amused. My dancing skills were nonexistent and Judi and I spent half the night looking down at each other's feet as she taught me how to dance to Roy Orbison's latest hit 'Dream Baby', which was played a dozen times that night.

During some of our regular hunting forays I noticed the odd dead sheep, some in full wool, being picked over by the crows. We asked Brother Howe if we could collect the wool from the dead sheep and sell it for pocket money. He agreed, so Chris, a schoolmate, and I began collecting wool, physically carrying it on our backs several kilometres back to the school. The crows were a dead giveaway, making our task of finding the dead sheep easy. After about three months, we had collected several heavy bags and Brother Howe decided that we had enough to sell to the Elders wool brokers, but first he wanted to sort the good wool from the bad. He used a stick to flick the best pieces into a heap, separating the wool into roughly two halves. He said, pointing to the best heap, 'We'll keep this lot and you can have the rest'. Despite our disappointment, Elders gave us seven pounds for our two bags of foul-smelling wool.

Soon after, we boarded the school bus to travel to Perth for the Royal Show. Brother Hewat gave every boy except for Chris and me one pound to spend, explaining, 'You boys don't need any more money. You've got sufficient funds from the wool.' It was a lesson that I did not understand at the time and haven't since forgotten. Still, we had three times as much spending money as the other boys.

Our entrepreneurial spirit was dampened briefly but not dashed. There were always ways to earn pocket money at Tardun. Six of us took off early one Friday morning in September in Percy's FJ Holden, which he had lent to Ned for a week, headed for the Murchison River to get some baby budgerigars from hollows in the stunted ghost gums that grew on the flood plain.

Percy, our old gang leader, had left the school in 1961 and was now working as a rail guard at Morawa. He got his first job working for a Catholic farmer east of Geraldton. His first week's pay was kept by the farmer to buy blankets for Percy's bed in a little cold hut by the main building.[1] Percy and Ned were still on good terms, despite Ned having sacked him twice in one day. John Ryall, a schoolmate, who described Percy as 'one of the more gregarious and interesting boys at Tardun', relates the story:

> *The Kelly–Faulkner duo should have been a good combination. Both were great raconteurs, both loved nature, both had an affinity for the bush, both had all the time in the world to do whatever needed doing. Despite these common attributes, however, it was Brother Kelly who sacked Percy twice in the one day. Before the start of work one morning Percy absent-mindedly, and in a quite loquacious mood, began filling the fuel tank of the Ferguson tractor, which Ned used to cart his windmill equipment and kangaroo dogs. Percy was too busy talking to notice that he was filling the diesel tank with oil. When he observed what was happening, the usually affable Brother Kelly was momentarily speechless. 'You're fired,' he bellowed. After cleaning out the tank and refilling it with the right fuel Ned had sufficiently calmed down to see the funny side of things. Percy, re-employed, rejoined the crew as it was heading out to fix a windmill. There the party set to dismantling the pump rod. Percy was atop the mill using a small shifting spanner to dismantle some links. Ned was below directing the removal of the casing and spearhead. He took his hat off to wipe his brow. As he did so Percy's hold on the spanner slipped and it dropped on to Ned's bald pate. 'You're fired,' roared a numbed Ned Kelly.[2]*

On the way to the Murchison River, we stopped at the Mullewa Shire Council office where Ned asked me to cash in a bag of goats' tails. I told the man sitting behind the desk that the bag held 43 tails, which therefore was 43 shillings, and began tipping the tails onto the counter so he could count them. He jumped up from his desk, 'I believe you, I believe you. Don't tip …, don't …' Too late. The awful smell drifted through the office as half the rotting tails, alive with maggots, lay scattered on the counter. The rest of the office staff fled the room as I pushed the tails back into the bag. He quickly gave me 43 shillings and told me to leave the bag outside.

Ned's driving was frighteningly erratic on the way there and he almost lost control of the car on a couple of occasions. We found out later that he didn't have a driver's licence. It had lapsed some 20 years before.

In late September, we were all off again to no man's land, this time to get an eagle chick from a wedge-tailed eagle's nest that Ned had discovered during one of his bush holidays. Jack, being the best climber, scaled the large York gum tree that cradled the enormous nest. The parent birds, equal to the task, attacked Jack, who bravely held them off with a stick as he snatched one of two chicks out of the nest and thrust it down his shirt. Still under attack he reached the ground and proudly presented to Ned the two-week-old chick. Ned raised it and called the enormous bird Horatio. Tommy built a giant cage in the middle of the schoolyard and soon the eagle was everyone's favourite. He was so quiet that even the children could handle him.

Horatio joined us on every hunting expedition, perching on a rail at the front of the trailer. Sometimes he would fly off and we wouldn't see him for several hours but he always returned to his perch on the moving trailer, coming in like a kamikaze aeroplane with his 2 metre wing span, while we ducked and scattered to let him through. Ned taught the eagle how to hunt for its own food by dragging a dead rabbit around on a string. He slowly increased the difficulty by twisting and turning the dead rabbit faster and faster and until Horatio could snatch it at any speed and from any angle. While Horatio was certainly a free bird when catching his own food, he still liked his cage and enjoyed travelling around the farm with Ned, the boys, the horses and the hunting dogs. He particularly liked football and interrupted a few matches when he swooped in to attack the football. He could get very savage and aggressive when he caught the large leather ball on the ground and the game stopped until he was ready to let us have our ball back.

His only unpopular characteristic was that when he was perched on the trailer he would excrete half a cup of gooey white liquid on the boy sitting just behind him. That position we saved for any visitors on their first hunting trip who were excited to sit so close to one of nature's greatest hunting birds.

During the year, Brother Hewat announced a shilling bounty for every galah egg we brought to his office. The noise from the thousands of nesting pink and grey galahs that had made the school their home was deafening. We couldn't believe our good fortune as the average galah's nest contained at least six eggs and, if you were smart, you would leave two eggs behind so that the hen would lay another four in no time at all. For the next month the race for eggs dominated school life, causing chaos. Brother Howe had to warn the boys who went hunting on horseback not to stand on the horse with one arm in a tree hollow, as many an Australian stockman had met his death this way, when their horse had moved away leaving them hanging with one arm stuck. With no other branches nearby, and no way of extricating their arm from the hollow, it was a painful way to die.

Boys went missing and normal school activity was disrupted. Three boys took off at 6 am one day and didn't return until midnight. They returned with hundreds of eggs having crossed paddocks strewn with double-gee thorns in bare feet.

Hewat had unleashed a monster that had grown out of control. In all, several thousand eggs were delivered to Hewat and he had to sell Echo, one of the school's bulls, to meet his debt. The galah population the following year remained about the same.

In November I sold several hand-reared white cockatoos and six pink and grey galahs to the pet shop owner in Piccadilly Arcade in central Perth. I had gained a reputation as the 'bird man' and was now in business. A couple of former students arrived at the school on motorbikes in leather gear, telling me to sell them some birds. I didn't know either of them and wasn't impressed with their standover attitude, so I told them that the white cockatoos were a pound each and the galahs ten shillings. One of them thrust two emu beaks into my hand as payment for two hand-reared galahs. I had to be careful as I was on my own and they were bigger and older than me, but there was no way I could let their bullying tactics succeed. Instead of taking them to my cages, I took them to the horse yard where the York gum trees were loaded with hundreds of noisy galahs. Pointing up to the branches I said, 'Do you see the one on the far left of that branch, the one scratching its head? You can have him. He's tame and nearly talking and the one sitting just above, you can have that one as well. He escaped this morning.'

I didn't wait for their stunned response. I fled as fast as I could to the main building and mingled with the other boys for safety. I never saw them again and laughed that they were probably still at the horse yards trying to talk the wild birds down from the tree. I realised later that I still had their emu beaks – a very satisfying end to the episode.

Ned had decided to get another eagle chick from the same family as Horatio, so a year later, in September 1963, we headed out to no man's land again to get another chick. This one Ned called Helen. The chick was four to five weeks old and had nearly all its plumage. Despite constant handling by Ned, it never really became tame and friendly like Horatio, preferring to stay in its large cage.

I had moved up a notch with my bird business. Hewat grinned as he handed me a telegram with an order for 20 white cockatoos and 20 galahs for the pet shop in Piccadilly Arcade in Perth. I had other orders too and needed to change my business strategy to meet demand amid growing competition from other boys who wanted a slice of the business. I recruited the new Maltese boys who wanted pet birds for themselves but were too inexperienced to know how to catch and tame them. We had only one chance each year to get white cockatoos and that was on All Saints Day, the first of November. We all went out to the Mills' farm, south of Mullewa, where the birds bred in the tall salmon gums scattered around the property in little forests.

While all the trees had hollows, only about one in twenty had an active nesting hollow and my experienced eye picked them out along the way. As we ran through the forests, I would ask a Maltese boy to stand by and guard each tree until I could return, climb the tree and retrieve the chicks. I gave each boy one of the chicks as payment. I arranged for John L. to deliver the birds to the pet shop; however, this turned out to be a big mistake. Near the shop, he dropped the thin timber box carrying the galahs. It split open and panicked galahs were flying up and down Piccadilly Arcade for the rest of the afternoon. Some of the shoppers took home free pets. Still, I got a postal order for 25 pounds. I had never had so much money in my life.

For years a pair of Major Mitchell cockatoos had nested in the same old York gum tree near the school's shearing shed. These birds mate for life and one of their first offspring, dating back to the 1930s, was now an old but loved pet kept by the nuns in the convent. Yet, one day in 1956, one of the boys riding in the back of a ute shot a single bullet from a .22 rifle at random into a flock of several thousand galahs. The birds, flying in tight formation, ducked and weaved as if in a strange dance. Scattered among this vast flock were the pair of Major Mitchell cockatoos. One of them fell from the sky and the following year, their nesting hollow was taken over by a pair of galahs.

Major Mitchell cockatoos were endangered and so were worth a fortune in the bird market. John L. said he knew the location of a rare pair of nesting Major Mitchell cockatoos that bred in the same tree every year on a farm near Canna. The only hitch was the tree was only a couple of hundred metres away from the homestead. His plan was to raid the nest at night with the help of a few of the boys. I refused to go, and the group set off one night while we were at the pictures with ladders, ropes and a torch. One of the boys was up the tree with his arm in the hollow when a spotlight suddenly illuminated the scene. The angry farmer, Dick S., had caught them red-handed and demanded to know why they were on his property. He was a conservationist and was well aware of the nesting pair. John L., panicked and stuttering, told the unconvinced farmer that he was trying to get some baby galahs for the orphans at the Tardun school.

In November 1964, we were back at the Mills' farm for white cockatoos. We were too late and most of the young had flown the nest. As I walked through the tall salmon gums with the Maltese boys, we stumbled upon a wedge-tailed eagle chick covered in meat-eating ants and near death. We supposed that it had been kicked out of its nest as so often happens when there are two chicks competing for food.

I took it home and nursed it back to health. Ned wasn't interested in a third eagle, so I asked one of the young Brothers to take it to the Perth Zoo and swap it for a Major Mitchell cockatoo. Wildlife officers were appalled when they discovered that Tardun boys were still taking galahs and white cockatoos from nesting hollows. A team of government officers came to Tardun to warn us not to take chicks from hollows. My lucrative bird business came crashing down with a thud and, at age fourteen, I had my first falling out with bureaucracy, as I couldn't see the sense or logic in what they demanded.[3]

1   At the time, the state government's protection laws required employers to put aside 25 per cent of the wages of child migrants and Aboriginal peoples into a special bank account. The government never enforced these laws and, even though some monies were deducted, few child migrants or Aboriginal people were given this money when they reached 21 years of age. Today, the Western Australian Aboriginal people are demanding this money, plus interest, from the government.

2   David Plowman (ed.), *Our Home in the Bush: Tales of Tardun*, Tardun Old Boys Association, 1994, p. 110.

3   In the many years since, I have seen these birds do incalculable harm to the ecology, ring-barking trees and destroying habitat throughout the whole state. Today the numbers of white cockatoos and galahs far exceed manageable levels and I believe that, while they remain protected, their numbers continue to increase at the expense of the more timid varieties that can't find nesting hollows and are now on the verge of extinction.

13 THE GREAT POTATO UPRISING

At the beginning of 1963, Ned taught me to bake bread and pies, which I figured was part of a cunning plan to extricate himself from the bakery to give him more time to go hunting. With more than 100 people to feed, I baked three times a week. The equipment in the bakery was primitive but adequate and I rolled the dough by hand. The preheating oven was a 2300-litre steel water tank with built-in shelves and an old-fashioned three-bar electric heater. The main oven was oil-fired and could be heated in 25 to 30 minutes – this was a vast improvement on the old wood fire.

My new boss was Sister Lawrence to whom, as I found out much later, I was likely related.[1] She wrote out orders for the week and supplied yeast, sugar, salt and meat and vegetable fill for the pies and pasties. She had never been impressed with Ned's flat doughy bread that was almost stale before it came out of the oven. Ned often cooked rabbits with the bread, causing the gamey smell to infiltrate the loaves. His lack of technique seemed deliberate and he shrugged off the complaints in his usual style, roaring with laughter and saying that his flat bread lasted longer, which meant that he needed to bake less often. Sister Lawrence was often at her wits' end but never took Ned to task.

I took a more professional approach and, with the help of Joe, an old boy who had been a baker with a big company in Geraldton, I learnt how to cook a decent batch of about 80 loaves at a time. Sister Lawrence was very pleased. Not only was the bread more palatable but also she had regained control over the quality of the bakery's produce.

I wish I had known then about my relationship to Sister Lawrence as I perhaps could have used it to gain preferential treatment at the time of the 'potato uprising'. Thursday evening was the best meal of the week. We had roast meat and vegetables, including a single baked potato. There was exactly one small potato for every boy and these were carefully counted so there were no leftovers. I decided to steal some potatoes and hopefully cause a minor uprising in the process to challenge this miserly rationing.

Sister Lawrence, who always served at the food counter, plopped a small potato on my plate. With the plate hiding my hand, I grabbed a handful of baked spuds. The boys at my table were greatly impressed, especially when we watched the drama unfold. Sister Lawrence demanded of Joe, the cook, why he had miscounted the potatoes leaving three boys short. Joe, who was by now in tears, cried over and over, 'I counted 83, Sister. I counted 83!' Sister Lawrence, not convinced, berated Joe as if he was a little schoolboy who couldn't count, causing a great deal of laughter in the dining room.

The following Thursday, buoyed by my success, we launched another attack with me in the lead. Our aim was to leave as many children as possible without a potato and so make a farce of the single baked potato policy. As I held out my plate for my serve, Sister Lawrence's heavy steel spoon suddenly came crashing down, shattering my plate into pieces and exposing my hand full of baked potatoes. Shards of porcelain lay scattered through the meat and potato trays, making Sister Lawrence even angrier. Before I could recover, she beat me over the head with the heavy spoon, sending hot gravy dripping down the side of my face, and shrilled 'Punish that boy, Brother. Punish that horrid boy!'

Hewat, for whom the Sisters could do no wrong, gave me 'six of the best' on my hands in front of all the other boys. Puzzled, he later asked why I had deliberately upset Sister Lawrence, especially as we got along so well in the bakery. I told him that we had been asking Sister for months to give us more potatoes, but she claimed one was enough and that we were greedy to demand more. The following week, the kitchen stopped counting potatoes and we got enough for seconds. Despite my brief falling out with Sister Lawrence, we got along well and I was always one of her favourite boys. I enjoyed working in the bakery and, even better, for the next two years, I was able to get out of 50 per cent of all night study using the bakery as an excuse.

The baked potato uprising was out of character for me. A diet of Catechism and discipline had cast me in a tight Catholic mould, conditioning me to never question authority, especially that of the

Catholic Church, and to be obedient and have faith. My growing confidence had given me strength to break the mould and see things for the first time as I wanted to see them. I had begun to realise that 'the truth' was highly subjective and, from then on, I was determined to subject it to critical scrutiny.

Early in 1963 a couple of new Brothers arrived at Tardun. Brother Rowbottom was a mild-mannered, easygoing young man who loved Australian Rules football. As Brother Howe had left Tardun the year before, Rowbottom took over the school's football team and was keen for the boys to join the local Mullewa under-18 side. Having orphanage children interacting with children from 'outside' on a regular basis was unheard of but, by 1964, the Tardun boys made up a third of the Mullewa side and travelled about on the back of a ute.

Mullewa had three very competitive football teams, including A and B men's sides, and an army of town supporters. We soon got to know most of the locals and fitted in well with the local boys in the team. Competition to be selected for the team every week was fierce and a lot of the local boys missed out on getting a game. In the Tardun boys' second year with the team, we won the grand final in the Great Northern Football League, fittingly beating our old nemesis St Patrick's College.

The local girls came to watch us play, attracted by the sudden influx of 'new talent', and waved, smiled and winked. This didn't always please some of the local boys, especially those few who looked down on us because of who we were.

In those days, Mullewa was a thriving, prosperous town with a large population. There were three machinery dealers, with associated workshops, and the second-largest Holden dealership in Western Australia. The companies Wesfarmers, Elders and Dalgetys had teams of stock agents and merchandise sellers. There were a clothing shop, three delicatessens, a restaurant and a hairdressing salon. 'Doughy' Wallace was the town baker.

Mullewa was the rail junction for the Perth to Geraldton and Meekatharra lines, and the government railways employed teams of workers and housed their families. A hospital, high school, pre-primary convent school and a drive-in outdoor theatre contributed to the thriving metropolis.

Like most towns, Mullewa had its share of legendary characters. One in particular was the local butcher, who had passed away some years before. He was known by the local police, who were convinced he had been stealing cattle for his shop. Mobs of cattle were driven to town from stations to the north and were rested on the town common overnight before being loaded onto rail trucks. The police set a trap to catch the butcher and one morning observed he and his helper shoot a cow from a slight ridge above the common. They sprang their trap and casually drove down to make the arrests. By the time they got to the crime scene they discovered the dead cow was missing an ear. It wasn't illegal to shoot a 'clean skin' – an unmarked or unbranded cow – and as most cattle were identified with an earmark, it was important for the police to find the ear. They never did find that missing ear as the butcher's helper had shoved it up the cow's backside. Years later when the old butcher shop was refurbished, it was discovered that the beautiful white polished Carrara marble slab the butcher had used as his workbench was actually someone's headstone.

Another character owned the local clothing shop. He and a few of his mates were busted at the Club Hotel for after-hours drinking. Before the police came in to take the offenders' details, the owner escaped up the chimney. Unable to hang on, however, he slid back down and stood in front of the sergeant, unrecognisable and covered in soot. 'And who are you?' demanded the sergeant. 'Father Christmas!' came the reply.

In July, Rowbottom took our team to Perth for the Institutions' Football Carnival, run by the East Perth Football Club, where we competed against our peers in a quick knockout competition. There were many fine football players in the institutions and club scouts were looking for potential recruits. I won the 'fairest and best' trophy for the match against Bunbury at East Perth Oval. One of the former Tardun boys, John Vella, was already playing league football at East Perth with his heroes Graham 'Polly' Farmer and Jack Sheedy.

Club supporters hosted us in their homes for the weekend and took us to and from each game. It was where I met the Armanasco family. Vic picked me up and took me to his home in Dianella to meet his wife Jean and three children, Brent, Robert and Vickie.

The boys were gifted athletes. Brent held the state schoolboy record for the 100 yard sprint and was being coached by Les Jamison, who was also coaching Raylene Boyle, a skinny girl who could run (and who later won silver at the Munich Olympics). I became close friends with the Armanasco family and stayed with them whenever I was in Perth. The family were patient about some of my more 'feral traits' and in time I adjusted to a more normal standard of social etiquette.

That same year, we formed the St Mary's basketball team and began preparing to compete the following year against the men's team in the Mullewa basketball competition. Young Brother Don McPherson, who became player and coach, was the driving force behind the team. While Brother Hewat was prepared to support yet another sports competition, he was reluctant to spend more money so we would have to build and pay for the new basketball court ourselves.

The only practical way to earn enough money was to catch and sell wild goats, which were now in demand for their meat. We caught hundreds of them and trucked them to Geraldton where they were put aboard a carrier ship bound for Singapore.

Every afternoon after school Tommy took as out on his Red Inter to collect large white ant (termite) nests. The clay-like texture made a uniquely hard playing surface and, after levelling and rolling the nest material, a thin layer of bitumen was put over the top to complete the job. We made backboards out of scrap metal and timber and fenced the court – we now had a professional basketball court and all we had to do was to learn to play the game. The local Mullewa postmaster, Don McDonald, visited twice a week to teach us the rules and pass on some of his skills. We practised daily and it wasn't long before we were ready to join the local competition.

In our first year in the Mullewa men's basketball competition we didn't win a game. Nonetheless, we were able to improve our knowledge and skill and there was no lack of the enthusiasm. The second year we played in the grand final, which was tied. We lost the rematch. But by the third year, we won the premiership easily. In the fourth year, the local association forced our team to disband, claiming that we were too strong.

Land clearing early in the year resulted in fire and smoke on the horizon in every direction. New farmers took advantage of the hot weather to burn the dry bush and scrub they had flattened the year before. Thousands of acres were on fire, day after day, in controlled burning. A strong willy-willy[2] meandered its way across John and Dan Grima's paddock, picking up hot ash along the way and starting a small fire on Crown land across the firebreak and the fence. This massive bushfire became known as the Grima Brothers Fire and it destroyed thousands of acres, burning out of control for more than a month. Every morning a wisp of white smoke could be seen in the east and by mid afternoon, the whole eastern sky would be boiling with jet-black smoke that seemed to reach to the stratosphere.

As it had the only communication to the outside world, the school became the centre of the enormous fire-fighting operation, which involved massive equipment, spotter aircraft and an army of volunteer firefighters from every town for 80 kilometres around. A single telephone wire ran 16 kilometres to the Tardun store, which also served as post office, railway depot, party-line telephone exchange, unlicensed pub and community centre.

Hewat was determined to keep us away from the fire and warned of dire consequences if we went near it. But that was where the action was and, just as determined, Ted, another student, and I managed to con a lift to a hot spot about 24 kilometres north-west of the old Mugga Mugga goldmine where outbreaks were occurring along a fence line separating Crown land from a farm. A bulldozer was parked up in the corner of the paddock and a dozen firefighters were watching from a slight rise, waiting for the next wind shift. A slight easterly was pushing flames towards a large patch of black mallee and Paddy L., a local farmer, decided to take a closer look in his ute. Knowing we were from the school, he said, after starting the small petrol water pump, 'Jump on boys and grab a hose each. We're going for a little drive.' We hopped on to the tray of the ute.

Before we were half way along the fence, the flames had moved into the top branches of the mallee and the wind speed had increased dramatically. Paddy, who had been drinking, couldn't decide whether to stop, turn around or keep going forward. The highly flammable eucalyptus oil was a perfect food for the fire, causing the top of the tree to explode rather than burn. The fire crossed over the tops of the mallee and on to the other side of the fence behind us. Suddenly it was all around us.

Paddy put his foot down, screamed something before winding up the window and took off. The heat was intense, as a roof of fire exploded over our heads. We turned the hoses on ourselves and prayed that Paddy's Holden ute, and the little Villiers petrol pump, would keep going. Our dash through 500 metres of inferno seemed to take an eternity. Firefighters on the other side were appalled that Paddy had taken such a risk with two children on the back. We managed to get back to the school, our absence unnoticed, but we were badly shaken.

Brother 'Tiny' Synan was responsible for all land-clearing operations and had two Caterpillar D4 tractors, which were used to tandem-drag 50 metres of heavy anchor chain, knocking over bush and scrub in the chain's path. A team of working boys did most of the heavy work cleaning up the fire debris lying around on the ground.

Tiny was from the old school of Christian Brothers: tough, uncompromising and fervently believing that strong discipline and prayer maketh the man. Despite his nickname, Tiny, though not tall, was powerfully built and had enormous forearms. He was very strict and deeply religious, but suffered bouts of severe depression that resulted in mood swings and moments of uncontrolled laughter. He was so paranoid as to believe everyone was plotting against him and had a streak of violence that, like a dormant volcano, could erupt at any time. He was best left well alone, but sometimes this was not possible. A couple of months after the Grima Brothers Fire, he took a large group of boys out one afternoon to do some root and rock picking.

Along a fence line less than a kilometre away, we spotted a fleeing mob of about 30 or 40 emus and excitedly called for him to drive the truck faster so that we could catch up. He ignored our yells of 'faster, faster' and our banging on the truck's roof and continued on at a leisurely pace. John Russell[3], who was standing alongside me, leaned his head toward the window and bellowed, 'Put your fucking foot down!'

Tiny brought the Bedford truck to a halt, jumped out and physically hauled me from the truck onto the ground and began punching and kicking me. I lay curled up like a ball. No-one dared say a word as he struck out in his rage. He then picked me up and threw me back onto the tray of the truck and drove on as though nothing had happened. Shaken and bruised, I was otherwise unhurt and a couple of boys helped me to my feet. I turned to John and said, 'You owe me one, you bastard!' He nodded, because we often covered for each other. We had become like a lost band of brothers, fighting to survive with honour and dignity in a strange land among strange people.

Around September, the school brought three new wheat harvesters (headers) and a new truck. It had been a good season. The wheat crops were as thick as the hair on a cat's back and, following near record rain, a record crop was assured. However, major disaster suddenly loomed. Little did anyone know that a silent killer fungus had penetrated wheat crops throughout the state and that there would be no harvest. Wheat stem rust was virtually unknown in Western Australia and none of the varieties of wheat grown there had any resistance.[4] Billions of wheat heads, bobbing about in the breeze across the state, were empty. An eerie red dust cloud followed the new headers as they went around the 5000 acre wheat crop searching for grain.

It was customary for Brothers Synan and Sullivan to go driving on Sunday afternoons to inspect the crops, taking one of the boys to open and close the gates. I was asked to accompany them one day and the car got stuck in the mud about 8 kilometres from the school. Sullivan asked me to run home and fetch a rope and one of the tractors. I was to stay on the road: 'Don't go off the road as the ground is saturated. Stay on the road!' he bellowed, as I took off running cross-country.

Over an hour later I arrived with the International Super Six tractor. As I approached the bogged car, he held up his arms to stop me going any further. I ignored his signal – of course, I knew best. I drove the tractor around to the front of the car, where the tractor promptly sank into the mud, bogged up to the axles. I ran cross-country again leaving two angry men to walk the 8 kilometres home.

I spent the Christmas holidays with Mrs Osborne at Walkaway, a few kilometres east of the old Greenough hamlet. She was a widow and ran the general store, which also served as post office. Every morning I travelled with her to Geraldton in her Zephyr car to pick up bread and supplies. The car had either a faulty battery or generator and, for the entire six weeks of the holiday, she had to park it on a slope so we could push start it.

The old railway station at Walkaway was still in use and Mrs Osborne, and her team of helpers, sold tea, sandwiches and scones to the passengers on the last leg of the journey from Perth to Geraldton. I became friendly with the stationmaster, who regularly took me shooting rabbits at night. His house had no electricity and he used Tilly lamps and candles to light his house at night. He lent me a half a dozen rabbit traps and I set off each morning, pedalling Mrs Osborne's pushbike to the sand hills west of the hamlet that were infested with rabbits. A skinny, stray brindle kangaroo dog I had befriended followed alongside. The rangy dog got the first rabbit every morning. The rest I 'dressed', removing their skin and innards, and Mrs Osborne handed them out to the locals.

I enjoyed my holiday at Walkaway but was soon back at Tardun, preparing for my final year at school. Most of my mates had left by early 1964 and only four of the dozen or so boys who started with me in Brother Ackary's class made it to the final year. With Brother Hewat in charge, and with the more benign influence of the younger Brothers, there was a degree of mellowing among the older Brothers.

Children from local families were now being accepted as boarders. Change was in the air. The realisation of this hit home one day when we were all out hunting with Ned in early 1964. He had suspected that the Maltese boys were up to something during our long walks through the bush. Always at the rear, they kept to themselves and chatted in Maltese. So Ned decided on an ambush. We all hid behind large granite rocks while the Maltese boys approached, chatting away and smoking cigarettes. Suddenly Ned jumped out, saying 'Little man, I'll have that and that', as he jovially confiscated all the packets of cigarettes. He lit one up in front of everyone, inhaled the smoke and said, 'Not bad, not too bad at all'.

We continued walking, amazed at Ned's behaviour, wondering what would be the fate of the Maltese boys. Hewat would be angry when heard about it and Ned would almost certainly ask them to 'back the cart'. As it turned out no-one was punished. The whole incident was hushed up and Hewat never found out about it.

Even Tiny was showing signs of mellowing. He bought the working boys a new hi-fi record player and a stack of new records that the man in the music shop had assured him were suitable for Christian adolescents. This was remarkable because Tiny fervently believed that modern pop music was evil and sinful and corrupted the minds of those who listened. The popular Doris Day number 'Que Sera, Sera' had been banned by the Catholic Church a few years earlier for its corrupting influence. ·

For the first time I didn't go anywhere for the May holidays. Brother Sullivan asked me and a couple of other boys to stay behind to help with the seeding program. It was back-breaking work as the seed and superphosphate were in 85 kilogram bags dead weight, which had to be manually loaded onto the back of a truck and then poured into the seeding boxes of the machines. In all, approximately 4000 bags of fertiliser and 2000 bags of seed wheat, barley and oats had to be sown into 6000 acres of prepared land over a three-week period. I was strong for my size and had no problem with the heavy work or the long hours behind the wheel of a tractor. There were enough of us to ensure that we had some fun along with the hard work.

Brother Ackary was worried about me passing my Junior Certificate because I was spending so much time working in the bakery. I was engineering more and more time out of class, and my absence often coincided with subjects I didn't particularly like, such as algebra and trigonometry. I was also organising the occasional midnight feast for some of the boys at the bakery, where I kept extra bread rolls, butter and a cooked rabbit. The hard part was sneaking out of the dormitory at night, but Tommy was often absent as he hardly ever slept and spent hours praying in the chapel or designing new models in the metalwork room or gluing pieces of film together by the light of a torch.

Four of us sat for our Junior Certificate examination and, just as Brother Ackary had predicted, I failed, managing to pass only four of the required five subjects for an overall pass. A few days later Hewat invited Chris and me into his office for a chat. He told us we had outstanding qualities and asked if we would consider a chance to become farmers.

1   Sister Lawrence was a Carroll, from Wexford, Ireland, and joined the Presentation Order as a young woman soon after the turn of the century. My grandmother was also a Carroll from Wexford, whose sister Minnie had joined the Dominican Order about the same time. The Carrolls in Wexford were all said to be related, so Sister Lawrence was probably a distant aunt.

2   'Willy-willy' is thought to be an Aboriginal word for a spiralling wind that collects dust and refuses as it travels across the land – hence they are also known as 'dust devils'.

3   Like many of the Maltese orphans, John was always angry at his treatment. He had three brothers and a sister, all of whom felt abandoned and cast adrift by the Maltese government. When John died in his early forties his wife approached me at the wake and handed me a beer, saying 'John owes you this'. I was proud to drink to the memory of a loyal friend and fellow traveller.

4   In 1964, the Department of Agriculture began trialling two new wheat varieties – Mengavi and Gamenya – which showed resistance to stem rust. Both varieties were planted on the school's farm with outstanding results, especially Gamenya as it had the potential to be used for noodle manufacture. This variety would feature in my later farming life. It also became the dominant variety used across the state until 1985.

14
WORKING BOYS

Prior to 1964, the Brothers had established thirteen boys on their own farms and were, that year, helping two others to get started. They proposed to us that Chris would take over Martin's farm. Martin had gone broke a couple of years before, leaving debts the Brothers were forced to pay as they had been guarantor for some of his equipment. It was an old property largely developed with a house and sheds and was fenced and had water. I was offered a small, undeveloped bush block north of Rowley's. Chris would pay the Brothers back at current land values and I would pay for whatever improvements I made on the bush block.

I was extremely reluctant to take this on at first. Some other boys in the past had refused such an opportunity and I couldn't blame them. I dreamt only of leaving the orphanage behind and starting a new life. Developing a bush block was not easy and the work would be hard – it would be a tough life with no guarantee of success. I needed time to think it over.

In 1965 I became a working boy, one of ten living at the opposite end of the main building. Brother Synan was in charge of us. We each slept in a small cubicle, which gave me privacy for the first time in my life, although on warm nights, as was customary, we moved our beds onto the balcony. We shared the recreational facilities: a billiards table, table tennis table and the recently acquired record player.

One of the boys had brought back a packet of cigarettes from a trip to Mullewa to play basketball. Once all was quiet, he offered the cigarettes around and a few of us were smoking and talking on the balcony. Tiny, who slept in a cubicle adjacent to the working boys' quarters, suspected we were up to something and began carefully walking across the timber floor. He was a heavy man and the boards creaked as he slowly made his way across. We threw the cigarettes over the balcony and feigned sleep. He looked over the balcony and saw a half a dozen cigarettes glowing brightly in the dark.

'Are you awake John? Are you awake Joe? Anyone still awake?'

Nobody moved. He went towards Jack's bed where he could see a glowing cigarette through the sheet. While Jack was copping the blows we could barely restrain ourselves from laughing out loud.

'Who else was smoking? Who else was smoking?' he angrily demanded while Jack kept repeating, 'Don't know sir, don't know sir!'

It was all the more bizarre because, a few years earlier, Jack had been given permission to smoke. He was a bad asthmatic and the doctors recommended he take up smoking as a cure. Ned, too, suffered from asthma and kept a carton of Rothmans cigarettes in his room. It was Harry's job to deliver Ned's meals when he was sick in bed. Whenever Ned was distracted, talking to one of his dogs lying on the bed, Harry would swipe a packet and share them around.

Approximately ten boys were divided up into working teams. Some worked with Brother Sullivan; some worked on the stock with Brother Thiel, who had replaced Brother Howe; a couple worked with Ned; and the rest with Tiny on his Caterpillar tractors.

My time working on Tiny's team got off to a bad start. The starter petrol engine on one of the Caterpillar tractors had a damaged front oil seal and it spewed oil from the crankcase during start up. Tiny dropped me off at the tractor one morning, and in a hurry, left me with a small quantity of oil and a waterbag, saying he'd be back later with my lunch. The idea was to not waste oil by filling the crankcase of the starter petrol engine, but instead just put in sufficient oil from the can to get the starter engine to fire the main diesel engine. But it was one of those days when the main diesel engine refused to start. I heard a strange noise coming from the starter engine and shut it down but too late to prevent damage to its crankshaft. Paranoid and suspicious as ever, Tiny accused me of deliberate sabotage and wouldn't talk to me for weeks. He told the other boys that the incident reminded him of the Virgin Mary's seven sorrows and wouldn't come out of his room for a week. Brother Sullivan and I repaired the damaged engine and, in time, Tiny got over it.

He was a brilliant mechanic and, as he was prepared to explain things and teach us, I learnt from him about welding and mechanical repairs. He was the best bush mechanic I have ever seen – he could hold a broken part together with fencing wire until he had time to make proper repairs. He never threw away a part he thought might be useful and had cupboards full of old bearings. He turned the large fully equipped workshop into his domain and most of the building resembled a junkyard, which annoyed other people who had difficulty finding anything. He had superb judgment in assessing the life remaining in an old bearing and he never changed one unless absolutely necessary.

Only once did his judgment about bearings fail. Three of us were helping him to completely overhaul of one of the Caterpillar tractors. The tractor had been split in half and the tracks were laid out on the floor. Tiny removed the spigot bearing from the clutch compartment, carefully examined it and declared that it had at least another 500 hours of service and didn't need replacing. He repacked the bearing with grease and put it back in. The bearing collapsed on the way out to the paddock. We had to tow the tractor back to the workshop, split it in half again and repeat the whole two-day process. On another occasion Tiny was welding something onto the tractor. The tractor wasn't properly electrically earthed and arcing occurred between the new bearings and the crankshaft causing enormous damage to the tractor. However, these were mere hiccups and he usually managed his enormous workload with great skill, repairing, maintaining and servicing all the farm equipment and machinery, in addition to the trucks, the bus and the diesel generators.

Tiny was also a handy bush engineer. He joined two old Wiles Standard 14 twin-disk stump jump ploughs together to make one large cultivator, eventually building three or four of these machines. This required a certain amount of knowledge of geometry to sort out the new link-point towing configuration. His mechanical and engineering skills were renowned in the district and farmers would come with broken bits and pieces, which Tiny would repair without charge.

I recall the day I struck his hand a painful blow with a 6 kilogram sledgehammer, having missed the punch that he was holding against the master pin on the Caterpillar tracks. He walked away, shaking his head and whistling a hymn. He didn't accuse me of doing it deliberately – a sign that he was mellowing.

Apart from Tommy, he was the busiest man at the school and had a prodigious appetite for hard work. By comparison, Brother Sullivan was the complete opposite. Even-tempered and quiet, he often mumbled his words and at times was hard to understand. He was responsible for the overall operation of the farm and oversaw the cultivation, seeding and harvesting of the crops with a team of five or six boys who drove the wheeled tractors. He set the depth of each plough or seeding machine and attended to the servicing and lubrication of plant and equipment, then sat in his ute in the corner of the paddock. He did manage to boil the billy for tea and fetch the lunches, as well as organise the movement of the machinery into the next paddock.

He would start the tractors at 8.30 am and shut them down at 5 pm. Unlike Tiny, he avoided long work hours, believing that the school had enough equipment to seed and harvest crops within normal work hours. A man of habit, he enjoyed two large bottles of beer after work and would spend the rest of the evening with the other Brothers.

During harvest that year, I badly injured my right thumb, which got caught up between a moving sprocket and chain and came out badly mangled. Sister Lawrence dressed the wound as best she could then sent me off to hospital. The new doctor, a Scottish general practitioner, had worked for a few years in Uganda and was a skilled surgeon. He was a gifted doctor who did everything: delivered babies, fixed and set broken bones and performed minor surgery. It seemed that there was nothing he couldn't do. He decided that the only way to save my thumb was a skin graft. He gave me a general anaesthetic and removed skin from my leg and stitched it over the thumb. For two weeks twice a day, he plunged the raw thumb into a bowl of red solution for several minutes and I howled in agony. 'I thought you Tardun boys were supposed to be tough!', he said as he grinned and again plunged my thumb into the fiery liquid.

Soon after, he took his family back to Scotland for a couple of months, saying that he wanted to see me first thing when he got back. On his return, I went to the hospital but showed him my other thumb. He repeated over and over, 'Beautiful! Absolutely marvellous!'

He wasn't impressed when he saw the injured thumb, which was still raw but definitely healing. The operation had been a huge success and I'm fairly certain it was his first skin-graft operation.

Shearing the farm's sheep was typically a chaotic process. The school provided the shed hands and cook for up to eight shearers at a time. We yarded and penned the sheep, and picked up, sorted and classed the fleece and baled the wool. The shearing of the flock of over 6000 sheep could take between two to three weeks, depending on the weather. Each shed day was divided into four sections, or runs as they were known, and after each run the shearers ate copious amounts of carbohydrates to keep up their strength.

John L. was usually a member of the shearing team and liked to ingratiate himself with the Brothers by coming back later to shear the stragglers or to kill and butcher some wethers. During one shearing season, Brother Sullivan noticed that the two bottles of beer he had placed in the fridge each morning were hot. Someone was swapping them over and suspicion fell on the shearers. Eventually John L. was caught red-handed one day after work as he was peeking through the keyhole to the Brothers' dining room. He had two hot bottles of beer in his hands. Stealing or swapping someone's beer was considered a 'mortal sin'. John L. was none too happy when the shearers named the first run of the day the 'Little Bo Peep run'.

'You can all get f-f-fucked' was John L.'s typical stammered reply.

He enjoyed being a larrikin and troublemaker and one of his favourite sayings was, 'At least when they're talking about me, they're not talking about some other poor b-b-b-bastard!'

One day, we walked into Mrs Mead's fish and chip shop and John L. insisted it was his turn to buy. The old lady was very strict and removed anyone who swore in her shop. John L. stuttered badly whenever he was nervous, annoying him greatly, and as he looked up the price board, he said very slowly 'I'll have f-f-fifty c-c-cents of c-c-hips … and I'll have the f-f-f-f … oh fuck, the fish'. Mrs Mead demanded that we vacate the premises at once.

In 1966 Chris and I took up residence in the hostel at the school where farm trainees and visitors were accommodated. We had stopped being working boys and were now farm trainees. There was nothing that we couldn't do on the farm. We unloaded and stacked 24 tonnes of bagged superphosphate before breakfast, until all the fertiliser had been delivered.

Hewat had left at the end of 1965 and was replaced by Brother Foley, cousin of Perth's Archbishop Foley. In his six years, Hewat had changed the culture at the school from a harsh orphanage environment to a more pleasant community, with a style different to the other orphanages such as Clontarf and Bindoon. The school had become the mail depot and meeting place for the old boy farmers and their wives or girlfriends.

In 1966, after working there since 1941, the three elderly Sisters left Tardun to go into semi-retirement at Stella Maris College in Geraldton. I would miss Sister Lawrence in particular, despite our little differences in the past. I often visited her in Geraldton, where she seemed unhappy. The times were changing: the girls at the college had little respect for the elderly nuns. She held my hand tightly the week before she died and, with tears, she said 'You boys, you Tardun boys, you were all good boys!'

We worked hard for a small wage that we would get back in kind in a couple of years. We borrowed one of the school utes to attend football matches and go to dances and social events in Mullewa. An old-time band would play on the stage in the town hall and the single young ladies sat on one side of the room with the young men on the other. It was a long walk across the hall to ask a girl for a dance and an even longer one back when she refused. My new clothes helped – I had been to Aherns department store in the city with a $50 voucher, the amount given to child migrants once they left the institutions. The government money allowed me to buy a suitcase, work clothes, dress clothes, shoes and socks.

BECOMING A FARMER

I began working in my spare time on my bush block known as Geoghegan's. I borrowed machinery and did a little clearing, fencing or whatever I could do that didn't require much capital. There were a number of problems with Geoghegan's. First, the block was too small. At 2600 acres, it was not considered viable on its own, unlike most of the blocks released by the Lands Department, which were between 4000 and 5000 acres. Second, the land did not belong to the Brothers and was passed over to them by the Lands Department under a conditional purchase agreement. Third, there were legal problems, as a block under conditional purchase could not be sold or transferred until the property had been paid for.

Brother Sullivan was painfully aware of these problems, but suggested that I apply when the time came for one of the adjoining new blocks: in particular the 4500 acre block that abutted the eastern boundary of Geoghegan's. If successful, my landholding under conditional purchase would then be in the order of 7000 acres – a viable size. The state had embarked on a program to release a million acres a year to new land farmers and 23 000 acres of bush and scrub, divided into five blocks, were due for release in the immediate vicinity. Interest was growing in these new releases and the competition to obtain a block was increasing. The Lands Department set up a selection panel and each candidate was scrutinised at length on their capacity, knowledge and financial resources to farm.

There was no requirement on farmers to have environmental knowledge or responsibility nor were there guidelines about how the land should be cleared or how much remnant vegetation should be protected. It was open slather. Some new land farmers with strong financial resources would flatten with a chain the bush on their entire block and set it alight on the hottest day, creating a huge firestorm of such intensity that nothing remained but rocks and burnt termites' nests. While this practice was acceptable to the Lands Department, those of us who had an affinity with the bush and the land and knew its limitations could only look on with deep misgivings. The destruction of native flora and fauna was colossal.

Tiny, who had more experience in land clearing then anyone else around, often talked about how the mistakes were being repeated over and over. He knew from experience what kind of remnant vegetation should be left because, once removed, the soil would turn saline. He also believed in providing shelter belts to protect newly shorn sheep and leaving attractive stands of trees and scrub.

In early 1967, the Brothers were able to transfer Geoghegan's into my name, bringing me under the umbrella of the Lands Department as a conditional purchase farmer, or 'Blockie' as we were commonly known. How they managed to achieve this when conditional purchase blocks were not transferable remains a mystery, but the Brothers had friends in high places. This did not please the selection panel, who saw me as a privileged intruder, slipping in under the radar.

I had cleared enough land for the Brothers to sow 900 acres of wheat, of which I would receive one-third. The money we earned was sufficient to keep me for a year and to put a deposit on a decent second-hand tractor. I signed a mortgage contract to repay the Brothers for seed, fertiliser and fencing, which came to $1900. The Brothers made it clear that it was all the help they could give me. This was disappointing as they had been far more generous to the boys who had left before me, but fatigue over settling boys on the land over many years had finally caught up with them. Chris and I would have to find our own new ways to survive. I also owed the Lands Department 76 cents per acre for the 2600 acres – the going price for virgin land. Nonetheless, the conditions from the Lands Department were generous: 2 per cent interest per annum on the loan over 30 years.

In 1968 the five new blocks were released and candidates were called to the selection panel for assessment. This was the moment I had been waiting for. Sullivan and I sat in a room with the five men who made up the panel. Sullivan, in his quiet way, explained that the

Brothers had a good record in establishing boys on farms and that they would assist me until I could 'get on my feet'. In addition, as my block abutted the new release it made sense to add the new block to make my farm viable. This cut no ice with the panel, however, who perhaps had long memories of the Christian Brothers from the bad old days when the Lands Department was the legal guardians of all child migrants. To my bitter disappointment, my application failed. It was also a great disappointment to Sullivan, but there was nothing he could do. I was left holding a small bush block that couldn't give me a future, but I was now determined to prove the panel wrong.

Tiny had spotted what he thought was a decent second-hand Countryman tractor at the Chamberlain dealership in Morawa and offered to drive me there to do a deal with the owner. Frank Roach, who knew Tiny well from previous business dealings, invited us into his office to complete the deal. Tiny was responsible for buying and selling all the farm equipment for the school and was known far and wide among machinery dealers as a hard negotiator. We settled on a price of $3800. I would pay $1000 deposit and take out a loan with a finance company to pay the balance over three years.

After the paperwork had been finalised, the dealer, Frank, said, 'There's only one problem, Brother. John is not 21 yet and will need a guarantor.'

Tiny thought for a moment and replied, 'The Provincial Council has banned the Brothers from acting as guarantors so what about you, Frank, why don't you go guarantor for John?'

Frank laughed his head off. 'I don't even know the young man, Brother, and even if I did … besides I sell tractors and machinery. I don't make guarantees to finance companies so they'll get paid in the event of a default.'

Disappointed, we left the office and headed towards the car.

Suddenly Frank ran out behind us and called, 'Bring the boy back in, Brother. I'll take him on.'

That one simple generous gesture by Frank, a man I didn't even know, was a critical factor in the future success of my farm. Had I not been able to purchase a tractor, and after my disappointment with the Lands Department, I would have given up and gone away.

For the first couple of years a Lands Department officer visited my farm to check on progress. The first year he laid it on the line without mincing his words: I was in breach of the contract as I had not cleared the minimum 600 acres. If I continued with this lack of progress they would confiscate my land. I pointed to the fact that I had no plant and equipment suited to land clearing and that even if I were able to clear 600 acres, I could not possibly clean and plough that much land in just one year.

He replied, 'Then just knock it down with a chain and leave it. We'd be happy with that.'

Under the contract, I had to provide a clean track around each paddock so he could negotiate it with his nice car and the bicycle wheel with a counter attached that he towed to measure the distance around the flattened bush and scrub. The following year, on the day before he arrived, I threw rocks and large stumps back onto on the tracks around the newly cleared land.

He grumbled loudly as his car bottomed out on yet another large rock. 'This track is not up to scratch!' he said, as he pulled up.

'I have no trouble in my old ute,' I lied.

'Then we'll use your ute,' he said.

'Can't,' I replied, 'it's broken down.'

He stood on the bumper of his car looked out across the flattened bush and scrub and said 'So you reckon there's 600 acres here?'

'Yup,' I replied.

'Okay, I'll take your word for it.' He never bothered me again.

I found the Chamberlain 18 disk plough was the ideal tool to tackle the short, thick scrub, sticks, white-ant nests and rocks and stumps that littered the ground. Punctures in the big tractor tyres were the biggest problem but their frequency could be lessened by putting another tyre on the outside, a job that could be accomplished by two strong men using heavy crowbars as levers and a sledgehammer. Even with the double tyres, I averaged three punctures a day. I carried on the tractor a portable compressor, patches and all the tools needed to make repairs. The outside tyre would soon be ripped to pieces and I was constantly on the lookout for suitable old tyres.

All the rocks and stumps in the paddock had to be removed by hand and even after many years the plough continued to drag more to the surface. The work was hard and hot and I was covered head to toe in thick dust at the end of each day.

It became clear to Chris and me that we would have to share resources if we were to survive. We had a tractor and plough each but that was all. I bought an old International 8-ton truck and now all we needed was a seeder. Harry Williams had an old Shearer culti-trash sitting under a tree that he let us have for $500, interest-free, to be paid for the following year. However, the machine was so old that we couldn't buy parts. Somebody suggested that we try old Carl Offzanka at the Canna store, saying that not only would Carl have the parts, but also we wouldn't get a bill for a year. Carl's store had a reputation of carrying anything you needed from this century or the one before. It was a treasure trove of old forgotten bits and pieces that were still sold at the old prices. Among boxes stacked on more boxes, Carl found our parts and we bought spindles, bearings, pins, bushes and other bits and pieces. We were able to rebuild the old machine almost like new – and we didn't get the bill until the following year.

Having no money and no borrowing power, as neither of us had title to property, we approached Wesfarmers to finance the main items such as fertiliser, fuel, sheep, windmill and fencing gear, plus a host of other requirements. This was done by means of a crop or wool lien – the cheque for the sale of produce went straight to the Wesfarmers, who took what was owed plus interest. We got the balance, if any. But without companies like Wesfarmers and Elders, it was unlikely that new land farmers could have got their farms off the ground.

We sowed 2000 acres of wheat and split the proceeds in half. Chris brought a header and I outfitted the old truck with new tyres and a wheat bin. Following the harvest, I equipped the bore Ned had sunk with a new windmill tank and trough and brought 620 pregnant ewes at a $1.92 each. I earned $12 457 from wheat and, after expenses, returned a loss of $200. The taxation value of my land and improvements in 1969/70 was $5398.

In November 1969, the Australian government announced wheat quotas for the following year.[1] The federal government's wheat sales and marketing agency, the Australian Wheat Board (AWB)[2], which had sole rights to market the national crop, was having difficulty finding markets. Since farmers were forbidden by law to sell or market their own wheat, we were at the mercy of the AWB, nicknamed 'the armchair sellers' for the widely held perception they had little idea about how to market grain.

The government appointed the State Wheat Quota Committee to oversee the allocation of the quotas. To my great disappointment, I was given a quota of 4000 bushels – a huge difference from the 14 000 bushels I had produced the year before – as the committee argued that I could not be considered a new land farmer because the property had previously belonged to someone else. I attended a meeting in Perth to argue my case, suggesting that my land still belonged to the state government and therefore technically the Crown was owner until the land had been cleared and paid for. Surely, I argued, the wheat quotas were designed to curb production, not to put farmers out of business but the committee were inflexible in interpreting the criteria.

Brother Sullivan transferred 2000 bushels of the school's quota into my name, but 6000 bushels was still not nearly enough. I sold the sheep, stored my farming equipment in the new shed and took work around the district in shearing sheds or wherever I could find employment. I leased the farm and the quota to friend and neighbour Naz Grima, a Maltese boy the Brothers had helped settle on the property next door.

For the first time I realised that the farming industry was as institutionalised, if not more so, than anything I had experienced as a child. There were numerous rules and regulations, and fines and penalties were exacted for every transgression. The proponents of government control cited stories of how, during the Depression, unsavoury merchants had ripped off the farmers and warned that these merchants would strike again unless the industry had government protection. Private sales of grain or other produce were forbidden except in exceptional circumstances, yet the various marketing boards that were responsible for selling our produce charged fees and levies at every turn. It was no wonder that farmers began to criticise statutory marketing of produce.[3] They were convinced that the many boards were filled with public servants who had little idea of marketing.

Every Saturday and Sunday evening, I would go to watch Tommy's heavily censored pictures, along with the Aboriginal boys and girls from the Pallottine Mission. Accompanying them was a handful of young female lay helpers, mainly from Victoria. One night, one of the children handed me a heavily perfumed letter from one of the helpers, so beginning a regular correspondence via hand-delivered mail that lasted several months. We couldn't be seen together as it would lead to her instant dismissal, so we waved and smiled at each other from a distance.

She invited me over to meet her in the mission kitchen at midnight one evening so we could have coffee and a chat. I parked my ute about a kilometre away and walked quietly to the mission in the dark. She was boiling the kettle for our second coffee when we heard a noise. She pushed me behind the door and the mission manager, Father Eddie, walked in and shone his flashlight around the room.

'What are you doing?' he asked, shining the torch on the two empty cups.

'Just having a late coffee, Father,' she said as she turned the gas off.

Eddie slowly moved the torch around the room until he spotted me standing very upright, trying to look as inconspicuous as possible behind the half closed door. He left the room abruptly without saying anything. The next day Brother Foley approached me with a sheepish grin, 'I have just been asked by Father Eddie to inform you that John Hawkins is forever banned from the mission'. The young lady was sent back to Victoria in disgrace and I never heard from her again.

Brother Foley was sheepish because one of the older lady helpers had taken a shine to him and the pair could be seen strolling together while the picture was showing. After serving four years as principal, Foley left the Brothers in 1968 before his six-year term was up and moved to Canada, where he married and settled down. Brother Bruno Doyle, who had gained a fearsome reputation at Clontarf, replaced him.

I turned 20 in March 1967 and tuned in to ABC radio to see if my number had come out of the lottery barrel for national service. Like all other young men at the time, I had compulsorily registered for conscription and, if the number chosen from 1 to 31 matched the date of my birthday in March, I was headed for the Australian Army. One number came perilously close but, thankfully, I was spared the ordeal of serving in Vietnam.

1   The quotas were created by adding up individual delivery figures for the previous five years, whereby a portion of that figure was removed and the balance divided by five became the new quota. The government guaranteed a payment of $1.70 per bushel (approximately 27 kilograms) or $61.20 per ton for quota wheat. Growers who exceeded the quota could not be guaranteed payment for over-quota deliveries. Special provision was made for new land farmers who did not have a five-year history of wheat production.

2   The AWB had been created under the National Security Act 1939 to protect Australian farmers from being exploited in the international grain market. The perception had been that farmers were being paid too little and the government was being overcharged for storage and handling. The AWB managed the marketing and export of Australian wheat but, by doing so through a 'single desk', it overrode the right of individual farmers to market their own produce.

3   The AWB controlled the sale of wheat for doing so imposed levies and charges. The Grain Pool of WA required permits for the private sale of all coarse grains other than oats and, of course, charged fees and levies for its services. Lupins later joined the list of statutory grains. Permits were required if a farmer wanted to use a contractor to cart fertiliser – this was designed to protect the government railways by minimising competition against them. Cooperative Bulk Handling had sole rights to handle store and ship grain – again with compulsory levies and charges. The situation wasn't much better in sheep farming. The Wool Board was responsible for marketing and promotion – and this too carried charges and levies. The WA Lamb Marketing Board controlled the sale of lambs – with levies and charges. In addition, there was the Potato Board, the Egg Marketing Board, the Meat and Livestock Boards, the Dairy Boards and so on – all levying fees and charges. The list was endless. In 1970, at a Farmers Union meeting in a town called Miling, 120 farmers called for the statutory marketing of all meat except poultry. In the same year, at a meeting in Katanning, 650 farmers called for the statutory marketing of wool. The following year they demanded a minimum of 40 cents a pound for their wool.

16

FORCED TO QUIT

The government-imposed wheat quotas had effectively ended my farming career, along with those of plenty of other young farmers. I got a job looking after Ollie Winters' property while he was away on holidays. Ollie, an old boy farmer, had leased Maurice Grima's property while he was away in the army. We decided to build a road along a gazetted line through Crown land. This shortcut would remove miles of travel for all around. I cleared a track of about 2.5 kilometres, carefully following the gazetted line.

The Department of Main Roads and the local shire council were appalled and Ollie and I were both wrapped over the knuckles. We had thought we were doing everyone a favour.[1] For the first time we heard the word 'conservation' used to justify an action. This made no sense to me at all – the land I had cleared for the road was no more than 5 acres, yet all around the district, tens of thousands of acres of trees and shrubs were being attacked by giant bulldozers dragging long and heavy anchor chains that destroyed bushland and habitat.

No man's land – our magic land of adventure and mystery where, in our imagination as children, dragons and monsters lived – had become a vast wasteland of flattened trees and scrub. There were no more magic pathways; no new animal or insect life we could gaze at in wonder. Gone forever was our old playground. The world seemed to have gone mad – and I was part of it.

I worked with Naz for the remainder of 1970, seeding, shearing and harvesting. A few hundred acres of self-sown wheat had emerged on my land and so we decided to harvest it and split the proceeds. I spent my money on a driving holiday to the eastern states.

In March 1971, I packed the old ute and headed north to try to get work on the Ord River Dam. My debts at the time equalled my assets. There were no petrol stations between Port Hedland and Broome, so I called into La Grange Aboriginal mission to see if I could buy petrol. Father McKelson, who ran the mission, noted the Mullewa number plates on the ute and asked if I knew anyone at the Pallottine Mission at Tardun. I told him I knew Father Eddie very well and some of the other Brothers and priests – but, of course, failed to mention that I had been banned from the mission.

Father McKelson had bought some new tillage equipment for their vegetable gardens. It was still packed in the wooden boxes and he asked if I would help to set it up. While I was there, he showed me recent photographs of an Aboriginal family in shocking condition who had come out of the desert and were believed to be the last of the local nomadic tribes.

A few days later I arrived at the dam site and, as luck would have it, the Dravo administration office told me I could have a job driving a dump truck. The site was a hive of activity, with a couple of hundred workers of all nationalities doing a range of jobs. It was hot and humid and the accommodation was substandard. But the food was good, as was the money, so it was worth a go.

About six weeks later my truck broke down. I was put on point duty at a blind intersection where dump trucks had right of way. The unpopular supervisor, an American, ignored my stop sign and raced through the intersection at high speed. The other workers told me that he always did this and would run you over if you got in the way. So one hot afternoon I took him on, standing in the middle of the road and waving the stop sign. He hit the brakes just in time. He jumped out of the vehicle and angrily told me he could have killed me. 'You stupid mother fucker!' he mouthed.

After some pushing and shoving – I can't recall who struck the first blow – in a moment we were both on the ground wrestling. Workers ran from everywhere to break us up.

Next day I was back on the road again, heading south to Mount Goldsworthy and hopefully a job at the iron-ore mine. I arrived at the Goldsworthy administration office, nicknamed 'bullshit castle', and landed a job as a driller's assistant. It was a filthy job and I was covered in oil, grease and dust. Naz's brother George was working in the powerhouse and showed me around, explaining the mining culture and the best way to get along. He told me that under no circumstances do you fight with a supervisor, or anyone else for that matter, as it would result in instant dismissal.

The Goldsworthy township had been built on the wrong side of the mine. Sirens blared warnings before each explosion so that people could take their washing off the line before a thick red cloud of ore dust, carried by the prevailing easterly wind, descended upon everything. The town was fully self-sufficient and the air-conditioned quarters were a welcome relief.

The German drill operator I assisted was looking for a way to make sure the machine would break down so he would have an excuse for a long holiday. I checked the oil in the V16 diesel engine and told him it was very low, suggesting that we call in the oil and fuel team. The operator, being a 'true blue' union man, told me it was not my job to call anyone and so continued drilling until the engine ran out of oil and blew up. 'They can't put me on another job,' he boasted. 'I'll have two months off on full money until they fix the machine!'

This didn't suit me so I was assigned to work on the cable gang, moving heavy electrical cable for the big shovels – the worst job on the mine.

Goldsworthy had its own better than average football team and competed in a strong local competition. I joined the team and began training with the other men. Captain Harry Newman, known as Mouse, was a gifted athlete and could play any position on the field. Mouse, played at centre halfback and was a champion player. It was impossible to get the ball past him. I roved and rested in a forward pocket. In one memorable game at Marble Bar, we couldn't see the ball for dust. The local council had built a new football ground over the old rubbish tip and the ground was still strewn with small rocks left behind by the graders. The blowing dust was so bad that it was impossible to see one end of the ground from the other. We won the game but no-one knew the real score as the ball sailed through the goalposts in a thick cloud of dust.

Some of the players were driving 180-ton Haul Pac trucks – the best job on the mine with the best pay. Wayne, the coach, was also a mine supervisor so I asked him if I could get a job driving a Haul Pac. A job was coming up but competition was fierce and I would need to learn to drive the truck first. I spent the entire nightshift in the cab of a truck driven by a footy mate. Neither the shovel operators nor the supervisors could tell that it was me in a white helmet behind the wheel of the giant truck. Next day at 'bullshit castle' I passed my driving test with flying colours and beat the other half dozen applicants for the job. We worked two 12-hour shifts and alternated dayshifts and nightshifts weekly. Strikes were a common occurrence and were often called for the most trivial reason. We had a fair bit of downtime, which a lot of us didn't welcome as we were only there to make money.

The mine manager was a German named Gunter. He drove around in his car urging the drivers and workers (both by radio and in person) to maintain production and berating them when he thought necessary. A strike was called over Gunter's attitude and the union delegates at a strike meeting told him there would be no further work until he apologised.

In his thick German accent, he asked 'For what shall I apologise?'

'Because you're a cunt!' rang out among the crowd.

The strike was resolved a week later when senior management apologised on Gunter's behalf.

One day on the bus heading up to the mine, a union representative asked to see my ticket and told me to have it with me the next day. I wasn't a member of the union. I didn't oppose unionism – it simply hadn't occurred to me to join. I told Wayne the problem and offered to leave my job, as I didn't want to bring the workers out on strike on my account.

I was surrounded by men from the football team when the union representative next asked to see my ticket. Two of the workers got out of their seats and took the man to the back of the bus for a chat. I was never bothered again.

I had had enough of the heat and dust and quit the mine in September 1971 to head south. I got a job with Toledo-Berkel, manufacturers of weighing equipment, and began a two-year training course to become a scales mechanic. I boarded at the Tardun Lodge in Barker Road, Subiaco, a suburb of Perth. The large Federation-style house was owned by Anne and Harry Brown and Tardun old boys, whether they had money or not, could always find a bed. Many held their 21st birthday or engagement or bucks' nights at Anne and Harry's place. Anne ran a catering business, while Harry was a parking attendant at Wilson's Parking in the city. Two other boys were boarding there at the time and the three of us were accommodated in the large sleepout at the back.

Harry was a typical alcoholic and began his day at 4.30 am with his first big brown bottle of beer, which he drank in the kitchen. He then went outside to the shrubs growing behind the sleepout and woke us with his coughing, farting, urinating and, sometimes, his throwing up. A heavy smoker, his cough had a death rattle.

The family pink and grey cockatoo lived in a cage near our room. This champion Tardun galah had learnt to mimic Harry's morning ablutions. Anne put on a special lunch one day for her business associates, friends and lodgers. A table for about 40 guests was prepared in the backyard. About halfway through the meal, the galah started up. Everyone stopped to listen. It sounded as though someone had suddenly started vomiting and had soiled his pants at the same time. Amid howls of laughter, a red-faced Harry walked over and kicked the cage to quieten the bird, declaring that Mario next door was sick with the 'flu and that the clever bird was mimicking his coughing.

My first job with Toledo-Berkel was to construct a shed at the back of the premises. I later built a mezzanine floor in the workshop. I progressed from there and learnt to fix broken shop scales, weighbridges and an assortment of other weighing devices. The company was situated in Hay Street, Subiaco, next door to an old house that had been the scene of an awful suicide. One of the young apprentices had spotted an old man hanging by a rope from a rafter at the back of the house. It took a few days before things were back to normal again in the workshop.

After a couple of months, Frank and I moved out of Anne and Harry's and shared a rented house in Campsie Street, North Perth, with two Irish men who worked with Frank as orderlies at Sir Charles Gairdner Hospital. Wally had been sent to Australia by his family to get him away from the troubles in Northern Ireland where he had some connection with the Irish Republican Army. He was certainly a small-time urban 'terrorist'. He was appalled one day when I brought the milk and paper from the delicatessen on the corner. 'The fucking street is full of newspapers and milk in the mornings,' he said.

Knowing I was British-born, he drove me up the wall with his constant haranguing about the British in Northern Ireland. I gave as good as I got and sometimes our heated arguments almost came to blows. I decided to quit before there was any bloodshed.

I found a room with a family in Cambridge Street, Wembley. Jack and Melva Mullins' eldest daughter had married and moved out and I was invited to take the large spare room at the back. This was perfect and at last I could settle down. Melva treated me like a son and did my washing and ironing and made me part of the family. Their youngest daughter, Trish, was a victim of the anti-morning-sickness drug Thalidomide. She was very pretty and I was immensely inspired by her courage in the face of her disability. She played sports, including hockey and squash, using a special way of holding the squash racket and hockey stick.

With a few of my Tardun mates who were living in the city, we dug by hand a huge hole in Jack's backyard for a swimming pool. We celebrated its completion with a keg of beer and a barbecue and, after that, my mates were always welcome to come around for a swim and to party, staying over if they wanted.

The work with Toledo-Berkel took me far and wide around the state, installing new weighbridges, making repairs and carrying out maintenance. One day I was sent to an Italian butcher in Osborne Park to make some repairs and walked out to the back of the shop where two men were butchering a young steer. 'I didn't know you could still kill your own,' I jokingly said to the two panicking men.

'How much meat do you want?' one of them asked. 'You can have some beautiful steak.'

I didn't take their meat and neither would I dob them in. The practice of butchering animals on the premises was still widespread in the early 1970s even though it was illegal. I chose to ignore it, as farmers had been doing it since the country had been settled without any problems.

One of the most unusual jobs I had to do was in Esperance in the south of Western Australia. The company sent me to investigate problems with the government railway's 30-ton weighbridge. The weighbridge operator was having difficulty zeroing the scale on the indicator dial, which mysteriously moved about by itself. I checked under the bridge with my torch and saw frogs sitting on the long lever that came from the centre of the bridge and hooked up to the scale in the office. Depending on how far along the sensitive lever they were sitting, the frogs were putting the scale out. I ordered the pit to be pumped out and cleaned, did some maintenance and drove home, wondering how much extra revenue the little green frogs had contributed to the state's treasury over the two years since the weighbridge had last been checked.

1   The road continues to exist today and is in constant use.

17
HAVING ANOTHER GO

The bush was still in my blood and after about a year in Perth I returned to the farm to decide my future. In March 1972, a cyclone destroyed my new machinery shed and quarters, which were uninsured. Chris, who was shearing for a living around the district, helped me to construct another shed using what we could salvage from the destroyed one. The 4500 litre fuel tank was found a half a kilometre away in the bush but was undamaged.

I had no money and was seriously considering selling the property and moving out, especially after the cyclone. Naz wouldn't hear of it, 'You boys should get together again and give it another go'.

He had some spare barley seed and fertiliser that we could use to plant a crop. We borrowed some equipment and sowed a late barley crop, which provided a small cash flow for the following year. Our creditors took us back so we planned a decent wheat crop for the following year. I had nowhere to live after the cyclone and so I moved in with Chris, who was now living in a mudbrick house on his farm.

After seeding, Chris went back to shearing and I took work as a shed hand or doing any other job I could find. Our harvest that year was average but the price of wheat had doubled overnight. We heard the news on ABC radio and were celebrating. The Russians had outfoxed the Americans by buying all their surplus wheat and a global oversupply had turned into severe shortage. The Russians put some of the wheat back on the market and sold it at inflated prices.

Fred, local farmer and born pessimist, came to see us and wasn't happy, observing that 'The bastards will double the price of bread. You wait and see!'

'How much bread can you eat, Fred?' I asked. He didn't seem to get the joke.

One night after a few beers at the Club Hotel in Mullewa, I was driving home with Percy and Irish Don, who I had grown up with at Castledare and Tardun. We were about 40 kilometres from my farm. We all had drunk too much and I was probably driving over the blood alcohol limit; however, I drove slowly so I could dodge the suicidal kangaroos that often darted across the road without warning. We reminisced about our childhood years, saddened by the loss of no man's land and other favourite places that had disappeared under the anchor chain in the drive to clear the land. Irish Don, like me, had inherited Ned's passion for nature and the bush. He suddenly asked me to stop the ute. It was about midnight, and we were adjacent to the old gnamma hole[1] and the Aboriginal soak, which had been destroyed and covered over with rocks and debris. Now part of a new farm, it had been one of our favourite childhood picnic spots. In spring the whole area was covered with colourful wildflowers as if brilliantly painted by an insane artist on a giant canvas. We could see only a sea of thick green wheat heads on metre-high plants silhouetted against the powerful headlights, stretching far into the black horizon. A record wheat crop was underway.

Intoxicated, Don stretched out his arms on the side of the road and, filled with emotion and determination, called on St Patrick and all the Irish saints in Heaven to place a curse on the wheat that grew in place of the flowers. St Patrick may well have been listening as the cold still night brought with it the first of three night frosts in a row.

My neighbour Joe, a big powerfully built Yugoslav, had sowed his crops too early and as they were flowering, they were therefore vulnerable to frost damage. Come harvest time, his promising golden wheat heads bobbed about on the slightest breeze – they were empty of grain. Frost at that time of the year was virtually unknown and Joe suffered more crop damage than any other farmer in the district.

The following year, Don went to Northern Ireland to meet his family.[2] At 22, Don was the first Tardun child migrant to discover where his family lived and we were all excited when we heard the news. Most of us dreamed too of meeting our own family one day. He was considered a true pioneer who showed that the impossible was possible. He had gone north in Western Australia to work in a mine and, by some miracle, met an Irish truck driver who, after hearing Don's story, was certain that he knew Don's family and that they lived in County Omagh. Accompanied by a Catholic priest, Don knocked on the door of his family home, which was answered by one of his younger brothers. On hearing the news, his father fled out the rear of the house and was found a couple of days later at a local pub. Don met his eight brothers and sisters, who had no idea of his existence and were shocked and horrified at his treatment. He learnt that he had been born out of wedlock and taken as a six-month-old baby to the Sisters of Nazareth in Belfast. Through the confessional, the local parish priest learned of the pregnant young Catholic girl and advised the parents 'for their own good' to give up the baby. His mother subsequently married his father and the couple began a family. Don was left at the orphanage until he was seven before being sent to Australia. He had no knowledge of his parents or his brothers and sisters. His guilt-ridden parents never spoke about their first son.

In a strange way Don may well have saved his family from further loss. In those days, it was tradition for the parish priest to recruit sons or daughters of large devout Irish Catholic families to devote their lives to the service of God. The families often felt compelled to do this and would push one of their children forward. The son or daughter would then reluctantly become a priest or a nun. Since Don's family had already 'sacrificed' one child, there was little chance the parish priest would ask the family to give another.

As an adult, Don could never shake the Irish sectarianism from his blood and could quieten a crowded room by singing the saddest anti-British ballad in his rich powerful baritone voice. The lyrics and the melody took him back to Northern Ireland as he remembered its tragic struggle for independence and his own personal loss and suffering. He had frequently suffered physical and sexual abuse at Castledare and this had affected his entire life.[3]

In 1974 my partnership with Chris came to an end. We were both financially strong enough to stand on our own feet. When Chris got married, I moved out into my own little dwelling that I was constructing at the time. The most common type of living quarters for new farmers was a small partitioned room in the machinery shed, which also housed equipment, seed and fertiliser and a workshop. Poisonous snakes were a common problem, as they fed on the mice that attacked the stored bags of grain. The best defence was to have cats – not only did they control the mice population but they annoyed the reptiles enough to send them on their way. While no-one we knew had been bitten, there were some close calls. Some of the farmers lived in old railway carriages that they converted into a bedroom and kitchen. By and large these were safe from snakes.

The government railways had put out a tender for the removal of a couple of houses at the Tardun siding. I brought the old stationmaster's house for the princely sum of $210 and was given a month to take it away. It was timber clad with an iron roof, two bedrooms, a separate lounge, kitchen and veranda front and rear. I removed the verandas and began digging two shallow tunnels into the hard ground to make way for the wheels of a hired jinker, a multi-wheeled transporter.

Using old 24 foot (over 7 metre) railway irons spaced just over half a metre apart, and borrowing every hydraulic jack in the district, I was able to sit the whole house on the jinker. Joe, the local storekeeper and postmaster, came every day to inspect progress. Like poor Hanrahan[4], the great bush pessimist who frequently observed 'We'll all be rooned [ruined]!', Joe told me often 'You'll never get that house back to your farm in one piece. They're not designed for travel you know. The way you've got that thing sitting on the trailer, it's bound to fall off, you know.'

The day of the big move, I instructed the truck driver to drive no faster than 15 kilometres per hour for the 25-kilometre journey. I told Mick, a local farmer's son who was helping, to follow the truck and use the container of petrol I had given him to burn the house if it fell on the main road. In the meantime, I slipped off with the ute to borrow a neighbour's front-end loader to dig a pit to lower the trailer into at the site prepared on the farm. As I drew up at the intersection with the loader, the swaying house and truck, which took up the whole road, whisked past at 80 kilometres per hour. However, this turned out to be a blessing in disguise, as it reduced the time the shaky house was moving about on the trailer. It survived the journey and, apart from some cracks in the walls, arrived in good condition.

In February 1974 a shockwave rocked Australian agriculture. The Whitlam government removed the superphosphate bounty that had been in place for as long as anyone could remember. At the time, the cost of the heavily subsidised superphosphate, used as fertiliser, was approximately $14 per ton. By May the price had increased to $32.90. A year later it had risen to $54 a ton, so becoming the highest single input cost to wheat growers. It was feared that without the subsidy the cost of fertiliser could rise to $70 a ton.

In March the Farmers Union called a mass meeting in Perth to coincide with an election rally at Forrest Place where Prime Minister Whitlam was to address his supporters. A couple of thousand farmers descended on Forrest Place to boo and heckle the speakers. It was the first time I had seen the farmers become so angry and militant.

In 1975 the newly elected Fraser government reintroduced the superphosphate bounty but Fraser's resolve only lasted until 1977 when he abolished it again after being constantly harangued from the Opposition benches.

My land was slightly more marginal than the school's land at Tardun. The country was generous when it rained but punished you when it didn't. Still, I was privileged to be part of a family of new land farmers who supported and helped each other. We lent each other equipment and never had to exchange money. You could always rely on someone to help with sowing or harvesting a crop in the event of a serious problem or bad luck.

This was crucial to my survival, as I was the youngest and least resourced in the community. No account was kept nor reckoning of value was put on the help I received. I tried to repay in kind with free labour whenever I could. I was often invited to share a meal at someone's place. When food and money were scarce, I shot kangaroos, wild goats, rabbits or ducks on the lake. It was easy to live off the land and old Ned had taught us how to make a decent stew.

In spite of a little frost damage, the harvest of 1975 was good but, thanks to Tiny, I continued to be frugal with farm machinery, buying old equipment in good condition and relying on the abundance of spare parts from old abandoned equipment. I was now financially strong enough to employ help and, with two tractors and seeders, we sowed a large crop. The farm soon became a frequent stopover for visitors, mainly old boys coming to stay for a few days. The welcome mat was always out and they could stay as long as they liked.

In 1975, the school sold 12 000 acres of land at a commercial price and gave the old boys first option. Naz's brother Sam bought the property next door and moved in with me until he could build his own quarters. I brought a small piece of land nearby, which added 1100 acres to my holding.

In November, I gave Naz a hand to shift some discarded railway iron from a cutting on the Mullewa–Meekatharra line. The stationmaster had told Naz he could have it if he was prepared to drag it out by hand. Percy and Naz's brother George came to help and the four of us began the task of lifting the heavy steel lengths out of the cutting.

George spotted a railway trolley with a flat top, which we lifted onto the railway tracks and used to run the steel to the end of the cutting and onto the truck. We assumed we were safe as the passenger train only ran once a week. About halfway through the second run with the trolley, we began to feel the ground vibrate. The train was very close although we couldn't see it around the bend. Three of us pushed the trolley down the slight decline at speed and we yelled to George to throw something onto the track to derail the trolley and its cargo of steel. George threw a length of railway iron across the tracks, sending the trolley and its cargo flying off down a slight embankment. George quickly grabbed the railway iron off the track and moments later the train raced past with the driver tooting his horn and waving his fist. We continued loading the truck and drove into town for a beer, a bet and lunch at the pub. In the meantime, the train driver had complained and the local police sergeant came to the pub to give us all a good telling-off for our foolishness. Fortunately he also saw the humour in what had happened, so we got off lightly. It was an experience we would always remember.

Another incident with the railways, while a little less dramatic, cost us the chance of winning a game of cricket one Sunday afternoon. As was customary, our team gathered at the 'ranch' (the residence for Elder Smith and Company employees) late morning to have a coffee and to relax before the game. Doug, the local Elders' manager, suddenly arrived and asked if we could help him to load some cattle into railway trucks. The trucks were sitting in the railway station on the hill and had to be pushed down to the cattleyards about a kilometre away. We began loading the first two trucks when Doug asked me to run up the hill to get the third one. I began walking slowly behind the big truck, pushing it lightly to keep up momentum. I could hear the boys whistling and shouting to hurry up. I pushed the truck harder until I was running behind it, then jumped up onto it, standing on the brake lever, which was lifted up onto a catch when in the 'off' position. The truck continued to gather speed. The only thing that could stop it was the brake lever on which I was standing, which had to be lifted up off the catch to apply the brakes – by now an impossible task. Doug spotted the runaway truck and ran towards me yelling, 'Stop that fucking truck! Stop that fucking truck!'

I spotted a heap of sand by the side of the track and launched myself into its relative softness. The truck continued at high speed until it collided with the two stationary trucks that were nearly fully loaded with cattle, but still had their doors open. The impact caused them to set sail down the track towards Pindar. Sensing freedom, the cattle leapt from the trucks and escaped into the nearby bush. Poor Doug was on his knees crying over and over, 'This is the worst day of my life! This is the worst day of my life!'

We should never have lost that game against Northampton as we were easily the more talented side. However, every now and then, as our fast strike bowler Bob Pearce ran up to the crease to deliver a thunderbolt, somebody fielding in the slips would cry, 'Stop that fucking truck!'

Bob would instantly lose rhythm and fall apart, holding his belly to stop laughing, while the batsman slogged another ball to the boundary.

1   Gnamma holes are natural water holes set in a granite outcrop, often containing vast amounts of water and covered over by a large rock. The holes were used by the Aboriginal peoples and by wildlife.

2   Most of the Irish orphans searched Northern Ireland for their families, as child migration had been illegal in the south. There were always some exceptions – using false paperwork some children were passed illegally across the border by unscrupulous clergy to bolster the child migrant numbers.

3   While Don's reunion with his Irish family had been very successful and he had raised his own family in Australia, his awful childhood continued to haunt his devout Irish Catholic family. Nearing retirement, in December 2007 Don was tragically killed in Perth by a drunken motorist as he walked home alone from a local Christmas party. He was 60 years old.

4   Hanrahan was the character in 'Said Hanrahan', an Australian bush poem by John O'Brien, the pen name of PJ Hartington, a Catholic priest from New South Wales.

IN SEARCH OF FAMILY

After the good harvest of 1975, I planned to travel to England and to North America. Mike Slawe, a young American schoolteacher employed at Tardun was a regular visitor to my farm and often spoke about American farm practice. His father was a doctor in the town of St Johns, Michigan, and had a lot of influence. I asked if he could arrange an invitation for me to attend a seminar conducted by the Michigan Farm Bureau.

I flew to London the following July after seeding a 3000 acre wheat crop. The season had started poorly, with barely enough rain to germinate the crops. Arriving at Heathrow, I was met by Percy's older brother, John, and his family, who lived in Newport, Wales.[1] We travelled to Wales and the next day to Alton, the town where I was born. The local Catholic Church had records of my baptism but no information that would help me find my family. However, the priest suggested that we speak to Charlie Hawkins, the local historian.

Old Charlie knew the town history well and, even though there were many Hawkins in the district, he doubted that I belonged to any of them. 'A few Hawkins children were sent away as child migrants to Canada but none that I know of went to Australia,' he said. 'It was only last year when I helped another Canadian lad link up with his family.' Charlie promised that if there was a chance that I belonged to any of the local families he would find out, but he had serious doubts.

Later we drove up to London to St Catherine's House, where all records of deaths, births and marriages were kept. My mother's address on my birth certificate was given as St Bernard's Hospital, Middlesex. With nothing much to go on, I asked the staff at a counter if they could search the files for details of my mother. When I showed them my birth certificate, they shook their heads. There was nothing they could do –

163

Hawkins is a common name. Yet, somewhere in that mountain of files, was a clue.

We gave up after about six hours and went back to Wales. I wanted to be in Belfast in time for 12 July, when the Protestants marched in the streets to celebrate the Battle of the Boyne, so, the following day, I flew to Belfast as a guest of Perry Morehead, who had a 600 acre farm about one hour's drive from the city. Perry was a cousin of Harry Morehead, whose daughter Julie had become my fiancée. He had visited my farm the year before and was impressed with the wide open spaces.

Perry picked me up at the airport and drove me to his farm named 'The Bridge' near Newtownards, Ballygowan. We turned off the road and crossed over a little stone bridge to drive to the farmhouse about 50 metres away. I inquired, 'Who owns that bridge?'

'Oh! I do,' he said, as we strolled back to take a closer look. I commented on a thin vertical crack that went all the way up through the elegant central arch. Like the bridge itself, it looked like it had been there a long time. Perry told me that the local council had ignored its responsibility to fix the crack in the heritage-listed bridge. I asked who built it and Perry replied 'The Romans!', while still fuming over the poor form of the local government. I giggled as I tried to conceive of any modern structure surviving around 2000 years of continuous use.

The old farmhouse was between 400 and 500 years old. It had a thatched roof, exposed beams and a low ceiling. Perry ran sheep and cattle, but was better known as a horse breeder. A couple of his horses had won the English Grand National. He owned the full sister to Shergar, a champion racehorse that the IRA had 'kidnapped' and shot in a failed ransom attempt a couple of years before.

The next day a reluctant Perry dropped me off at the Battle of the Boyne march, leaving me with two minders. He warned me not to tell anyone that I was a Catholic. I spent the day marching with the local Protestant chapter while filming with an 8-mm camera. On a number of occasions my two companions had to vouch to suspicious locals that my camera was exactly that, as everyone was on the look out for strangers with bombs.

We finished the day at the house of William Boyce, a huge barrel-chested, red-faced and red-haired Irish farmer. We settled down for a few drinks. As the evening wore on, his curiosity got the better of him and he began to ask 'What foot do you kick with?' questions. I knew exactly what he meant and told him that I was neither Protestant nor Catholic, just an Australian tourist. He continued to niggle, promising me that it would make no difference if I told him. A few drinks later, I foolishly admitted that in Ireland I was an Australian tourist, but in Australia I was a Catholic. Bill exploded at once, rising from his chair and spilling drinks over the table. 'I got a fookin' Cat-lic in me hoose!' he roared, as everyone tried to stop his menacing advance towards me.

I nervously reached for the purple sash around his shoulders, which had his name and Lodge number from the local Protestant chapter in silver lettering. I asked quietly if I could take it home as a souvenir. He calmed down instantly and gave me a bear hug. My two minders hastily made excuses and hurried me out of the house and drove me back to Perry's farm. Perry was furious at them for taking me to Bill's house and he wasn't impressed with the sash around my shoulders. Above all else, Perry avoided the 'Troubles' where possible and despised the violence on both sides.

Two days later we were on the road again, heading for Slane in the south of Ireland. Perry had a sister who, with her husband, owned a massive 'bed and breakfast' in a magnificent Georgian mansion. The family also trained horses on their 15 acres of prime real estate.

Perry decided on a back route, as the scenery was far prettier. About an hour into our journey I noticed what looked like a heavily camouflaged soldier lying flat on his stomach by the side of a narrow lonely road. I told Perry, who just nodded. Then I noticed more men and just around a corner an armoured military vehicle blocked the entire road. Within an instant we were surrounded by a dozen British troops with blackened faces, wearing camouflage clothing. We were ordered from the car at gunpoint. I was led to the opposite side of the road and searched by three British soldiers. I tried to explain that I was an Australian tourist, but was abruptly told to 'Shut the fuck up!' by a no-nonsense soldier, who was looking through my wallet and passport. Poor Perry, who loathed violence, was forced to empty our bags onto the road with a submachine gun close to his head, while other soldiers searched his car. A military helicopter was circling overhead in a wide arc. It appeared that Perry's green Volvo station wagon had been followed for quite some time.

The soldiers found nothing and without apologising allowed us to continue our journey. Perry apologised for their behaviour, but didn't appear to be concerned for himself. I gathered that what had just happened was a hazard of life in Ireland that he had learned to accept. I was more curious than fearful and stored away the incident as another to remember.

A couple of days later I flew to Detroit in North America. I asked the bus driver on the way from the airport if he could recommend a good hotel close to the Greyhound bus terminal, as I had heard that Detroit was a mean city. He dropped me off outside the front of a hotel a block away from the terminal and told me to get a cab in the morning to take me to the bus.

'Don't walk, it's not safe,' he said. I ignored his warning and, early next morning, walked to the terminal to buy a ticket and was nearly mugged on the way back. A tall black American came out of a doorway and asked for a cigarette. Another appeared from behind me. They approached from opposite directions. Although the footpath was empty, the wide street was busy with traffic. I shot across, narrowly missing a car amid tooting horns, but made it safely to the other side. From now on I would heed the advice of the locals.

At the hotel, the obvious suddenly hit me: I should have contacted St Bernard's Hospital while I was in London. I phoned from the hotel and the hospital receptionist put me on to an orderly who had worked there for many years. He told me that there were three Hawkins sisters who had worked at the hospital and two of them were still there. He mentioned Elizabeth, or Betty as she was known, who he thought had left the hospital around 1946. I asked if there was an Anne Hawkins. He thought Betty's first name was Anne but wasn't sure. He put me on to Queenie Hawkins, who sounded quite excited. We spoke for a little while and she said the family were Irish from Wexford. I explained I was doing some research work for a friend tracking family relatives and asked if her sister Betty (or Anne) had a child in 1947. There was a brief pause and in her lilting southern Irish accent, she said, 'No, you've got the wrong family'.

I assumed that was the end of the matter. They were Irish and I was English – or so I thought. I had no idea that I had just spoken to my mother's youngest sister.

I arrived in the town of St Johns, and was met by Bill Kissane, his wife and their two little adopted children. Bill had agreed to act as my host for the duration of the five-day seminar. They had a 300 acre farm on the outskirts of town and grew corn and wheat and raised about 100 head of cattle. I met most of the local farmers, who saw me as a bit of a curiosity with my strange accent. They had difficulty understanding why it was necessary for broad-land farmers in Australia to hold so much land and plant such vast acreages of wheat to earn a living. I was in demand to give talks at meetings and the local newspaper wrote stories about my visit.

I learnt that there was a 'friendly' animosity between the farmers in Texas, where everything was the biggest and best, and the farmers in Michigan, where landholdings were far more modest. At one memorable meeting attended by 100 or more farmers, I began my speech by relating the story of the Texan rancher who came to Mullewa. The rancher, wearing a big hat, walked in to the pub one day and began boasting to the publican about the size of his ranch. The publican told the Texan that Mick, who would be in soon, was the best person to talk to as Mick owned Tallerang sheep station, which also covered a lot of land. When Mick walked in, the Texan told him his ranch was so big it took him all day to ride his horse from the ranch-house to the front gate.

Mick thought for a moment and said in his raw Australian drawl, 'Funny thing that, I had a horse like that too. Bastard of a thing. I had to shoot it!'

The room erupted with howls of laughter followed by long applause. After the short speech came questions. They were as keen to learn about Australian agriculture as I was to learn about American farming practice. In fact, at one point, I found myself in the boardroom in the midst of negotiations with oil companies who supplied farmers with fuel. They too wanted to meet the wheat farmer from Western Australia.

One difference that stood out to me above all else, especially in Michigan, was that the farmers hardly ever repaired their own machinery, preferring instead to employ town mechanics. I helped Bill repair his corn-chopper, which he used to make silage that he fed to his cattle. I also convinced him to concrete the floor of the big barn, which housed his cattle over winter and helped with the preparation and the big concrete pour.

Bill was a proud American and took me everywhere to show off his own great state. On one occasion this caused enormous embarrassment. We drove to Lansing, the state capital, where he said he would show me something that would fairly blow my mind. We entered a large department store and walked to the middle of the huge room. He said, with his arms outstretched, 'What do you think?'

I didn't know what he meant and began looking at the price tags on the clothing rack. Suddenly his wife realised and said, 'Oh my God, you have these things in Australia?'

'What things?' I asked.

'Superstores,' she replied.

'Yes, everywhere,' I said to the embarrassed Bill and his wife. They had been planning their surprise for days.

Time was slipping by. I'd spent three weeks in Michigan and I hadn't seen much of the country, apart from my two-day business trip with the vice-president of the Michigan Farm Bureau to North and South Dakota.

Bill arranged a meeting with the president of the Michigan Farm Bureau. He wanted to know the rest of my travel schedule within America. I replied that I had no particular schedule but wanted to see the Rocky Mountains before I went home. Later he handed me an envelope, saying that there would be someone to meet me at Denver airport. Inside the envelope was an airline ticket and tourist information on Colorado.

I was met at Denver by a farmer, Stanley, his wife and their son. They had a sprawling wheat farm close to the foot of Pikes Peak, one of the highest mountains in the Rockies. The harvesting contractors were just finishing stripping his 2000 acres of wheat, which was yielding 2.5 tons to the acre. A vast difference to the half ton per acre I could expect in a good year.

Stanley and his family took me on a long drive through the Rocky Mountains and to the top of Pikes Peak, where there was still snow on the ground in mid summer. Later Stanley took me to lunch at a restaurant with a group of about 30 farmers. The establishment specialised in 'Rocky Mountain oysters'. A large plate of these supposed delicacies was placed in front us. The farmers kept an eye on me as we began to slowly chew through the rubbery substance covered in sweet sauce.

'How do you like the oysters?' they asked.

'A bit chewy, a bit rubbery,' I said, now realising something was up. 'What are these things anyway?' I asked, putting down my fork.

'Balls. Hogs' balls!' they cried, roaring with laughter.

I thought that maybe this was payback for my little joke about the Texan farmer that I had made in Michigan.

By our standards, Stanley's farm was overcapitalised in plant and equipment and he was using his new John Deer header to harvest small areas of particularly heavy crop left behind by the contractors. He took me to a few field days where I was able to compare input costs. This shocked me. New tractors were selling at half the Australian price. The cost of the new Steiger tractor in Colorado was US $28 000. The same tractor was selling in Australia for more than Australian $60 000.[2] The cost in parts to overhaul an International 806 tractor in America was around US $700. In Australia the cost was about $2050, due mainly to import tariffs on parts. In America, herbicides such as 2,4-D cost only a fraction of what we paid and fertilisers and fuel were considerably cheaper. The American farm lobby was powerful indeed. It negotiated the price of its main input costs with governments and companies and had a strong presence in Congress. It made me realise that something was very wrong at home and I was determined to find out why.

After a week or so in Colorado, I flew home and went to the office of the Farmers Union in Adelaide Terrace, Perth, to speak to the editor of the *Farmers Weekly*. I told him that as America was our biggest competitor in the wheat markets, we should be aware of any cost advantage they had over us. I asked him to provide a monthly column showing American input costs for a comparable state such as North Dakota, which had crop yields similar to ours. The column should include the prices of all American plant and equipment in wide use in Australia, as well as the costs of grains, livestock, fertilisers, chemicals, fuel and oils, and services such as grain handling and transport and selling charges. The amount of subsidies farmers received should be included, as well as the import duties our government charged on essential items.

I explained that apathy was the main cause for the huge disparity in costs and farmers needed to be shocked into applying collective pressure on government if we had a chance to reduce costs and become competitive. Little interest was shown in running the column. Perhaps it was seen as far too radical and that it would upset government and other bodies who had vested interests in setting transport prices and other charges.

The problem of lack of competitiveness was largely home-grown. In my view, rampant inflation, combined with unnecessary rules and regulations, strangled efficiency and competition. The Farmers Union was incapable of leading a challenge, as its own conservative leadership mainly supported the status quo in the interests of 'orderly marketing', the ramifications of which it never fully understood.

While I was overseas, I had kept up with weather information from home. Things were looking ominous – little rain had fallen in the time I had been away. Disillusioned and disappointed, I returned to the farm to find the crops faring badly. Everyone was talking drought. The harvest was barely enough to cover my costs but, as I had little debt, I was sure I could bounce back the following year.

1   Percy's staunchly Protestant mother had handed him over to his aunt when he was a baby and he finished up at the Sisters of Nazareth orphanage in Belfast and was promptly baptised a Catholic. No records exist to explain how this came about. He had been welcomed back into his family the year before, even though he was a baptised Catholic, and had a brother and sister still living in Wales. He got along particularly well with his uncle Jim, who was running a safe house at his little farm for British troops on patrol. Percy and Jim had similar characters. When Percy bought Jim a TV set as a farewell present, Jim had to point out that it was no use as the farm had no electricity. The family had held a welcome party for Percy at a local Protestant pub when the IRA tossed a bomb through the window. Fortunately no-one was seriously injured, although the explosion caused the ceiling to collapse. Rescuers removed part of the ceiling and it fell on an old man who was lying flat on the floor. He was covered in dust but still managed to hold his pint of Guinness with one hand with his other covering the top of the glass. The rescuers had thought he was dead. Percy was taken to hospital with about a dozen others for observation but, apart from a few cuts and scratches, he was uninjured.

2   At the time, the exchange rate for the Australian dollar was fixed. $1.28 would buy US $1, making the tractor almost three times more expensive to buy in Australia.

LOVE AND DUST

I had first seen Julie, my fiancée, on a fishing trip to Kalbarri in early 1975. The small fishing village was located about 130 kilometres off the Great Northern Highway, well north of Geraldton in north Western Australia and was accessed by a rough gravel road. Ollie and Naz had built a new holiday shack there and the Tardun boys were always welcome. We had been out deep-sea fishing and Ollie stopped the boat in the river to chat to Harry Moorhead. His two beautiful daughters, Julie and Helen, were sunbathing on the deck of his boat.

I officially met Julie in Harry's fashion shop in Mullewa some months later when I went in to buy football shorts. My institutional background still carried a lot of stigma – being born out of wedlock was bad enough, but being abandoned by your parents, and your country put you in a special 'untouchable' category, especially by the well-to-do, who frowned on the likes of me. It wasn't information that you volunteered freely to a stranger, least of all to a girl you were trying to impress. Fortunately Julie already knew who I was, so there was no need for me to pretend.

She was quite shy and I was staggered when she agreed to come to the movies with me. My only idea of romance was what I had learned from Hollywood in heavily censored Cary Grant and Doris Day movies. I played it cool and picked Julie up in my newly cleaned ute with a six-pack of beer.

Soon we began dating on a regular basis and fell in love, although Julie's parents, Harry and Margaret, weren't too keen at first. A suitor's family background was always an important consideration and for all they knew I could have been the son of an axe murderer! All I could offer their daughter, who was training to be a teacher, was a bush block and lots of enthusiasm.

However, by the time we had decided to marry and raise a family, Harry and Margaret fully supported us. Unfortunately, the life we had planned together would clash with the most severe drought in the state's history and surviving would be a test for our relationship.

A common catchphrase about farming in those days was 'get big or get out'. It was used by farm consultants and economists who believed the cost price squeeze[1] could be defeated by expanding operations to achieve economy of scale. Many of those who heeded this advice and bought extra land and new farm equipment had the banks breathing down their necks. Eventually the banks began a culling process that shook the industry to its foundations. The three years from 1977 would prove decisive for all and disastrous for some.

In 1977 the rains came late and the frosts arrived early. I sowed two-thirds of the planned acreage into cold ground, which stunted early plant growth. With little rainfall, the crops grew thin and weedy.

Optimistic Chris shrugged his shoulders, saying 'Oh well, I'll be able to tell my kids I went through two droughts in a row.' We all tried to be optimistic but little did we know there were two more droughts on the way.

The federal government, fearing a mass exodus from farms amid the collapse of land values, began warning the banks not to foreclose on farmers. The government introduced an interest subsidy of 2 per cent, which was of little help while interest rates were 16 per cent and beyond.

The state government introduced a transport subsidy so that farmers could agist their sheep elsewhere, although properties that could take them were few and far between. Sheep, already in poor condition, began dying like flies and it became clear that an organised process to destroy livestock was required. Local councils provided bulldozers at disused gravel pits to bury the truckloads of carcasses that were delivered daily.

The best sheep were sent to the Midland livestock market, but many farmers received a bill as the return from the sale of the livestock didn't even cover the transport costs. While farmers virtually gave the animals free to the abattoirs, the price of lamb and mutton for Perth consumers did not noticeably drop.

Rumours began to circulate of farmers turning the gun on themselves, distressed after days of slaughtering animals they had carefully bred over a lifetime. A late rain in September caused some farmers to joke grimly that it had ruined what had been a beautiful drought.

Not all the state had been affected by drought and land several hundred kilometres south still had plenty of grass. The manager of Elders at Morawa, Kevin O'Neill, put together a consignment of 15 000 sheep to send to a single farmer at Boyup Brook. About 45, 000 sheep were available for selection but only 15, 000 made the train. The rest were shot – too weak to travel.

From the beginning of the drought, starving emus migrating south had been massing along the rabbit-proof fence in their tens of thousands. Huge numbers began pouring over the nearly 2-metre-high fence by walking over dead and dying carcasses piled high against it. The crops were so thin and the ground so bare, nothing could hide. It was said that you could 'flog a flea around a paddock all day'! A single emu walking around in a paddock yielding one ton of wheat per acre could perhaps destroy half a ton a day. The Agricultural Protection Board began supplying farmers with free ammunition and, when their guns wore out, free barrels.

By 1978, most farms had de-stocked, keeping only a small flock from which they could begin again when the drought finally broke. It was just as well, because in April, Cyclone Alby hit. Most cyclones bring good rain when they cross the coast of Western Australia north of the agricultural areas, but Alby followed the coast all the way down bringing destructive winds but very little rain. Topsoil from bare paddocks took off on the wind, blackening the sky. Fences were buried so deep, only the top wire remained visible. Severe damage was recorded in most of the state's agricultural regions. Farmers had to hand feed what little stock they had kept until it rained again.

In September, Julie and I got married in Geraldton. Father Eddie performed the service. I had asked him to marry us as we had become good friends again and I was no longer banned from the Pallottine Mission. It was a typical Catholic wedding with about 100 guests. Father Eddie broke convention with Catholic tradition when he offered Julie, a non-Catholic, Holy Communion at the altar, something I had never seen before as non-Catholics were barred from receiving the Holy Sacrament. Many of my old schoolmates attended and the party dragged on well into the night. We spent our two-week honeymoon at Kalbarri in her family's holiday home. One evening we went fishing from a sandbank near the mouth of the river and my first inexperienced cast with a fishing rod resulted in a good-size fish. We were alone yet, as more fish came in, anglers came running towards us from opposite directions. Soon it was shoulder-to-shoulder fishing as people jostled to cast their line. We beat a hasty retreat as it was far too dangerous to continue. Still we had enough fish to last a few days. We spent the rest of the honeymoon exploring and just relaxing.

We moved into an old house with a shopfront in central Mullewa, which had been empty for a couple of years. Once owned by Julie's grandmother, who ran a delicatessen in the shopfront in the heady days of the 1950s and 1960s, the house definitely had seen better days. Julie's parents now owned it and Harry used it to store his bits and pieces.

The old house was infested with wild cats in the roof and under the house. The new bank manager, who lived next door in a house at the rear of the bank, had a similar problem and was using a cat trap he said was useless as the canny animals refused to go in. I went to the police station to ask the sergeant, a redheaded Scotsman known as Scotty, if I could shoot the cats.

'Don't shoot toward the street and shoot only when you've got a clear shot,' he said, 'and let me know when you do it so I can tell the other police officers.'

After getting rid of the cats, we began the task of cleaning out the house, which had been used by squatters and was in deplorable condition. We painted it inside and out, fixed the plumbing and put some new floor coverings down. In a few weeks, we had a house we could live in.

The drought and the low price of commodities had affected business confidence in town. Empty shops and boarded-up windows were beginning to appear in the streets and the town was becoming a shadow of its former self. Many businesses relocated or just shut up shop and walked away.

For the third year in a row, we sowed our crops after a false break in the weather in May, but there just wasn't sufficient rain to germinate and sustain the crops. There was little to be done on the farm. It was 40 kilometres out of town, the crops were dying and I was glad to be away from it.

The local council had embarked on employment schemes for farmers but there was a limit to how far the scheme could go. Julie was fortunate enough to have a job teaching at the high school. To keep myself busy I began constructing a large shed at the rear of the house from materials Harry had picked up from somewhere. Scotty could see me working from the police station and, whenever he saw I needed a hand, came down to help. I got on well with him. He was a tough nut from the old school and took nonsense from no-one. He once got into trouble from his own department for shooting out the tyres of a stolen car he was chasing along the Mullewa North Road. The thief had eluded a police blockade on the Geraldton–Mullewa Road and Scotty was determined to stop him.

In 1979, the last year of the drought, after another dodgy break, the farmers threw their money and themselves back into the fray. We were unaccustomed to making individual decisions and didn't know how not to plant a crop – the unwritten law was that farmers should always sow a crop and pray if it doesn't rain. We were given no advice or formula from authorities that would have helped us to make a calculated decision based on weather data from previous years before committing ourselves to a new crop each year.

Living in town was a blessing in disguise. I did not have to witness wilting crops on my walk to the shop. I tried to focus my mind on more mundane things. Julie and I had become good friends with the new bank manager, Colin, his wife Pat and their two little children. The Bank of New South Wales had many bad accounts and Colin was worried about what might happen. Our situation was bad enough and I began to doubt that the Commonwealth Bank in Geraldton would finance us again for another year.

One morning I ate a bad mushroom I found growing in the garden and became violently ill. The doctor gave me a shot of Pethidine to ease the violent pain and kept me in hospital for most of the day. Before I left he gave me some Valium.

'What are these for?' I asked.

'Aren't you depressed?' he inquired.

'No. It was the mushroom that made me crook.'

He admitted that he was treating most of the farmers for severe depression.

In an attempt to lift the gloom, local machinery dealer Bob Mann invited Ron Barassi, the superstar of Australian Rules Football, to give the town a pep talk to lift the spirits of the farmers. It would be like the coach trying to lift a side that hadn't won a game all year and was well down at half-time. That afternoon the town hall was packed as Barassi gave his address. He was about 10 minutes into his speech when an elderly and somewhat inebriated Aboriginal woman wobbled onto the stage, put her arms around his neck and planted a large kiss on his cheek. A startled and embarrassed Barassi called through the microphone, 'Hey Bob, can you come and get your mum?'

It brought the house down. Photos of the incident appeared on the front page of nearly every newspaper in Melbourne. However, it was Barassi's message that worked. He reminded us that we couldn't be blamed or be described as bad managers if our finances were tight. We couldn't be blamed for something beyond our control. We shouldn't punish ourselves or our families by thinking that we could have done something different or better. Most importantly, he reminded us to take holidays or time out for recreation and social activities. It was important that we not lock ourselves away and bring down the shutters.

1   The term 'cost price squeeze' refers to when the price received for a commodity barely covers the cost of its production.

THE HIGHS AND LOWS

In 1979, Julie's parents, Harry and Margaret, travelled to London to visit their daughter Helen, who was living there. Before she left, Margaret offered to check the records at St Catherine's House for me. She was as keen as Julie and me to discover my background. It was something we desperately wanted for our own family history, for the sake of our unborn children and for my peace of mind. Like most of my schoolmates, I had, once I left Tardun at the age of 17, contacted Catholic Immigration in Perth asking for my records. They had none and strongly advised me, as they had done to other old boys, to not go looking for relatives as I would be bitterly disappointed. Ignoring their warning, I wished Margaret luck, never thinking that she could possibly surpass my wildest expectations and that I would be blown away by her news when she got home.

Harry and Margaret arrived in London on 27 July 1979 with almost a blank sheet of paper containing only my date of birth and my mother's name, Anne Hawkins. The only other information I had been able to give them was that Anne may have worked for a short time at a priest's house in Shanklin on the Isle of Wight. I had given them a packet of photographs to pass on in case they found my family. Margaret wrote a journal while she was away – it became a treasured record of their search.

Saturday July 28. London was a hot 85 degrees so the Isle of Wight looked a good option to begin the quest to find Anne Hawkins. Left for the island, train to Portsmouth, hovercraft to Cowes, train to Shanklin. First call was to Father Donelly at the Sacred Heart Catholic Church. He had no recollection of Anne and introduced us to a nun, a long-term resident of the convent. [She said] 'Yes I do recall the name but have no idea of her whereabouts.' Next move was to phone all persons with the name Hawkins on the island. This produced a negative result.

On the following Monday, Harry and Margaret, along with their daughter Helen, set off to Ryde to visit the town council. With the help of the staff they checked the marriage records to find out if Anne had married there, but to no avail.

Tuesday September 4: To St Catherine's House, London, to check journals of birth records; ordered a birth certificate in the name of John Patrick Hawkins. This would be available in two days. Telephoned the historian at Alton. He had no further information since John's first visit. Phoned Nazareth House, a place where many of the boys left from, on their journey to Australia. A friendly nun from Australia apologised for the lack of information, wished us luck and prayers for a happy ending. Next phoned Hammersmith Hospital. Spoke to a person who may have had information; she became agitated so the conversation was terminated.

Thursday September 6: To St Catherine's House to collect birth certificate of JPH. It revealed that his mother was a 24-year-old student nurse, Anne Elizabeth Margaret Hawkins. Checked her birth date in the journals. It was decided to view the marriage registration journals from 1947 onwards. Perhaps Anne eventually married. The name Hawkins, there were so many would this be an impossible task. We each took a journal. Three hours later a breakthrough. An Anne Hawkins with three Christian names had married an Edwards, also with three Christian names. This would narrow the field down; now to double-check an Edwards with three.

Harry and Margaret had planned to leave England for home on 10 September but as all the flights were fully booked they decided to stay on in London and continue the search.

Thursday September 13: The decision was made to go to Ealing to get the feel of things. Maybe they still lived there. Any leads at all. Left by bus for Ealing approaching our destination with much trepidation. Passing the church, we decided to call in and met a friendly priest who let us view the book of wedding records. This was confirmation of the document seen at St Catherine's. The priest said 'The Edwards family have left the district and I have not seen any of the Edwards family for some time.' Continued on to Hope St [the address that had been listed in the wedding document], knocked on the door and waited a minute or two. The door opened and we were greeted by a most apologetic gentleman, 'So sorry but I have just got out of the shower. You're lucky to catch me in. I was about to go out in five minutes.' Did he know the Edwards family?

'Sorry, I can't help you. I have only lived here for about five years.' We must have looked downcast as he sensed our disappointment. 'Well you may get some information from the man in number 11 across the street. He is one of a few long-term residents.' There we were greeted warmly and he told us he had not seen the Edwards family for several years and he believed that they migrated to Canada twelve years ago. Once again the bar had been raised. Disappointed and resigned to the fact that the trail may end here, we thanked him and turned to go. He called us back. 'A Miss Edwards, possibly a sister to Mr Edwards, returns to this street now and again to visit friends. Perhaps I could pass a message on to her.' Then he told us in much detail how the Edwards Sheet Metal Works was well known for its superb manufacturing quality. We gave the gentleman a self-addressed postcard, which would be given to Miss Edwards. This would enable her to contact us in Australia. We said goodbye, returned to the city centre. During lunch, we assessed the situation. We would go to the council offices, finally, to confirm that the Edwards family were not ratepayers in Ealing. On the walk to the council, glancing across the road at a building familiar to us in Australia, the Citizens Advice Bureau, the following words were spoken in jest 'That's where you go find out most information. There is no harm in a visit.'

It was 1pm and we were told that the council offices would not open till 2pm. We were given new telephone directory, which was only delivered yesterday, and browsed through it, flipping the pages to the name Edwards. There in bold print was Edwards Sheet Metal Works. Much excitement, as the council visit was cancelled. We phoned the works and were greeted by the friendly voice of a lady and asked to speak to a member of the Edwards family. 'The Edwards family have

*retired from the business and it is now managed by their son-in-law.'
'Do they have a family?' 'Yes, they have three daughters.' 'No sons?'
'No.' 'What part of England have they retired to?' 'They have retired
south to Selsey. I will give you their phone number.' All this information
was given, without my Australian accent being questioned. The
exhilaration was unbelievable. Hurdles can be jumped so, to celebrate,
we returned to no. 11 Hope St., to thank the man for being one of the
keys to our success and to present him with a large plate of cakes.*

*Returned to London and that night rang Anne at Selsey. I told her I
was from Australia and had a package from John Patrick in Australia.
'Who is he? Do I know him?' Then a long deathly silence. A feeling of
guilt was overwhelming that I was intruding into her life, after thirty-
two years. Goodbyes were said, with a promise I would call again
before leaving for Australia.*

*Friday September 14: 8.30am phoned Selsey, a busy line, then
at 9.30am busy, at 10.30am, the phoned was answered, 'Sorry, but
Anne Edwards has gone away. I have no idea when she will be back.'
Realising the stress she was under, I decided not to call again.*

As there were still no available Qantas flights to Australia, Harry and
Margaret decided to travel to Selsey the next day.

*Sunday September 16: Arrived in Selsey at midday, after a stopover
at Chichester. Decided that knocking at the door at Anne's home was
not an option; wandered pass their house ... just to take a photo of it.
Had lunch at the hotel then walked to the RC Church of Our Lady of
Mt Carmel and St Peter to meet the priest. He was willing to deliver the
package of photos from John. After a discussion, it was decided this
would have a negative effect and the best thing to do was to go back to
Australia to tell John the outcome. Any further decision would be made
by him.*

In her last entry about finding my family, Margaret wrote:

*The hurdles were high, there were a few stumbles, but the quest to find
Anne had been achieved. Helen stayed in London and at John's request
visited his mother and sister in Selsey. In Anne's words, it was the
worst day of her life, when a couple came to the home [the Sisters of
Nazareth orphanage in Romsey] and took her son away for adoption.*

Helen visited my sister Susan, who lived in the same village, and gave her the photographs. Margaret finished her journal by describing my reaction when they returned home.

I came back to Australia to visit John and Julie. John was stunned when I told him the news. He clasped his hands to his face, turned, and in true Aussie style, walked to the fridge and asked, 'Does anyone want a beer?'

In early 1980, not knowing his name, I addressed a letter to 'The Catholic Priest, Selsey'. I sent a copy of my birth certificate and asked if he would speak to my mother. About six months later, Father Price replied and said my mother was a well-known businesswoman and a personal friend and that he would find it difficult to talk to her. He asked that I be patient and felt sure she would write to me one day. I wasn't much surprised at the tardiness of the response and tried to imagine what it would be like for my mother after all these years. I had time on my side, but patience was another matter.

Her letter was a great disappointment. In a one-page note she asked that I not contact her or the family as she was happily married and had no wish to see me. I felt at this time that I was on a rollercoaster of highs and lows. Julie was pregnant with our first child, which was about the most exciting thing that could happen to me, yet I was on the verge of bankruptcy – and now my mother had rejected me. I decided to put as much as I could behind me and concentrate on planning for and surviving our perilous future on the farm.

21

SETTLING DOWN – WITH DOUBTS

'We got some good late summer rains, which is always handy in our neck of the woods. It provides subsoil moisture for the winter wheat crop,' I told our bank manager in early 1980, as he mulled over the budget. Summer subsoil moisture was always an advantage for a winter crop and I put a bit of spin on it, hoping to convince him that he wasn't taking a risk. He personally managed the worst cases on his books and mine wasn't looking positive. The banks were getting nervous – the droughts were seriously compromising the viability of farming, and with them, my future career.

'The thing with you is that you haven't gone out and purchased expensive plant and equipment and your debt–equity ratio still falls within our limit,' he said, with a broad smile. Bemused but filled with a sense of relief and foolish bravado, I said, 'Aren't you being irresponsible?'

It was an outrageous thing to say, especially as we had just signed off on the loan facility. Sitting back in his chair, with a puzzled look, he asked, 'What do you mean?'

'Well, I was just thinking what chance a bloke would have if he walked into a bank seeking finance for a business plan that had failed four years in a row, and he had no business strategy other then to adopt the previous one, and he was up to his neck in debt. How far do you think this gentleman would get?'

'Wouldn't get past the bloody teller,' he replied, roaring with laughter. It must have affected him – we always got an invitation to the bank's Christmas party after that.

Good, strong winter rains came in May and, on top of summer rainfall, meant that prospects for a good crop were excellent. The crops were thick and lush and God smiled again on our country. The good harvest enabled us to pay off some of our debt and buy a second-hand car. Colin, our neighbour, was worried though. He had also received instructions to weed out the worst cases on his bank's books and he didn't relish the job of being the hatchet man. The political pressure on the banks had eased somewhat but the culling of farmers would begin now that the drought had ended. Banks didn't like selling out farmers in droughts. I thought, cynically, that the image of a mother holding a child in her arm, a suitcase in her hand, with the homestead as a backdrop and surrounded by dead and dying livestock isn't good advertising for a bank. The banks prefer to take a more subtle approach, making farmers quit by squeezing their finances, forcing them to sell the farm 'voluntarily'.

Driving back from the farm one hot Sunday evening, I noticed a scuffle outside the front of the Club Hotel. A policeman was on the ground yelling for help as a group of Aboriginal men, one on top of him, was working him over. I got out of the ute, casually walked over and said 'Righto boys, there's five against one here. Let him up and let him go.'

I knew a couple of the men from my football days, which helped. I told the new policeman, whose face was bleeding, that the men were drunk and he should go home and sort it out tomorrow. The cop was having none of it. He quickly handcuffed a man called George and threw him into the back of his car, demanding that I get in with him. I refused, saying I lived in town and got on well with the Aboriginal people.

I had no idea about how the scuffle had started, but he was safe and I wanted no further involvement. He then threatened to charge me for failing to carry out the instructions of a police officer. I reluctantly got in the back with George. Being Sunday there were no other police officers on duty, as they had all gone away for the weekend. I could see why he thought he needed me – he was clearly frightened of George. I was furious when he ordered me to take George, who was now threatening me with all kinds of things, into the lock-up cell.

The policeman dropped his trousers and exposed his bare buttocks, saying 'See anything here? The bastard bit me. He'll get three months for assault.'

I could see an exact replica of George's teeth marks around a red welt, but replied, 'I can't see anything. There's nothing there.' I walked out the door.

I refused to attend court as a witness, instead giving a written account of what happened. The policeman asked his wife to take photos of his posterior, which he presented as evidence to the amusement of his colleagues and the judge. George got three months for assault. The police told me that they would warn me when he came out of jail and I was to report any problems. Unfortunately, Scotty, the police sergeant who I got along well with, had moved on and I didn't know anyone else I could talk to.

Within days of George's release, a terrifying hail of rocks began landing on the tin roof of our house in the middle of the night. In the morning I told Julie that he'd be back the following night. I wanted to sort it out without the police involved so I went to bed with my running shoes on and kept a small wooden club and a torch handy.

Scruffy, our little Australian terrier, would lead the way once the rocks starting landing. Sure enough, about 1am, the rocks came crashing down against the side of the house and on the roof. I followed Scruffy into the vacant block next door, which was littered with old cars and rusting water tanks – the perfect place to hide. I walked around, yelling for them to come out and face the music. Next morning I spotted George and two of his mates outside the post office. I explained to George that it wasn't me who locked him up and I had been forced into getting in the police car. I warned that if he wanted to continue his silly game, he should come again that night with his mates. This time I would be more than ready. That evening, George came over to apologise. It was all over. A vendetta had been avoided and we got along famously after that.

Late in 1980, I hired a young man to help with the harvest. He had just left the Australian navy and had a drinking problem. Driving back to the farm one Sunday night he was pulled over by the traffic police and asked to 'blow in the bag' to check his blood alcohol limit.

'Where are you going?' the policeman asked him.

'I am driving a truck for John Hawkins.' The policeman let him go with a warning, but followed behind him to the turnoff at Williams Road. Again he demanded that the young man get out of the car and blow in the bag: 'You are driving all over the road. What do you think is going to happen when you blow into this bag?'

'You'd better stand back, because I'm gonna blow it to smithereens!' replied the young ex-sailor. The policeman let him go again and the next morning he told me how lucky I was to have such a great mate in the police force.

Every year after harvesting, we went to the Moorhead's holiday house in Kalbarri, swimming, boating and fishing for most of January. We caught more than our fair share of Spanish mackerel, which in those days were plentiful to the north and south of the town. There was an abundance of smaller fish in the river and tourist anglers could catch a feed just about anywhere.

In January 1981, Joanne, our first child, was born at the Mullewa Hospital. Dr Docherty delivered her and allowed me in for her birth. The most incredible thing a person can watch is their child being born and I was stunned and overjoyed at the same time. I was still somewhat in a daze when Docherty called out 'What you think you're doing? Get down to the pub and bring some champagne so we can all celebrate.' Having a child was the greatest moment of my life and I had never dreamed of experiencing such a happy event, especially after my sad childhood. I determined then that my child would have a different life – she would never feel the sting of abandonment and the pain and indignity of old-fashioned discipline. This beautiful child, and any more to come, would be loved and cared for as long as I lived.

Fathers being present at the birth of their children was a new phenomenon at the time and it took a while to catch on. Gerry had been the first in town to do it, but he fainted at the critical moment. Unable to do much about it, the nursing staff shoved him under the table to get him out of the way. He had to be treated later for a couple of cracked ribs.

Soon, it was Scruffy's turn to get pregnant. We mated her with an Australian silky terrier, but when we brought her home a large stray dog also got into the act. She successfully gave birth to one puppy, but a much larger one remained behind and the mother and pup were in serious trouble. Julie had been up half the night and Scruffy was weak, exhausted and in great pain. Fearing it was too late to drive the 100 kilometres to the vet in Geraldton, I took Scruffy to Jack Murray, who ran the local zoo. Jack had often bought birds from me when I was a boy at Tardun. He suggested that I take Scruffy to the doctor immediately. The doctor had helped Jack on numerous occasions with his animals. I took Scruffy to the hospital in a basket early in the morning and waited my turn with the other patients. When Docherty came out of his room and saw the 'patient', he bellowed, 'This is a hospital not a veterinary clinic'.

I held my ground, to the amusement of the other patients, pleading that the dog would die if he didn't help.

'Take the thing outside and wait,' he grumbled and strode back to his room. Moments later he came back with a syringe and said, 'Inject it under the skin. It'll relax the muscles.'

An hour later, little Scruffy gave birth to an impossibly large pup. Both the pups were given to good homes in town.

The rains came again the following year and, once again, we managed to pay off some debts. I began to involve myself more with the Farmers Union, which by then had changed its name to the Primary Industry Association, becoming local branch secretary. The association was heavily bureaucratic from top to bottom. A motion passed at a local branch could then be passed or failed at a zone meeting and then at a conference, creating a river of paperwork. Head office dealt directly with the issues raised from branch motions. Farmers who regularly criticised mindless government bureaucracy couldn't see that this was as bad as it could get. I figured that a lot of the issues raised at our meetings could be sorted out at the local level, where we had intimate knowledge of the problems, without the involvement of the vast bureaucratic machine. At times, only three of us attended the branch meetings and we would hold them at the hotel bar and have a beer.

Although two generations of wheat growers had known no other marketing system, the performance of the Australian Wheat Board was still of major concern and the memory of the disastrous wheat quotas was firmly fixed in our minds. Incompetent marketing had sent some farmers broke. It happened once and it could happen again. But the majority of growers still believed that single-desk marketing delivered maximum results and challenging this view was difficult.

Most wheat was sold as Australian Standard White (ASW).[1] Gamenya made up 80 per cent of ASW wheat in Western Australia and was the best wheat for the manufacture of udon noodles, for which there was a huge market in Japan. The Japanese market was importing 10 per cent of its wheat from Australia. The rest came from America and Canada. Australian grain was noted for its quality, which came from the high concentrations of the variety Gamenya and, later, Eradu. Neither North America nor Canada could match Australia's quality, although they had won a much bigger slice of the Japanese market through bilateral trade agreements.

I believed that the AWB was not aware of the potential of Gamenya to be sold at a premium price to Japan, a rich and quality-conscious market willing to pay for consistently high-quality wheat. This lack of market knowledge was costing the farmers dearly. Our main markets continued to be Russia and China – both opportunistic markets that bought solely on price. The Chicago Wheat Exchange set the daily price for wheat and AWB wheat was subject to the vagaries of the broad market. Whenever I raised these issues I was simply told not to rock the boat.

Before 1980 the grading system was based on 'fair average quality' (FAQ) of wheat. Samples of wheat were collected from various reception points across the state in the early stages of harvest and, when mixed together, formed a 'representative' sample to be used as a yardstick to assess the quality of wheat for the season. I felt that the system had us locked in to producing low-quality wheat for low-quality markets and created a unique double standard. While a farmer had no objection to his neighbour receiving more money for his wool, he would not tolerate him getting more for his wheat. For me, the most troubling and frustrating thing was that the single-desk system denied progressive farmers the freedom to market their own grain and this gave us little sense of ownership when we delivered our grain.

From 1983 to 1988, the combined sowings of the low-yielding Gamenya and Eradu fell significantly. The Japanese, who paid a substantial market premium, began complaining. In response, the AWB began looking for bins that held higher concentrations of these varieties, but growers had swung away to other varieties that gave higher yields.

To attract growers back to Gamenya and Eradu, the AWB offered us a small varietal bonus of $4–7 per tonne – a fraction of the premium the Japanese were paying. The production of these two varieties continued to fall.

It took until February 1985 before the first threat to the monopoly powers of the AWB came. A joint committee was set up by the Queensland Minister for Primary Industries to investigate how Queensland could secede from the AWB. Farmers proposed that they could do better marketing their own grain, complaining about the excessive selling costs, poor marketing and uncertainty over price and returns. The AWB threatened that should Queensland break away, it would not receive the protection of the guaranteed minimum price (GMP). The federal-government-backed GMP was like a bank guarantee and, without it, in uncertain times, growers could struggle to finance their crops.

In April 1985, 8000 farmers marched on Parliament House in Perth. There were no federal ministers to hear the complaints and minor state ministers were howled down when they tried to speak. Some 40 000 farmers invaded Melbourne in the biggest demonstration of its kind ever seen. The Hawke Labor government was seen to be as unsympathetic as the previous Whitlam Labor government. The issues that had caused the riots in the earlier protest – high costs, unfair tariffs on imported equipment and chemicals, high levels of excise levies and climbing interest rates – were still damaging the farmers.

There was also concern over the looming trade war between North America and Europe over subsidies, the fallout of which, it was felt, would seriously damage the viability of farms in Australia. Australian wheat growers, caught in the middle, could only watch as their traditional markets collapsed and, as the AWB was unable to protect them, were forced to sell at the going price. No farmer could compete against the crippling American and European subsidies.[2] The federal government soon announced plans to enable marginal wheat farmers to quit agriculture with 'dignity'.

Other issues – such as how the state government controlled the movement of fertiliser by road thus stifling competition and increasing our expenses, and the excessive costs of transport grain – occupied my mind. Rising freight rates were uncompetitive, in spite of repeated government assurances to the contrary, and legislation required the grain to be transported by rail. I told a gathering of local farmers that the only way we could test the government's claim was to place an advertisement offering the tender to transport wheat at the Pindar wheat bin. This was a radical plan and it involved a degree of false advertising, as we had no legal power to contract a transporter. However, we all agreed it was a plan worth pursuing.

In 1985 I placed an advertisement in the business section of the *West Australian* newspaper calling for the transport of 24 000 tonnes of wheat from Pindar to the port of Geraldton, a distance of 130 kilometres. Approximately 30 bids came in, some from the largest trucking companies in the state. I phoned each company and admitted why we had placed the advertisements. They were all happy for us to use their quote to pressure the government. The quotes were substantially lower than what the government was charging, a couple of quotes by 50 per cent. I presented the evidence to the Minister for Transport, demanding that he do something. The freight rate at the Pindar bin the next year was reduced by 35 per cent, making it one of the cheapest bins in the state. It caused distortions in the system as farmers carted their grain backwards, away from the port, to get the cheap freight benefit. It also caused problems for Co-operative Bulk Handling, as extra facilities had to be installed to handle the overflow, which nearly doubled the normal deliveries. There was no more talk of closing our 'uneconomic' bin; instead the government invested money upgrading the tattered Pindar railway line. The following year, the government reduced freight rates across the state.

A couple of years later, I found myself in court with fifteen other farmers charged with illegally transporting fertiliser by road. It was illegal to contract freight companies without a permit from the Road Licensing Authority and inspectors had followed the trucks to our farms in the dead of night and busted us all. The penalties were heavy – and we could expect the maximum. We had breached an act designed to protect the more expensive government rail from competition.[3]

I arrived late at the Geraldton courthouse where the farmers and their lawyers were waiting. I had decided to represent myself. The lawyers informed me they had already plea-bargained with the judge that their clients would accept the lesser penalty of a fine of about $1700 each. To their horror I told them I was fighting the case and asked if anyone had read the legislation. None of them had. I pointed to a loophole in the legislation that I was intending to use to argue my case. So convinced was I of winning that I took my two young daughters along to the trial for a bit of fun – this was why I was running late. The lawyers rushed back into the chamber to change their plea. In little more than an hour, the judge threw out the charges and awarded costs against the Crown. One of the inspectors threatened, 'Be very careful Hawkins, we'll be watching you closely from now on.'

I countered the threat, saying, 'It is my ambition to see you all out of work and when you re-enter the workforce, you will hopefully be doing something constructive!'

After the 1986 McColl Royal Commission into Grain Storage, Handling and Transport recommendations were handed down in 1988, it was no longer illegal for farmers to use contractors to cart fertiliser.

1   ASW is described as a multipurpose wheat suitable for the manufacture of bread, including flat breads, noodles and a range of other products.

2   The subsidy war continued into the early 1990s. The farmers' only relief was a crop disaster in the northern hemisphere that caused a tightening of world stocks. In effect, we had become predators waiting for a drought somewhere else to be able to sell our wheat at a decent price. The only market to hold up for the entire period was Japan, yet I felt that its need for quality wheat was being ignored.

3   I was asked to give evidence to the McColl Royal Commission into Grain Storage, Handling and Transport (1986–1988), a federal government initiative to weed out inherent inefficiencies throughout the entire industry. The WA legislation was one of the Royal Commission's many casualties and the transport industry was freed of unnecessary regulations.

22

'THAT'S HER, THAT'S MY MUM'

In 1980 I decided it was time to go back to England with the hope of physically seeing my mother, perhaps with the help of the priest in Selsey. Julie supported me in my plan as she knew how much it meant to me. My mother's letter of rejection was still firmly in my mind and I had sent a copy to the priest. I intended to respect my mother's wishes, even though I felt them to be awfully unfair. All I wanted was to just see her.

A few months before, I had received a letter from my sister Susan, who was so excited to have a brother. She had responded to a letter I had written to her where I had mentioned how disappointed I had been about my mother's letter. Susan filled me in on some of the family background, and even through I was very excited about communicating with one of my siblings, my feelings were tempered by my mother's objection to meeting me as it would be many years before I might actually meet Susan, or anyone else from the family. So I decided it was best if I kept my trip a secret from my English family.

I contacted Percy's brother, John, in Wales, telling him to expect me some time in August. We had finished seeding the crop by the end of June and I was in London by late July. I caught the train to Chichester and took a taxi to Selsey and booked in for a few days at the Thatched Roof Hotel right on the coast, where, as the publican told me, the Australian tennis team often stayed. The village was a popular tourist destination, but the holiday hadn't started so the hotel was quiet. The friendly publican wanted to know the purpose of my visit.

'Just looking around, a bit of history that sort of thing you know,' I said, ordering a beer at the bar. I noticed large brass binoculars fixed to a stand looking out across the English Channel and, before I could ask, he explained, 'Lots of retired navy chaps live around here: you know, captains, even the odd ex-admiral. They like to look out, identify the ships and talk about old times.'

Next morning, I knocked on the presbytery door of the parish priest. Father Price was a little shocked. A tall thin man with a clipped upper-class accent, he invited me in to share tea and biscuits with his counterpart, the local Anglican priest.

'I'm not here to barge in on my mother's life,' I told them . 'I will respect her request not to see me. I just want to see her in the flesh, see what she looks like, then I promise I will go away.'

Father Price explained to his friend that one of his parishioners was my mother and he had the devil of a job to counsel her. He pulled an envelope from a drawer and said, 'I've got some photos here that I can show you.' He offered a photo of three women and prompting me to guess which one, he said, 'One of those is your mum'.

My eyes kept returning to the blonde woman on the left. I felt that I had seen her before and my eyes were drawn to her image. A minute later, I pointed and told him, 'That's her, that's my mum'.

Father Price replied, 'I suggest you come to nine o'clock mass in the morning. She'll be there. She never misses mass. Take the photo with you – and by the way you have three sisters.'

I spent the rest of the day agitated and unable to concentrate on anything. I needed a diversion and found it at the pub where the navy chaps were talking about the current cricket test between Australia and England. Being Australian, I copped it from all sides as friendly banter was bowled up and hit back. The subject turned to fishing, and someone asked what it was like in Australia. I mentioned the coastal town Kalbarri and the mackerel there. One man said, 'Mackerel's a shit fish; well, at least here it is.'

It didn't help when I stretched out my arms and told them 'Ours are this big'. Amid laughter, I went to my room to find the picture of me holding little Joanne in one arm and the tail of a Spanish mackerel in the other, which nearly reached my head.

I had great difficulty sleeping that night. But, next morning, I was kneeling at the very rear of the 450-year-old Saints Peter and Paul church, observing the three women who knelt together at the front. Apart from us the church was empty. Before the service was finished, my mother left her seat and began walking towards me. My heart was pounding. I thought Father Price must have told her, but she walked past me, dropped some coins in the box, lit a candle and then was gone. I sat for a long while to catch my breath and think about what had just happened. Father Priced joined me, but he didn't say anything. He just knelt and prayed. Before I left the church, I told him I'd be back in the morning for one last look. For the rest of the day I toured around the historical landmarks of Chichester and tried hard to forget my pain.

I had gained some credibility at the pub after showing the photo of the mackerel, and the publican was determined to take me to the beach early in the morning for a taste of freshly caught local lobster. About 6 am the next day, he took me to where the fishermen were cooking the morning catch in large iron pots, and asked for an especially big one for his Australian friend.

I didn't see much of my mother at mass, as she went out through a side door, got into her car and drove away. Father Price asked me where I was staying and what my plans were. I told him I was satisfied now that I had seen her and would be off to Wales first thing in the morning.

I phoned John in Wales that evening and said to expect me some time the next day and went to bed about 9.30 pm. Half an hour later, I answered a knock on the door and an attractive young woman looked at me momentarily, before bursting into tears. She told me that her name was Susan, that she was my sister and that I was coming home. With these simple statements, my heart nearly burst and I cried freely as I got changed and packed my bags. As I went to pay the account, the publican inquired if we were all right as we were both very distressed. I replied that we were okay and I would see him again before I left the village. Susan and I stayed up until 3 am, talking, crying and hugging. She had recently divorced and had two young daughters, Nicky and Amanda, who were asleep in bed.

Susan told me the story of my family and the pieces began to fall into place. She was shocked when Father Price had told her about me and at first didn't know what to do. Our mother had married Fred Edwards a year after I was apparently 'adopted' and they soon started a family. Fred had inherited his father's smash repair business in London and the couple had quickly built it into a large precision engineering company, employing between 60 and 100 workers, including some of the finest toolmakers in the country. Business had flourished and soon they bought a house in Buckinghamshire, a few doors down from Chequers, the prime minister's country residence.

While her son was growing up in a British orphanage, my mother had become a socialite and wore furs and fine jewellery. She was pretty and glamorous, and mixed with the top end of town in business and politics. She had natural wit and charm and an infectious laugh. Everyone loved her.

She and Fred rubbed shoulders with the Foreign Secretary and, on occasion, the Secretary of State, who, unbeknown to her, was my legal guardian and would be in charge of my future migration to Australia.[1] I thought about how my mother had socialised with my legal guardian while her seven-year-old boy marched up a gangway on a ship to Australia to the tune of 'Auld Lang Syne'. It seemed almost comical – like a Charlie Chaplin drama.

She had her second child when I was two years old. Her three girls – Joy, the eldest, Susan and Liz, the youngest – attended the finest Catholic schools and my mother drove a Rolls-Royce.

More recently, Fred had become ill and had made some bad business decisions. The family had sold off most of the factory's fleet of vans and trucks. Susan's former husband, Michael, was managing the business. My mother and Fred had retired to their favourite holiday village where my mother was very active in the local social scene.

Susan asked me about my life and I told her it was just fine. I couldn't tell her then – and didn't know if I ever could – about my upbringing. I quickly diverted her back to her life story. The contrast between my life and hers was so great that any guilt she might feel would just add to the enormous pain she was feeling.

Next morning Susan phoned Joy and Liz, my other two half-sisters. Joy was too upset to come down from London to see me. Liz, who was only 19 years old, was excited to meet her new brother and caught the first train south from Sunderland Art College. Susan drove to my mother's house and privately told her the news. My mother came around a couple of hours later to meet me. Neither of us expressed much emotion – we just shook hands and sat in chairs at opposite ends of the room – but she couldn't keep her eyes off me as we engaged in small talk. I obviously reminded her of someone, but just who I couldn't tell.

She told me that she was worried about having to tell Fred and felt that she needed help to do this. She phoned her aunt Minnie, an elderly nun who apparently Fred admired and respected. Minnie arrived the next day with a bottle of Irish whisky – surprising given that she was a teetotaller. She was very close to my mother and had almost certainly been aware of my mother's pregnancy. She had probably offered advice she now regretted, especially once she had learned that fellow Catholic nuns from a different order had betrayed her niece. Behind her glasses, Minnie's eyes were damp. She gave me the bottle she had opened and sipped on the way down by train. She said she'd heard I had a touch of flu and that the whisky would help. It would help her too – she would need Dutch courage to confront Fred.

Liz arrived about the same time, telling everyone in the room that she had always wanted a brother. A couple of hours later, Minnie and my mother went back to break the news to Fred. He exploded in a violent rage, forcing them to retreat to Susan's house to spend the night. It was my worst nightmare. Everything I had set out to avoid was happening and I felt a sense of helplessness as the family began to unravel. Minnie and my mother managed to calm Fred the next morning, telling him that I had left the village and was never coming back. For Fred, who had provided a lifetime of love and support to my mother, this seemed the ultimate betrayal and he lashed out like he had never done before. The pressure wasn't good for him as he was still seriously ill and was in and out of hospital. I offered to go to Wales, but Susan and Liz wouldn't hear of it. It was family business and we had to sort it out together. I didn't see my mother for a couple of days but spent the time getting to know Liz and Susan, as well as my two nieces.

We went driving together and took in all the tourist spots in that part of southern England. One day, my mother turned up unexpectedly and took me out for lunch. I showed her the photographs the others had seen of baby Joanne and Julie, our holidays at Kalbarri, as well the farm. I tried to present an image of happiness and contentment, but she could read between the lines. She reached out, took my hand with tears and said, 'It was not meant to happen. I saw that lovely couple take you away in their pram. How can I ever believe the nuns again? I loved you. I didn't want to give you away.'

Left *The first photo taken of me three months after arriving in Australia. Invited by my holiday family to Christine's birthday party, I was allowed to blow out her candles for the second time.*

Below *Early 1960s: My biological mother (right), my aunt Queenie (left) and my sister Joy (middle).*

Top *1957: Tommy calming the wild donkey soon after its capture.*

Bottom *The captured donkey about to be hauled onto the back of a truck.*

Top 1958: *Just after our arrival at Tardun from Castledare. I'm standing in the back row, last on the right.*

Bottom 1959: *Riding a bucking steer at the first (and last) rodeo at Tardun.*

Top *1959: Me, Jim and Chris
on Rodeo day.*

Bottom *1960: The boys prepare
to go hunting with Ned.*

Top *1963: Ned and Horatio, our pet eagle.*

Bottom *1958: Visiting boys inspect our morning catch.*

Top *Early 1960s: The
Christian Brothers
Agricultural School, Tardun.*

Bottom *Early 1990s:
After forty years, nothing
much has changed.*

8/40/93.

For all persons, sixteen years of age and over, and those under sixteen not accompanied by parents.

COMMONWEALTH OF AUSTRALIA
DEPARTMENT OF IMMIGRATION, AUSTRALIA HOUSE, LONDON, W.C.2.

MEDICAL EXAMINATION.

Declaration by Applicant.

NAME _____ John, Patrick, Hawkins. _____
Full Name in Block Capitals

ADDRESS *NAZARETH HOUSE, HILL LANE, SOUTHAMPTON*

1. Have you ever had any serious accident/illness or surgical operation ? If so, please furnish details
   No   *No*

2. Have you or has any member of your family ever suffered from or been suspected of Tuberculosis?
   No

3. Have you ever had Enuresis or any sign of disease of the Genito Urinary Organs ? *No*

4. Have you or has any member of your family ever suffered from **mental disease or epilepsy** or been
   treated in an institution of any kind for these Diseases ? *No*

5. What medical attention have you required during the last twelve months ? *None*

   I hereby certify that the information supplied by me to the Medical Examiner is correct in every particular :—

Signature of applicant which must be made } *John Hawkins*
in the presence of the Medical Referee

Results of Medical Examination.

AGE *7 yrs.* HEIGHT *3 ft 10 ¾ ins* WEIGHT *3 st.*

A. Heart *Normal*   F. Genito Urinary Organs *Normal.*
                                 Urine *Normal*
   Blood Pressure *Normal*   without glasses RR. LE
B. Lungs *Normal*   G. Sight { with glasses (if worn) RE LE
   (Particularly Tuberculosis)   (Snellen's Type)
   X-Ray report ____   Cause of defect in sight ____
C. a. Nervous System *Normal*   H. Hearing *Normal*
   b. Mental Condition *Normal* I. Physique *good*
D. Intelligence *Normal*   J. Skin *Normal*
                                 K. If pregnant, period of pregnancy
E. Digestive Organs *Normal*   L. Teeth *good*

REMARKS **(include particulars of any departure from normal conditions not fully set out in above)**

In cases where the Medical Examiner is unable to describe the applicant as being in perfect health, he should state under " REMARKS " the exact nature of the defect which he finds and whether it is of temporary or permanent nature. The presence of Pediculi should be noted.

Any disablement received on Active Service or otherwise should also be noted and commented on, and if a Pension is received the amount of it should be stated.

I certify that I have this day examined the above-named and am of opinion that the applicant is/is not in good health and of sound constitution, and is/is not suffering from any mental or bodily defect which would cause inability to earn a living as a *a citizen*

State Occupation

Date *5/4/54* Signature and Qualifications *B. Bourke* *Jack Burke.*
DR. B. BOURKE

Address 61. OXFORD STREET
SOUTHAMPTON

TO :—
CHIEF MIGRATION OFFICER, AUSTRALIA HOUSE, STRAND, LONDON, W.C.2.
(FORM K.)   **PLEASE TURN OVER.**

Above 1954: *The official immigration document with my signature, aged seven, is accepted as proof of consent by the Department of Immigration in Australia. I was tricked into signing this false medical record – the test findings were fabricated and signed by an 'approved' doctor.*

68 Kinross Road.
Rushington.
Totton
NR Southampton
Hampshire
England.
SO40. 9BN

8. July 02.

My Dear John,
        I am absolutely over the moon at
finding you at long last. Every time a friend
or relation visited Australia, I wrote letters
for the "where are you now" page in the
papers, hoping ~~that~~ by sheer chance that
you might be in that area - But I never
gave up hope that one day I would hear
from you again.
    Going back to the time you were in
Nazareth House, the Mother Superior had
promised, that although our faiths were
different, (We are C of E) there was no
reason why we could not adopt you.
and, that last weekend, that we went to
pick you up we were shattered just
to be told "He's gone." They Flatley refused
to even tell us which country at

Above *2002: The first page of the first letter sent to me by my would-be adoptive mother in England. She died in 2005.*

The description of me as a deserted child that had appeared on my entry record to the Sisters of Nazareth flashed through my mind. Instinctively I knew the woman sitting in front of me was incapable of such desertion. She was still visibly upset, but I asked her quietly who my father was. She smiled slightly, affectionately patted my cheek and said, 'I loved your father and would have married him. Don't worry, John boy, you are well-bred.' I gathered that she still loved him and wanted to protect him, even after all these years.

Something was awfully wrong with the script. A mother and son reunion was meant to be full of happiness and joy. It was not turning out the way I had practised in my mind – that we would fall into each other's arms, full of sorrow, regret and tears.

Here I was, a dry, unemotional desert, unable to respond to her. I had to keep reminding myself that the woman in front of me was my mother. Conceived in love, I was of her flesh. We shared the same genes and had similar personalities – yet we were total strangers with nothing much in common.

She told me about her life growing up in Ireland and paused as though she remembered something else. 'Mum would have loved you and raised you as her own,' she said almost in a whisper. 'You would have loved her too. We were poor but you would have loved Ireland and you're a nice looking Irish boy.' She patted the back of my hand.

She talked about how her family were strict Catholics and the potential scandal caused by her having a child out of wedlock, and the dilemma of her own conscience. I could imagine that, as a single mother, she would have had little prospects for marriage and how hypocritical and judgmental Irish society could have been at the time.

She asked me about my life. 'Catholic orphanages are much the same, mum,' I replied defensively. I didn't mention Castledare, but told her about Tardun, knowing this would be easier for her. I couldn't tell her anything about my adoptive family in Southampton and my sudden removal. She was shattered enough by the nun's first betrayal.

It was a long time ago and I had banished it to a dark and distant past. I felt that I had to hold it together for the sake of everyone. The worst part was, try as I might, I couldn't feel love towards my own mother, although I had forgiven her and felt no ill will towards her. I began to doubt my own humanity and capacity to love and be loved.

I was unsure who I was and feared that long-term institutionalisation had corrupted my capacity to respond emotionally. I loved Julie and my baby daughter in Australia, but did I love them enough? Could I ever be a real father? I was in deep and uncharted waters. I felt that the developing love between me and Susan and Liz was real and I gained enormous strength from that.

The next week, my mother had arranged for what she described as a Chichester harbour cruise, just for the two of us. We boarded a large boat and set off. Along the way she pointed to the little bay where King Canute had ordered the incoming tide to turn around and go back. 'He tried to defy the natural order of things,' she chuckled. I thought how appropriate it was that she should say this at that time.

Eventually we arrived at a private mooring further up the river and walked to a large harbour-side house where a large gathering of people was waiting. My mother had chosen this moment to come out of the closet. About 80 people – my mother's Chichester friends, among them lawyers and doctors but also ordinary folk, some of whom she had helped along the way – had formed into a semicircle. She led me around by the arm like a prize bull, introducing me to each in turn as her son, nervously laughing and joking. One old woman was too shocked to even look at me. She turned to my mother in horror, crying my mother's name.

The host provided a magnificent barbecue and we were surrounded by people who wanted to hear our story. My mother held on to my arm for most of the afternoon. Tears filled my eyes when we walked back to the boat arm-in-arm: she was proud of me and I was proud of her. We were mother and son at last.

We travelled to London to meet the rest of the family. I reminded my aunt Queenie, who lived with aunt Agnes, of our conversation when I had rung from Detroit in 1976. She had no recollection of talking to me. These two younger sisters lived together in a house they co-owned, but they didn't get along.

Debbie, the only child of my aunt Peggy, asked her mother if she too had any skeletons in the closet, as she wouldn't mind a brother or sister. I met Marie, another of my mother's sisters, who had come over from California. She was a Catholic nun in the order of the Sacred Hearts of Jesus and Mary and worked full time with victims of AIDS.[2]

Uncle Joe had migrated to New Zealand after the war and had served in the New Zealand army for a time as an explosives expert. He married a local girl and they had quite a few children. Uncle Billy was up north somewhere and hadn't been seen for 20 years; that's all the family would say about him.

During my last week with the family, Fred took a turn and ended up in hospital. I sat in the car in the carpark, while the others went to see him. Before I left, I went to say goodbye to the publican of the Thatched Roof Hotel, who was curious to know what had happened to me.

A couple of hours before my departure we all went to mass in London. The family took up two pews towards the back. About halfway through the service, I heard a noise and looked up. I saw the electrical wires attached to a large chandelier fitted with dozens of lights fuse and burn and, seconds later, the whole chandelier came crashing down on the vacant pews in front of us. Anyone sitting under it could have been killed or badly injured. Naturally superstitious, my aunts thought this was a bad omen and promised to say the rosary while I was in the air.

At the airport I finally met my sister Joy and her husband, John. Joy was still upset, but she had accepted the reality of her mother having a child out of wedlock and promised to write to me. It was incredibly hard to wrench myself away from the family – it was like being abandoned all over again. I boarded the plane home an emotional and psychological wreck.

1   My sisters and I verified my mother's political connections when I was in the UK in 2000 from the dozens of letters and invitations she had kept until her death. I quietly learned to accept the hurtful irony that probably the only person with enough political influence to save me at the time when I was in the orphanage was my own mother.

2   In 2007, Sister Hawkins was awarded 'woman of the year' in St Jerome parish in the diocese of Oakland, California, in recognition of 60 years of outstanding work in the community.

SETTLING DOWN AGAIN

My family reunion in England had been both exciting and unsettling and it would take some time for my emotions to settle down. Julie, Joanne and I moved into our new house on the farm, along with our second daughter, Belinda, soon after her birth in 1983. Again I was at the birth to witness the magic all over again. At first I thought she was a boy. Immediately after she was born the nurse swung her around for me to see before hurrying her off into another room. I caught a glimpse of the nurse's finger protruding in the obvious place and again went to the pub to buy champagne, telling a few people that we had a little boy! It made no difference to me when I found out we had another girl – we welcomed Belinda into the world with as much joy and fanfare as when Joanne was born.

We were able to move into our new place because of a far-sighted program called the Rural Housing Scheme, which gave hundreds of farming families with school-age children the opportunity to move out of tin sheds and hovels into decent accommodation. The Rural Housing Scheme took second or third mortgages, and the interest rate was 2 per cent lower than that of the banks. The primary lender, the bank, always took the first mortgage and any equity left after that was mortgaged through the Scheme.

I had rejoined the local Pindar Progress Association soon after we moved. It was an annual gathering of the clan in our district. Most of the farmers and their wives attended and talked about the Christmas tree and who was going to be Father Christmas. The other issue was the election of the chief fire officer and his deputies for our voluntary bushfire brigade. It was important that everybody be given a title and, being the newest and youngest, I was made sixteenth lieutenant.

Presumably it meant that if I were the *only* person at a local bushfire, I would be in charge.

The Bourke government had put a moratorium on land clearing when it came to power in 1983. Two years later, it banned land clearing altogether. By then it had become obvious that the campaign of previous governments to clear one million acres a year had been disastrous. Soil salinity was now a serious problem and, lacking understanding and guidance, we had all been major contributors. We had removed trees and scrub from vulnerable areas and the ground turned poisonous in front of our eyes. Foxes and cats proliferated and the small colony of rat-kangaroos near my railway cottage had disappeared. The bush turkeys that bred in the scrub behind the house had also gone.

By 1984 we had most of the basic farm infrastructure in place, including a new fully equipped workshop, machinery sheds, new sheep yards and silos. New windmills and fencing had also been added. The children soon turned into typical farm girls with pet rabbits, a joey and a pet emu named Hooly, who was no ordinary bird.

I rescued him as a tiny two-week-old chick soon after Belinda's birth. He was stuck in the boundary fence at Bob Gregson's farm. In no time he outgrew the chickens in the chicken yard, took charge and chased them around the pen for something to do. We had to take him out of the yard after the hens stoped laying. Hooly soon grew into a confused adult bird and followed me everywhere, even chasing after the ute when I went to clean the sheep troughs or when I drove the tractor. He was a constant distraction in the workshop and would often sneak up behind me and peck me on the shoulder at the most inopportune moment. He could run at 40 kilometres an hour and had no difficulty keeping up with me. One day he disappeared and I told Julie and the girls that, thankfully, as he was now an adult male, he was probably looking for another mate instead of me. About two months later, while taking rubbish to the tip, I took a closer look at what looked like a normal clump of spinifex grass growing nearby. It was Hooly, cleverly camouflaged among the trees and scrub, sitting on some empty beer cans thinking they were eggs. Male emus brood the eggs and takes care of the chicks and Hooly was obviously following his destiny. He was in very poor condition, as he had been sitting on the cans for many weeks without a break. The following year he disappeared again but this time he arrived back with six day-old chicks, who all sadly drowned after following him into the fishpond.

About the same time the state government had introduced legislation for the commercial farming of emus. The government demanded expensive licensing fees and imposed tough rules and regulations about infrastructure on those few brave enough to enter this new industry. Expensive fencing was supposed to stop farmed emus from escaping or wild emus breaking into farms. The government also imposed strict controls on the removal of birds from the wild and heavy penalties were imposed if caught. This seemed to me to be a typical bureaucratic nonsense, as farmers were still allowed to shoot emus in large numbers whenever they attacked their crops.

Hooly had again wandered off, but this time brought home six half-grown chicks, who went berserk after seeing humans for the first time. Word soon spread as far as Geraldton and, in early 1985, I had an unexpected visit from two uniformed officers from the Department of Conservation and Land Management, the department that controlled and monitored emu farming. They told me they had information that I was running an illegal emu farm with wild birds. I pointed to Hooly, who was in the horse yard with half his chicks while the other half were panicking outside the fence trying to get back in. I suggested to the embarrassed officers that if anyone was to be charged, it should be Hooly as it was all his doing. I added that someone must have got in early with an April Fools' Day joke.

This was last time that Hooly brought back chicks. His attention had now turned to Sorum, our brood thoroughbred mare who had just returned home after a long absence. Because she was pregnant, I fed her a special mix of grain and pellets that I poured into her feed trough. While Sorum's head was in the trough, Hooly took advantage by pecking her on the rump. This caused Sorum to lash out with her hind legs to keep the annoying bird at bay. This turned into a bad habit and she would lash out when feeding even when the emu wasn't around. In the normal mating procedure, a male emu pecks the female on the back as a sign to sit down and he then sits behind her to mate. Just how he thought he might manage this with Sorum doesn't bear thinking about. Hooly spent his day following the horse around the paddock like a shadow. It was clear she was becoming paranoid and perhaps even psychologically damaged. She managed to bite him one day after trapping him against the corner of a fence. She spent the next two days coughing up a feather that had lodged in her throat.

One evening I got a call from Merv Fegan, who had a farm about 10 kilometres away, to tell me that my horse was at his house. I told him it couldn't be Sorum as I had fed her at 6.30 pm, just before dark, and she had settled in for the night. He replied, 'I know it's your horse because it's a grey thoroughbred mare and there's an emu with it'. With her head downcast Sorum reluctantly and slowly followed me home next morning with her halter rope tied to the ute's tow bar, followed, of course, by Hooly. A couple of passing vehicles stopped to look at this strange procession – one man saying that he wished he had a camera.

The story of Hooly's antics had spread far and wide, and local farmers were reluctant to shoot a quiet emu in case it might be Hooly. Hooly eventually lost interest in Sorum and took off again looking for a mate. A farmer turned up at our farm one day with an emu tied up on the back of his ute. I told him it wasn't our bird and that he should let it go free. I had to warn visiting farmers to keep their sheepdogs tied to the back of their utes, as Hooly would attack them. He had no respect for dogs no matter what their size, except for little Scruffy who he towered over but who had bossed Hooly around when he was a little chick.

One day, while looking for a mate, the nearly two-metre-tall Hooly walked into the kitchen at Tardun, forcing the staff to flee. The principal, Brother O'Driscoll, phoned to demand that I retrieve the bird, but Hooly spent the next two days wandering up and down the verandas looking into the classrooms to the amusement of the students. Eventually the sheepdogs ganged up on him and chased him away from the school. Hooly lived to the ripe age of 16 years and we gave him an appropriate burial when he died. We were sad at his passing as he had given us all so much joy and fun and had enriched our lives.

In late 1983 my youngest sister, Liz, came to stay for a few weeks. We picked her up at Perth Airport on a typically hot day in February. She wore a thick black overcoat, which contrasted spectacularly with the bright shirts and shorts worn by a holiday crowd returning from Bali. She had graduated from Sunderland Art College, and while she was in Australia spent time drawing Aboriginal children and John L. shearing sheep. Her journey had the full blessing of my mother but because Fred could never accept me as a stepson, her trip was kept secret.

I dropped her off one morning at Wally Keefe's shearing shed, after warning her that John L. was a rough shearer – probably the roughest. Liz was a young, petite 'English rose' and I thought that the rough and tumble of an Australian shearing shed might offend her sensibilities. Shearing was tough, hard work and shearers sometimes lost their temper and beat the living daylights out of a difficult sheep with their handpiece.

The shearers were nervous as Liz set up her canvas near John L.'s stand. They hated having women in the shed and yelled 'ducks on the pond' when any came near. The shed was a tough man's world and women were seen invaders, requiring an intolerable shift in language and behaviour. This time, however, they had no choice but to put up with Liz's presence, as John L. was the boss and paid their wages. He was popular in the district as he paid all his shearers in cash, after he had cashed in the cheque from the farmer whose sheep they had shorn at the pub. He epitomised the black economy: he kept no records and never submitted a tax return. It had taken the taxman a few years to track him down – little wonder because he had arrived in Australia with no records and only his name as noted on the ship's passenger list.

I went back to the shed about 3 pm to pick up Liz. She said as she packed her things, 'You were wrong about John L. He's just the gentlest man with sheep. It's the others who are cruel and rough.' Puzzled, I went outside to check his pen. There were six neatly shorn wethers, the sum total for his run. All the other pens held between 30 and 40 sheep each. John L. had obviously spent the whole day posing and trying to impress Liz. In typical fashion he asked her, 'S-s-see if you can find my m-m-mummy, so she can t-t-tuck me in at night!' and roared with laughter as we walked out of the shed.

In three short weeks Liz and I grew very close. We talked about anything and everything, sharing our most intimate thoughts. She was in popular demand and everyone wanted to meet her. She met quite a few of my school friends and listened to their stories. I took her to Tardun and showed her around. She met the Brothers, who treated her like royalty. It was a sad but beautiful parting at Perth Airport and we would all miss her very much. In the time she was with us, Liz had been impressed with the way Julie and I treated our two children as respected individuals and she was determined that she would raise her future children in the same way.[1]

In 1982 the taxman finally caught up with John L. as part of an audit of farmers who hadn't deducted sufficient tax from the wages they paid their workers. Two tax inspectors set up office in the town hall at Mullewa and all the farmers were called in. Flipping through my cheque butts, one of the inspectors excitedly exclaimed, 'Here he is again!' He was looking at a payment that I had made out to John L. for shearing my sheep. His look of satisfaction indicated that he thought he had finally tracked down a real villain. I asked them what the problem was and they said that they had never heard of him. According to their records he had never paid tax in his life.

I warned John L. to expect a visit before the week was out. He later told me how the inspectors knocked on his door late that Friday night, demanding to see his books. He met them at the door, deliberately dressed in his smelly shearing clothes that he'd worn all week. Stuttering uncontrollably, as he did when nervous, he invited them into his house, but they refused. They demanded that he hand over his books. He returned with a stack of *Playboy* magazines. 'Not those books,' said one of the inspectors. 'We want your accounting books!'

John L. claimed that his cleaning lady had accidentally thrown them out with the empty beer bottles. The unsuspecting tax officers had little idea that they gone into battle with a rat with a gold tooth. After considering the length of time that John L. had operated as a shearing contractor, the tax office conservatively estimated that the amount owing to them was $38 000.

Three weeks later, a meeting with the tax inspectors in Perth ended prematurely because of the smell coming from John L.'s shearing gear. A subsequent court case went even worse for the authorities. While the prosecution held forth to the judge, John L. was rolling new cigarettes from butts that he kept in a tin. The judge warned that he was in contempt of court. John L. rose to his feet. When the judge asked, 'Is your name John Leslie Sullivan?', John L. replied, 'G-g-g-g-guilty, Your Honour!'

'No! I am asking you, is your name John Leslie Sullivan?'

'G-g-g-g-g-g-guilty, Your Honour!' came the same reply.

The court fiasco continued until the judge, finally fed up with John L., who the judge suspected was a stuttering idiot, fined him $2000 and demanded that he get out of his court. John L. walked out, grinning like a Cheshire cat.[2]

In 1987, Queen Elizabeth II returned to reopen the civic centre after extensive renovations and to proclaim the Port of Geraldton a city. I had first seen her in 1963 when she came with Prince Philip to Geraldton to open the then new civic centre. Children from all the district schools were invited to gather in an orderly formation on the football oval. Seated in an open car, the royal couple slowly were driven up and down the grassy field through the blocks of children who lined the way. She barely glanced at the Tardun boys, as her attention was suddenly drawn to a rowdy group from Geraldton High School who hooted, squealed and whistled. The presence of Brother Tommy ensured that we were the most subdued of the thousand or so excited youngsters who waved flags and cheered.

Her second visit was an opportunity to take our children to see her. We often read stories about kings and queens, princes and princesses, knights in armour and dragons and castles. I foolishly told our girls to collect some wildflowers to present to the Queen of England, so off they dashed into the bush and returned with some pink, white and yellow everlastings, which they wrapped in foil. The girls were unusually quiet during the drive to Geraldton and sat expectantly in the back of the car, tightly clutching their little flower arrangements. I always delivered on my promises, but this time I feared that I had raised the bar too high.

Several thousand people stood in a large roped-off area in front of the Geraldton airport terminal. A long red carpet was already laid and a line of local dignitaries, with their wives, was waiting to greet the Queen, dressed in their splendid best. Keeping order were dozens of security guards and police, who took their positions in front of the barrier a few metres apart. I would need to find a weakness in the security so that my daughters could give the Queen the flowers. I spotted it just before her plane landed. At the far end of the barrier, where the view would be poor because of the sharp angle, stood a lone security officer chatting to a handful of people. I crouched down and told my girls that on the count of three I would lift the rope and they must sprint to the bottom of the stairs coming down from the aircraft. At the moment the doors of the aircraft opened, I yelled 'Run!' The security guard ran after them and caught Belinda, who struggled and began to cry in distress. The Duke of Edinburgh had watched the scene unfold and called to the security guard to release the little girl. Poor Belinda was still visibly upset as she handed her posy of everlastings to the Queen, whose face opened with a broad smile as she graciously accepted the modest offerings. Fortunately, the magic moment was captured forever on film.

1   Today Liz has three beautiful children of her own and our families have grown close, especially the children.

2   John L. died suddenly in 1995 at one of our old boy get-togethers at Tardun. He had been in ill health and about a month before he died, I visited him in hospital. He told me that he had a near-death experience and was no longer afraid to die. The school chapel was packed on the day of his funeral. I was asked at the last minute by Brother O'Doherty to give the eulogy. Having nothing prepared, I scribbled a few notes during the first part of the service. I began by describing the incredible hardships of his earlier life and how this had influenced his later years. He may have paid no tax, but he certainly knew how to redistribute wealth. Most of the people in the congregation would have been aware of his enormous generosity. I described how he was a larrikin who displayed irreverence to all authority and related instances of his incredible and outrageous sense of humour. The congregation was in fits of laughter. I finished by describing my visit to the hospital and how, before I left, I asked the Irish nurse who was caring for him what kind of patient John L. was. Without blinking an eyelid she said, 'He's definitely the worst patient this hospital has ever had!' I asked her if she would like a telephone number 'just in case'. She replied that it might be handy. I wrote down '000', telling her that this would bring the police, the fire brigade and probably even the armed forces if necessary. I ended the eulogy by saying that that John L. 'was now with God, but not too close as even the Almighty had a limit to his patience!' The eulogy received a standing ovation. Even O'Doherty stood to applaud. The dark humour continued at John L.'s graveside. I was standing near Ricky Ridley, one of John L.'s shearing buddies, and commented on the unusual depth of the grave. Ricky replied in a laconic fashion, 'Yeah, they never want to let this bastard out again!'

24
HONESTY AND DISHONESTY

There are moments in life when raw honesty catches everyone off guard, even a judge. The harvest was shaping up well and I employed Percy to cart the wheat to the bin. About a month before he was due to start work, he lost his driver's licence for drink-driving and he had to apply to the court for an extraordinary licence so he could keep his job. The magistrate on the day was known to be particularly hard on drunk drivers and rarely gave out extraordinary licences. However, proceedings seemed to be going particularly well, especially after my letter as referee and employer had been read to the court. George, the solicitor, looked across in my direction and winked and gave the thumbs up. It seemed we had the case won already. Suddenly the magistrate looked over his glasses and said 'I've heard everyone else. Now Patrick [Percy's real name], in your own words could you tell me why you need this extraordinary licence.'

This was just the worst possible thing. I cupped my hands to my face.

'Well, your honour, you know, so I can drive John's truck, cart the wheat, you know, drive to town, get supplies, pick up parts, you know, go to the pub, have a beer.'

The court fell silent as the magistrate digested what he had just heard. Everyone's eyes were cast skyward. Suddenly the magistrate laughed – something no-one had seen him do before.

'I'm going to give you your licence, Patrick, and strongly recommend that you don't go to the pub for a beer. You are probably the first person who has ever told the truth in my court.'

Luckily he was due to retire and, as it was one of his last cases, he was in a good mood.

For some years, neighbour Sandy Barnetson and I had been leasing Bob Gregson's farm. At nearly two metres tall, Sandy had the longest legs of anyone I've known. He could swing one leg over the side of a ute and plonk it down, keeping his other leg on the ground, and yarn this way for as long as you liked. The chance came to buy Bob's place jointly and Sandy and I made the two highest bids at the auction. There was little money about but Bob's bank at Goomalling wanted more for the property. We travelled there to negotiate the price, settling on $190 000. The bank manager ducked across the street to get an offer and acceptance form from the newsagency. We were almost home before I realised that he had made a big mistake. According to the contract we had actually bought the farm for $90 000. We joked about it for the rest of the way home. Sure enough, as we had predicted, the telephone was just about ringing off the wall as we walked in the door. The panicked bank manager was pleading for us to correct his mistake and fax the document back. He was greatly relieved when he received the corrected document and couldn't thank us enough.

A year later we applied to have the property subdivided. Sandy would take the northern portion, which he had always leased, and I would take the southern part, which we leased. Part of our section included 600 acres of pristine remnant vegetation that had never been cleared with attractive rocky outcrops and stands of sandalwood. In winter the whole area was splashed with brilliantly coloured wildflowers. It was our favourite picnic spot and our daughters and their friends played among the giant granite boulders.

Our application to subdivide the land arrived back with a demand to fence off these 600 acres and virtually hand them over to the government. The cleverly worded contract, drawn up under new legislation designed to protect the environment, stripped away meaningful ownership but made us responsible for the land's upkeep. We were required to put in a firebreak between the fence and the land and to keep it free from vermin, erecting a 7 kilometre fence around the land before we would be granted permission to subdivide. We were given instructions on what type of fence was required, the cost of which would run into many thousands of dollars, wiping out what little equity we had in the land.

I spoke to the unsympathetic chief of Conservation and Land Management (CALM) in Geraldton – the law was the law and it was CALM's job to enforce it. I managed to track down the woman who was responsible for drafting the new legislation and asked her if she thought it was a bit harsh, especially considering that it was already illegal to clear remnant vegetation. I suggested that many farmers had left pockets of remnant vegetation on their land and they should not be punished for doing the right thing by the environment. Even though Western Australia had suffered devastating environmental damage, in recent years farmers in every town were forming landcare groups to tackle the problem, planting trees and putting in contour banks. The legislation could kill all this goodwill and I was the first farmer in the state to suffer its effect.

She replied that the legislation had been carefully considered and was designed to protect the environment for all time. She then said how wonderful it was to leave something so precious for the future.

For a moment, I pondered her comment before replying, 'I wonder if you could conjure up the same warm inner glow if somebody nicked a third of your block in the city and charged you for the fence.'

I faxed a copy of CALM's contract for our land to ABC radio in Geraldton. Paul Thompson, who for years had presented rural programs, suggested that we get the Minister for Agriculture on air the next morning to explain it. The Minister refused. A couple of days later I got a call from his office saying all the relevant departments had been advised to allow our subdivision to go through. A month later, I got a call from the Minister for the Environment, who apologised, explaining that 'Sometimes, dodgy legislation gets through under the radar; obviously we will need to change part of the legislation.'

One day I drove to Tardun to collect my mail and spotted Brother Synan working alone on a tractor in the main workshop. I stopped for a yarn. We were good friends and often discussed issues that were affecting us. I casually mentioned that a few of us were thinking about forming a Tardun Old Boys Association, especially now that more of the former students were returning to look at their old home and catch up with their mates.

Brother Synan, or 'Tiny', thought for a moment and said, 'I'd like to help you. I'll put in 200 acres of wheat to get a fund established.'

This was indeed a generous gesture, because despite the low price of wheat, it was still a lot of money.

We formed the association at a big barbecue at the school. About 60 old boys turned up with their wives or girlfriends or just on their own. All the Brothers were present, mingling and chatting with the happy crowd. Whether we liked it or not, they were the nearest thing to parents that we ever had and they were glad to see us back. Some negative memories were unleashed when one man spotted Tiny and, in a torrent of swearing and finger-waving, accused him of brutality. Pointing to me he said, 'You beat the crap out of John, you beat the crap out of me and you beat the crap out of all of the kids!' The crowd hushed. Head bent, Tiny absorbed the torrent before turning and slowly walking away.

Like many others, I had long banished my negative memories to a distant corner of my mind. Most of us simply wanted to get on with our lives. We came back because we wanted to see our mates with whom we had grown up – we were like brothers. The next morning, I stopped to talk to Tiny while he was working again on the tractor.

Before I could say anything, he thrust his hand out to stop me and said, 'Jim's right about what he said and I've known it for a long time. I did treat some of the kids very badly, and I pray every day for God's forgiveness. I only hope the hard work I do is accepted as penance.'

I could see in his damp eyes that he was suffering from guilt and remorse. I'd never seen him this unhappy before; he was seriously depressed. He remained a man deeply troubled by his past. While most of us forgave him, he was unable to forgive himself. But, like Brother Sullivan, he had devoted his life to settling migrant and Australian boys on their own farms.

A LOOSE CANNON

In the late 1980s and early 1990s, American wheat subsidies notched up a gear. Compounding the hardship caused by low wheat and wool prices, the federal government had removed the guaranteed minimum price (GMP). The timing couldn't be worse. World wheat prices had fallen to $112 per tonne, while the cost of production was $150 per tonne. The GMP had been in place for many years to protect against such a situation and the government was now bailing out.

In 1989, I wrote to the AWB complaining about the poor wheat prices. Most of my production was Gamenya, but the AWB system of equalising income penalised me for producing quality wheat. The AWB insisted that the varietal bonus was compensation enough for low yields. I was incensed. The only way I could financially survive in my area with its poor rainfall was to be rewarded for quality production. I spoke to my neighbours, who were in the same boat. We formed a group and began to lobby, writing letters to the rural press accusing the AWB of putting the growers and the Japanese market at risk. We demanded a fair go for those growers who were prepared to support the quality criteria of the Japanese market. A public brawl began to heat up.

While we had strong local support, it wasn't the same everywhere. But the message was gradually getting through via radio interviews and press articles. Support became more widespread and even included some government ministers. Eventually the AWB gave ground. Our demand to meet our markets face-to-face was realised. We began to host official buying delegations from Japan and Korea, who inspected farms and storage and handling facilities.

In January 1991 a strong splinter group of farmers from Morawa threatened to blockade wheat shipments out of Western Australia unless the state government instituted an equivalent of the GMP. The group's young leadership was highly articulate and motivated and their commitment to action – so unlike the conservative approach of the peak farmer body, the Primary Industry Association (PIA) – appealed to many younger farmers. The membership swelled. They now had the numbers and the determination to carry out a blockade. At a meeting of several hundred farmers in Morawa, they called for a vote on a blockade.

Heavily outnumbered, I asked to speak against the motion and was refused by the committee. I strode to the front of the hall and asked the farmers, most of whom I knew, if they would hear me out. I explained that I too was running a splinter group of farmers trying to get a better price for wheat. I told them that it was crucial to guarantee continuity of supply to the Japanese and Korean markets and that we couldn't afford to shoot ourselves in the foot. There had to be other ways to get our message across. The vote on the motion to blockade wheat movements was overwhelmingly lost. I joined the splinter organisation, resigning from the PIA the next day.

In March 1991, a public meeting attended by 500 farmers was held in the Morawa Town Hall. Farmers voted to take militant action, although nothing specific came out of the meeting. After the meeting, four of us gathered at the local pub to formulate strategies and to share ideas. We knew the state government would never introduce a GMP without direct pressure. One farmer proposed an outrageous plan to blockade Perth. He had been thinking about it for a long time and had worked out every detail. After considering all the implications and public safety, we decided to proceed with this risky protest. Only certain farmers who we felt we could trust would be contacted and asked if they would drive a truck in the demonstration. I organised the Mullewa contingent and the others would come from Three Springs, Morawa and Mingenew.

On a Sunday night at a meeting in a motel room, the farmers were told the plan for the following morning: five critical arterial roads leading into the city would be blocked. The shocked farmers were given the option to quit. None did, and on Monday, at exactly 7 am, a driver pulled his truck over at a set of traffic lights, blocking two lanes of traffic. He locked the truck, threw away the keys and escaped in another vehicle. This action was repeated fourteen times in different locations around the city at exactly the same time. The entire city of Perth was effectively blockaded until the police organised to get the trucks towed away. None of the drivers was apprehended, but they all copped fines. While public opinion seemed to go the way of the farmers, and business groups in the wheat-belt towns raised money to pay for damages and fines, the main daily newspaper was not so sympathetic.

A week later, Premier Carmen Lawrence, standing on the front steps of Parliament House, announced to a throng of 3500 farmers that her government would underwrite a GMP of $150 per tonne. A couple of weeks later she flew into town to join in the celebrations. The Morawa Shire Council brought kegs of beer to the town oval and hundreds of farmers from all over the district joined in a victory celebration. The introduction of a state GMP was a smart political move and a huge morale boost for the state's wheat farmers. It came at a critical time and it enabled the banks to finance another crop, something they had not been prepared to do when the price of wheat was so low.

The following year, the price improved beyond the $150 per tonne, saving the government from any financial liability and, most importantly for me at least, ensuring continuity of supply to the anxious Korean and Japanese markets.

About a month after the blockade we decided that a formal structure was needed to carry the interests of our splinter group forward. We became the Rural Action Movement.[1] I was reluctant to join the committee as my hands were already full running another splinter group, which, in February 1992, would become the Western Australian Noodle Wheat Growers Association. The association was established at a meeting in the Mullewa Town Hall. Farmers came from all over the state, some in light aircraft. More than 200 joined up the same day. A committee was formed and I became inaugural president. Before the year was out we had close to 600 members. Later that same year, the AWB announced a market premium for those growers who produced wheat for a separate noodle pool. It had taken four years of hard slog to achieve our objective.

The largest trading company in Japan brought a proposal to pay a quality premium for our wheat and they wanted a trial shipment of pure Eradu wheat but they first needed to evaluate samples of Eradu and Gamenya, which they asked us to supply. They offered our organisation the premium but I had to tell them that, as we would be acting outside our legal parameters, we couldn't accept the offer. However, we supported their proposal, as it had the potential to set a precedent in the market and other Japanese companies would want the same.

I arranged to collect 20 kilograms of the two varieties from different farms across the state. Every 2 kilo bag was analysed to ensure there was no chemical contamination. I delivered two suitcases to a Japanese man at Perth Airport, who disappeared as mysteriously as he had appeared. I had to remind myself it was only wheat that we were dealing in. The company faxed the test results back to my farm, and they were better than they expected. They wanted to go ahead with the trial shipment. The company made a formal application to the AWB, but it was refused. At a meeting with the AWB, we threatened to go to the press with the story if they continued to refuse. A couple of months later a ship arrived in Geraldton and left soon after with its cargo of Eradu wheat.

We had been supplying the Japanese market for more than 40 years and it was time the growers talked to their customers face-to-face. We bypassed the AWB and went straight to the Premier to sanction our plan to take a delegation of growers to Japan. The AWB weighed in and took control, offering to organise a market tour and provide an escort for the delegation. This was exactly what we didn't want, but the matter was now out of our hands.

In February 1993 we spent 14 days touring flour mills and noodle manufacturing facilities in Japan and Korea. Their mills and manufacturing technology were second to none. There was no doubt about what Japanese wanted: samples for testing and another trial shipment of pure noodle wheat.

Every night, a large company hosted dinner at a restaurant. Mitsubishi took us to what was reputed to be the finest seafood restaurant in Tokyo. On either side of me sat senior executives of the company. During the meal I explained to one of the executives how frustrated some growers like me were about having little say in our industry. I pointed out that the directors of the AWB were not elected by the growers, but were appointed by the government. Discreetly pointing to AWB staff seated at the end of the table, I casually stated that we farmers now knew why Jesus wasn't born in Western Australia – they couldn't find three wise men from the East. For a brief moment, I thought he was going to choke on his fish as he tried not to laugh.

For five days we toured flour mills and processing facilities in Korea, some where noodles were being manufactured by hand by large groups of women who worked sitting on the floor. We were invited to hold discussions with the largest noodle manufacturer in the world. The company bought mainly American flour but wanted to talk to our farmers. For the first half hour, we answered questions on the usual topics and then came the hard part. Through his interpreter, the chairman, Mr Kim, told us that our prices weren't competitive. I quietly explained that we actually were competitive but he was buying subsidised American wheat, probably of very low quality. He was angry, but he allowed me to continue. I told him how we wanted to trade in fair and open competition and, although we weren't subsidised, we could still compete on price because our quality was far superior. The meeting ended politely with handshakes all around and Mr Kim offered to host our farewell dinner, where he made the sweetest announcement: his company would resume buying flour from Australian wheat for their factory.[2]

That same year, I was awarded the prestigious Rural Achiever of the Year award, by the Royal Agricultural Society, for helping to develop the Japanese and Korean noodle wheat markets.

Although the state government had earlier stepped forward to provide the GMP, it had steadily been reducing its financial contribution to research and wheat breeding so that, by the mid 1990s, it was barely a trickle. It no longer considered wheat breeding a priority. Graham Crosbie, the chief cereal chemist with the Department of Agriculture, had dedicated his whole career to researching and developing quality grain for the Japanese market and his work was recognised internationally. Crosbie warned we could lose our competitive advantage unless we lifted our game and suggested that farmers should take control over the funding for wheat research and wheat breeding on a commercial basis. This was difficult for some farmers to swallow as breeding had always been a government responsibility.

By now, the WA Noodle Wheat Growers Association had a degree of political influence and, in 1996, we met with the Premium Wheat Growers Association and the Soft Wheat Growers Association. This was the beginning of the Council Of Grain Grower Organisations (COGGO). Since then, 2000 grower members have contributed more than $10.6 million to research and development. The growers now own patent rights on four canola varieties, three wheat varieties, one lupin variety and two Kabuli chick pea varieties.

1   As proof that good often comes from adversity, RAM evolved into the United Farmers Co-op, now the second-largest fertiliser company in the state. In addition, it is marketing coarse grain.

2   The noodle wheat markets of Japan and Korea have returned many hundreds of millions of dollars in extra revenue to Australian growers and the economy. In December 2006 the price difference between noodle wheat produced for the Japanese and Korean markets and Australian Standard White was $38 per tonne, or an extra $60 million in income.

THE AFTERMATH

In 1987 newspaper reports had begun to appear about life for the former inmates of Bindoon. Shocking stories of sexual and physical abuse were related. These stories were added to by other orphans from all the institutions run by the Christian Brothers and the nuns. Soon, stories about homes run by the Salvation Army, the Anglican Church, the Methodist Church, Fairbridge Farm School and others began circulating. The British government's chickens were coming home to roost. However, not all child migrants were critical of the scheme and some came to the defence of the Christian Brothers, stating that they had not been abused and praising the Brothers for helping them to establish their lives in Australia.

Although child migration had long since ended, it wasn't until the 1980s that the calls for justice and compensation by child migrants finally stirred up media attention. Television stories and drama documentaries such as *The Leaving of Liverpool* shocked British and Australia viewers.

The Australian Catholic Church was reeling, as it copped most of the blame. Small groups of former students began to tackle their old institutions. VOICES, an organisation of former inmates from Bindoon, took the Christian Brothers to court in 1994. Ultimately the action failed on appeal as the statute of limitations in Western Australia prevented the Christian Brothers from being held accountable. As the offences had taken place many years before, most of the accused were dead.

Pastoral letters of apology were read to parishioners all over Australia. The Christian Brothers publicly apologised and set up programs of compensation and counselling. For those who had found relatives, the Christian Brothers paid for their travel to Britain and their expenses.

The Brothers employed one of their own to conduct an investigation into the running of their homes. In his report 'The Scheme', Christian Brother and historian Dr Barry Coldrey vindicated many of the complaints made by former inmates. He told the investigating British Health Committee in 1997, 'at times savage physical abuse and fairly widespread sexual abuse occurred'.

His book *The Scheme: The Christian Brothers and Childcare in Western Australia*, published in 1993, outlined examples of serious abuse at Bindoon under Brother Paul Keaney's regime between the late 1930s to 1956. Keaney had been admired by many of his peers, and some were inclined to follow his example.

The Australian senate inquiry into child migration in 2001 revealed widespread serious abuse across all the institutions in Australia.[1] Abandoned children, uprooted from their country, had been psychologically scarred and suffered from trauma and disorientation. The kind of specialist care they needed then was not provided in any Australian orphanage and the tough regimes run by untrained disciplinarians only added to their burden.

Yet the Christian Brothers had run some of the most elite and egalitarian colleges in Australia and were recognised nationally for their high teaching standards. Unfortunately they had allowed some abusive Brothers to enter their orphanage system where they did enormous damage, destroying the Christian Brother's credibility and proud history of childcare dating back to their founder, Edmund Rice.

We Tardun boys were now adults and some, possibly in a state of denial, were unable to empathise with allegations of the boys at Bindoon, even though many of us had travelled to Australia on the same ship and came from the same place in England. Our experience was different to theirs and we had long ago lost contact with them. Some ex-Tardun residents even doubted the veracity of the claims of abuse as few of us had experienced the brutality that was being reported in the press. Our upbringing had been tough, yet nothing like this. Many of us had buried the fact that we too had been emotionally and psychologically scarred by the whole system and had forgotten the pain caused us by being wrenched away from everything we had known. However, I wasn't surprised that Castledare was mentioned. I was glad that most of my old teachers at Tardun, including Acky and Tommy, had passed away – the scandal would have been enough to kill them.

A social worker in Nottingham, Margaret Humphreys, set up an organisation known as the Child Migrant Trust in 1987, which mainly concentrated on tracing families, counselling and reunification programs. Reunification was a critical issue, as very few child migrants had found relatives because tracing was extremely difficult. Even if families were found, there was no guarantee that any reunion would be successful. The Child Migrant Trust in Nottingham had made good progress in tracing families but, unfortunately, few people in Australia had the means to afford the travel and expenses to return to the United Kingdom, so the travel scheme run by the Christian Brothers, which applied only to their ex-residents, was very useful. None of the other organisations offered this service. I felt strongly that the responsibility for family reunification rested squarely on the shoulders of the British government and pointed this out at one of our Tardun 'old boys' meetings. I suggested the only way we could achieve this was to shame the British government into doing something, but in the meantime we could begin by raising money to send child migrants from other orphanages back to Britain. We set up the Australian Child Migrant Foundation (ACMF) as a separate entity from the Tardun Old Boys Association to lobby governments, church groups and other institutions that were part of the child migrant scheme and to provide support and assistance to child migrants. I was elected chairman and we approached the Chief Justice of Western Australia, David Malcolm, to be our patron. He readily agreed. It was good to have support from a person with a legal background who was a willing helper.

The whole area of child migration had become a political and legal minefield. Some organisations were vigorously opposed to accepting help from the churches, as they blamed them for the wrongdoing, and others, like ACMF, recognised the joint culpability of church and government. We were willing to go to the churches for help and were determined from the outset not to involve ourselves in any political fighting but instead to focus on raising money for family reunions.

We took our plan to the Archbishop of Perth, Barry Hickey. For a long time, Hickey had been on the defensive about the issue and was cautious at first. Gaining his trust was our first hurdle. He suggested that we write a motion to put before the Australian Catholic Bishops' Conference and that he and Bishop Bianchini from Geraldton would sponsor it. I drafted letters at night in free hand and faxed them to the ACMF secretary, who knocked the letters into shape. We began lobbying in Britain and Australia.

A month after our motion was passed by the conference, we received funding from every parish in Australia. Soon we had several hundred thousand dollars and we began sending child migrants, irrespective of their religion or background, to Britain. We paid for the flights and gave a small amount to cover expenses. Our criteria did not include a means test, only proof that the applicant had relatives to meet in Britain. We figured most of those who could afford it had already met their families.

We were accused by some of accepting blood money. I told critics that we would accept money from the devil himself if it meant that the child migrants, many of whom were elderly, could act on their first and probably only chance of ever meeting their relatives.

We lobbied the British and Australian governments for funding. The reception was mixed. The Liberal–National government of the time claimed that the Australian government was doing enough by funding the Child Migrant Trust.

In Britain, in addition to seeking finance, we lobbied for a parliamentary inquiry into child migration. The British Prime Minister, John Major, acknowledged receipt of our letters but never actually responded to our request. Tony Blair, then in opposition, promised an inquiry once he took office. We also wrote to the British Minister for Health a number of times reminding him that the issue of child migration came under his portfolio. We believed that it was now Britain's responsibility to run family reunification programs, not ours. The Minister did not respond personally to any of our letters but instead handed our correspondence to minor bureaucrats.

We wrote letters to all the British churches reminding them of their involvement and seeking their financial support. While some responded with sympathy, only two sent cheques in support of the Foundation: then Irish Cardinal Cahal Daly and Cardinal Basil Hume, then head of the Catholic Church in England and Wales.

Cardinal Hume quickly responded in April 1995 to our plea to send three Tardun boys – brothers Frank, Des and Jim – back to their family. His letter was sympathetic to the plight of the child migrants and promised that he would consult widely about the issue and take advice. He finished, 'I am anxious to do what I can'.

On the same day, I received a letter from the Queen's secretary at Buckingham Palace expressing the Queen's understanding about why ACMF felt prompted to write and her interest in ACMF, but reminding us that her position as constitutional sovereign restrained her from intervening publicly in matters where the responsibility rested with government ministers.

A short time later a letter arrived from the head of the Church of England, who was also sympathetic and was prepared to consult with fellow church leaders, including Cardinal Hume and the Anglican Archbishop of Perth.

I phoned the Anglican Archbishop of Perth to ask his support, as we were sending back child migrants who had been raised in orphanages run by the Anglican Church in Perth. There seemed little desire to help, possibly because the issue was seen to be a Catholic one, but also because the Anglican Church in Perth was autonomous and had no money.

I travelled to Britain in August 1996 to catch up with my family and to meet with Cardinal Hume and the leaders of some of the other churches. The Western Australian Premier, Richard Court, asked me to deliver a message asking the churches to cooperate in a recently announced state government parliamentary inquiry into child migration. I mentioned this to Cardinal Hume at the beginning of our meeting, which apparently alarmed one of his staff, who said, 'We'll open a can of worms!' Hume firmly insisted otherwise and asked me to take back a message to Premier Court that the Catholic Church in England would fully cooperate and provide any information as requested, saying 'We have no secrets'.

I discussed how the ACMF would soon be out of money as the demand for our services was growing. Cardinal Hume agreed to discuss with the Bishops' Secretariat the idea of putting a motion of support to the Catholic Bishops' Conference of England and Wales, and another to the Scottish Bishops' Conference. I raised another idea that might help to force the British government to conduct a parliamentary inquiry. All the churches that had been involved in the child migration scheme could take out a full-page advertisement in the British newspaper the *Daily Telegraph*, expressing their deep regret for their involvement in child migration and calling on the British government to launch an inquiry. Hume agreed to speak to leaders of the other churches. I finally asked the Cardinal if he would intercede on my behalf with the Minister for Health, as I was keen to meet with the Minister while I was in England.

After the meeting Cardinal Hume took me on a tour of his headquarters at Westminster. He was still having problems coming to terms with his church's involvement in removing children from their families and said, 'I was a young priest then. I didn't know. I should have known.' Before I left, I gave him a small bottle of emu oil, a remedy used by Australian Aboriginal peoples for thousands of years, to ease the arthritis in his hip.

'Does it have any side-effects?' he asked, as he gazed at the yellow liquid.

'None that I know of,' I said, 'although with too much use, you might grow feathers around the affected area!'

The following day I visited Lambeth Palace. The Archbishop of Canterbury was out of the country so I discussed the same issues with senior church officials. The idea of the newspaper advertisement appealed to them, and they said they would talk to the Catholic Church.

Unfortunately the advertisement never appeared. It was my view that the other churches would not have seen it as in their interest to admit to their involvement as long as the media heat was being applied to the Catholic Church. Who knew what might get found out if a parliamentary inquiry did go ahead?

I visited the Sisters of Nazareth at their headquarters in Hammersmith. I had been invited to lunch and sat alone at the head of a very long table. Two Sisters served lunch, which included a bottle of wine, and then disappeared. There was little conversation and the atmosphere was uncomfortable and eerily quiet. I was told that Mother Bernard would be along shortly. I was determined not to raise any personal issue I had with the nuns – this was strictly fundraising, as the Sisters had indicated they would donate to ACMF.

Finally Mother Bernard entered the room and sat down. She cut to the chase, asking 'How much do you want?' I told her I couldn't answer this question, as it depended on her generosity. I explained how there were a lot of women coming to the Foundation for help, many of whom had been little girls when they were sent to Australia by her organisation. She agreed to send a cheque for 35 000 pounds and told me that we could come back for more if necessary.

Unlike the Christian Brothers, the Catholic nuns were more reticent in admitting that abuse occurred in their orphanages. This made raising funds from them far more difficult. Most of them were in a state of denial. It was said to me, 'Isn't it great to see you've done so well in Australia, aren't you glad we sent you there?'

The ACMF later approached the Sisters of Mercy and asked them if they would match the donation from the Sisters of Nazareth to help fund the 'sentimental journey' of 40 women back to Britain to be reunited with their families. This was to make a big statement to the British government and, as predicted, it attracted a great deal of media and the story was carried on the front pages of the British tabloids. I took calls from British journalists for several days and repeated over and over the need for a British parliamentary inquiry.

The next stop was Dr Barnardo's Homes, the children's charity and the biggest of the child migrant organisations, with records stretching back to the 1850s. Most of their children had been sent to Canada and relatively few had been sent to Australia in the postwar period, mainly because parents would not give their consent, a requirement under the Children's Act 1948.[2] They were the only organisation I had seen that appeared to operate within the letter of the Act and, as a professional organisation, kept far better records than the religious voluntary organisations. They would not admit a child into their homes unless they had comprehensive details of the child's family history. Barnardo's were prepared to help us by using their extensive network across Britain to provide accommodation into private homes. In addition, Clarence House School, which had an earlier involvement in child migration, offered accommodation free of charge to visiting child migrants. This generous offer was a result of the efforts of the WA Chief Justice David Malcolm.

I stayed with my sister Liz in Harrow during my two weeks in England. In my second week I got a call from Cardinal Hume's office, passing on a message from the office of the Minister for Health. It was short and to the point: 'The Minister is aware Mr Hawkins is in the country, and he has no wish to speak to him.'

Ultimately it took a change of government to bring about an inquiry into child migration. In 1997, British Prime Minister Tony

Blair announced a parliamentary inquiry to be headed by MP David Hinchcliffe.[3] In my view the investigation was too narrow, most likely to protect the British government from claims of legal liability, and ultimately did not prove useful to the cause of child migrants. The inquiry collected many stories of abuse in Australian institutions, and found much wrongdoing on the part of the sending and receiving agents in Britain and Australia, but stated that there was no evidence of major negligence. The British government was apparently just carrying out its duties within the relevant Acts of the time.

The good news for the ACMF was the inquiry's main recommendation that the British government would fund all future family reunions. The Foundation was now redundant. We had sent back close to 100 people to meet their families in Britain and now we could all get on with our lives.

I spent half my time in England dealing with child migration issues and the other half with my mother and the family. I couldn't spare any more time, as I had my own family in Australia to consider and crops to spray. It was time to go home.

1 Read a detailed account of the Australian government inquiry in Part II, pages 286–290.

2 Part II, page 286, explains the position taking by Dr Barnado's Homes and why this resulted in fewer child migrants being sent from this organisation to Australia.

3 Read a detailed account of the British parliamentary inquiry in Part II, pages 282–285.

MEETING MY OTHER MOTHER

In 2002 I received a letter that shocked me to the core. It was from the Child Migrant Trust. By now a frail old woman, Joy Broom had sent a letter to Sarah Womack, a journalist working for the *Guardian newspaper*, after reading an article Sarah had written about child migration. Joy explained that she and her late husband Roy had tried everything over the years to find the little boy who had been snatched from their arms, including placing advertisements in the 'Where are you now?' sections of newspapers in different states of Australia. She had heard stories of brutality in Australian institutions and wondered if I was still alive. She felt somehow that she had failed me and was still haunted by the memory. She asked in the letter, 'John was an orphan. Didn't he deserve a family life?'

Sarah put Joy in touch with the Child Migrant Trust and, in a heartfelt letter to the Trust, dated 31 May 2002, she wrote:

John had started calling us Mummy and Daddy and my daughter Wendy of the same age referred to him as her new brother. He had his own room and his own toys. He told us he was unhappy at the Home and mentioned the cruelty of the nuns. Even basic food like tomatoes, biscuits, cakes etc. he had not eaten before he came to us. Rather reminiscent of Dickens Oliver Twist. After John was given oats I noticed the remains of the nuns breakfasts one morning: bacon and eggs, fruit etc. For a special treat we had made for him a large Easter egg with our present inside. He never received it. When we asked the nuns about it they told us the mice had eaten it (the gift as well?).[1]

The letter rekindled dormant memories of the saddest time of my life – memories I would have preferred remained buried forever. Phoning Joy was difficult as she was quite deaf and the telephone interfered with her hearing aid. Within days she sent me a letter. She told of the family's heartbreak when I disappeared that day in 1954. She related how the family had searched the world, as the only thing the nuns had admitted was that I was somewhere overseas. Joy thought it was because they were Protestants that they were so helpless and she was sorry the family couldn't have done more to protect me.

She remembered me as a loving child and told stories of Wendy and me and how Wendy had cried when she lost her brother. Each letter, each story stoked my memory and my past came tumbling back. Missing pieces of a jigsaw puzzle were finally falling into place.

It wasn't enough – I wanted to know more and asked her many questions in my letters or over the phone. As the truth emerged, I became more and more angry. I sent to the Sisters of Nazareth at Hammersmith a copy of Joy's letter to the Child Migrant Trust, demanding an explanation from the Sisters. They replied that German bombs had destroyed their records in Southampton, but that it was wonderful that Mrs Broom had kept in touch with me all these years. It seemed remarkable that they couldn't explain to me what had happened in 1954 because their records had been destroyed in 1941. It sounded far too convenient. They mentioned an adoption register where the names of children adopted out of their homes had been recorded, although this document too seemed to have disappeared. They regretted that I didn't enjoy my time with them in England.[2]

Disgusted, I wrote to the new English Cardinal, expressing how utterly gutted I was about the Sisters of Nazareth's response and the role of the English Catholic Church. He didn't reply. I felt somehow cheated that Cardinal Hume had passed away, as I felt that he would have been more compassionate and honest and perhaps would have directed the Sisters of Nazareth to respond more openly.

By now my mind was consumed by anger, but there was nowhere I could turn. I began writing page after page of furious drivel, emptying my head onto paper, and then burned each page as a way of exorcising the demons that had begun to emerge. I couldn't understand what would motivate ordinary Christian people to deny a child the chance of a decent family life, deciding instead to send that child to an overseas orphanage. They were playing God, incarcerating me to save my soul, but surely they couldn't expect that God would smile on their work. My own idea of Christianity was badly shaken but not destroyed. I tried to understand why the nuns failed to grasp the extent of the pain and suffering they inflicted on innocent children unlucky enough to have fallen into their hands. I felt that my life and soul had been kidnapped and wondered how many other children had suffered the same fate.

I decided to write my story but, first, I knew I would need to expunge my anger and pain, so I began to research the story of child migration. This journey would take nearly four years and benefitted me beyond my imagining.

About eight months after my first contact with Joy, I took my two daughters, Joanne and Belinda, to the meet their English family for the first time. The girls had been writing to their cousins and aunties since they were small children, so they had some idea of their overseas family. The family resemblance was staggering. Liz's little daughter Ellie and Joanne looked like twins, and Uncle Billy's granddaughter Emma looked like Belinda. Unfortunately, my mother had passed away two years before, dying halfway through mass on New Year's Day in 2000, in the same church where I had first seen her nearly 20 years before. She died in the arms of the family doctor. The parish priest called for the church bells to be tolled as a mark of respect, the first time the bells had been rung part way through a service in the 400-year history of the church. If my mother could have written her own script, this would have been it. She is buried with her husband, Fred, in a church cemetery on a hill just outside Selsey.

We travelled south to Southampton to catch up with Joy and Wendy. My sister Susan came with us – I felt like I was about to enter uncharted territory again and I would need all the emotional support that I could get.

Joy had told me in one of her letters that the family had moved house soon after I was sent to Australia. Their old home in Bugle Street seemed sad and empty and she felt that a new house would help her forget the pain – it was as if she and Roy had suffered the death of a child but there was no burial, no closure. I had become a ghost who haunted their lives and in their minds I was still a fragile, frightened seven year old that had never grown up – I had never had the chance.

Top left *1961: Standing outside my bird cages. John L. squatting in front.*

Top right *1963: Riding a stock horse at Tardi Station.*

Left *Working boys picnic. I'm standing near the door in a white shirt.*

Top left *1963: At Tardi Station with my new sandals – before which we mostly went barefoot.*

Top right *1969: Proud of my first ute and tractor.*

Left *1971: On holiday in Queensland.*

Top *1980: Meeting two of my sisters for the first time, Susan (left) and Liz (right).*

Right *1982: Me and Joanne.*

Top left *1982: Hooley the emu.*

Top right *1983: Julie with baby Belinda and Joanne.*

Bottom *1984: Aerial view of my farm.*

Top *1992: In Tokyo meeting with senior Japanese executives to discuss trade issues with the Australian Wheat Board.*

Left *1993: Rural Achiever of the Year.*

Opposite *1996: A record wheat crop.*

Top *1996: The head of the English Catholic church, Cardinal Basil Hume and I discussing issues on child migrants finding their families.*

Bottom *1997: With Premier Richard Court and Archbishop Hickey sending off 40 women on a Sentimental Journey in 1997 to visit their families for the first time.*

Top 2003: *Seeing my adoptive mother, Joy, for the first time after 48 years.*

Bottom 2008: *With my daughters Jo and Belinda at Christmas.*

I brought a small gift: the official Australian 2000 millennium gold coin. I wanted something precious and rare – but there was nothing in this world that would ever be good enough for this woman who had once reached out to save me. I wondered how I would react once I was face-to-face with her and I feared that our meeting would leave me feeling almost indifferent and sterile, like I had felt when I first met my mother. We had exchanged recent photos, so we knew what to expect. I tried to imagine what this encounter would mean for Joanne and Belinda. Would it affect them in any way?

Joy and Wendy had prepared a special 'welcome home' lunch. They were waiting at the front of the house when we arrived. Joy was quite overcome. Tears welled in my eyes as she held my arm and declared to pedestrians passing by in the quiet street, to the world, to God Almighty: 'My boy's back. I've got my boy back.'

She repeated this over and over, as tears flowed down her face. This was indeed a true mother–son reunion and, like a weeping child, I fell again into her comforting arms. We held each other on the side of the footpath for a long time in sadness for all those missing years.

Joy still regarded me as her only son and I felt a bit like the prodigal son who had just returned home after a lifetime of banishment. She was so sorry that Roy wasn't here to see his boy. I could still recognise Wendy, although she had only been six years old when I last saw her. After lunch she opened the family album and the photos took me back to the happiest time of my childhood. There was Roy standing proudly by his big black car, the same one he used to pick me up from the orphanage. There were photos of the old house where we lived – photos of a loving family together. My head was spinning.

Joy said maybe it was for the best that I had been sent to Australia, as I had done so well. I told her that it wasn't really fair for her to say that – many child migrants had not fared well from their experience.

'You gave Wendy a university education, mum. Would you have done the same for me?' I asked.

'Oh yes,' she said, 'you were very bright as a young child.'

'Who knows what I might have achieved in England if I was raised by you,' I told her.

We talked about the child migration scheme and I related to Joy and Wendy what I had found out – how I felt that good people had used false argument to justify policies that led to cruelty and abuse. I could have had a mother and father, but those were hypocritical times. I tried to be fair in my account and tell it to the best of my knowledge. I wanted Joy to know the truth, as she too carried deep scars.

Joy explained how other families in Southampton had desired to adopt children from the same orphanage but had run into trouble with the nuns. A couple she had known wanted to adopt a boy. She still remembered his name: John Holloway. At age six, he was put on the same ship as me and sent to Castledare. We grew up together until he was sent to the Clontarf orphanage five years later.

Joy managed a wry smile when I told her how the British parliamentary inquiry in 1997 had essentially exonerated the British government and how the Australian senate inquiry did the same for the Australian government in 2001. It was always someone else's fault.

'You were only eight years old when they stopped sending children,' she whispered. 'They could have sent you back to me if they wanted to.'

I explained, trying hard to contain my anger, how I felt that I had been part of a social experiment and was exploited by a whole system under the guise of it being both legal and charitable. Joy paused for a moment while she absorbed my comments.

'They should have left you behind. You had a loving family. For more than a year that Mother Superior tricked us into believing we could adopt you. You had no other home, no hope. No-one else cared about you. I remember afterwards, they walked into our shop looking for donations. What cheek!'

She paused again to gather herself: 'You had a loving family,' she said, as tears again welled in her eyes.

'The officials at Australia House in London would have known that, mum,' I quietly replied. 'I was frightened and scared. I told them everything I knew about my new family and begged them to listen. They knew I didn't want to leave England, but that was no excuse for the people at Australia House. I'd been earmarked since the age of six months and I'd been promised to Australia by the nuns. There was no way they would let me go.'

Joy asked, 'What drove those nuns to do this awful work. Surely they were human beings too. How could this be God's work?'

'That's a question they've never been able to ask themselves,' I suggested. 'If they had, they would have apologised to us both by now.'

I had been taught as a child that the basic meaning of Christianity was to share each other's pain, yet the Catholic Church had created pain.

The old adage that time heals all wounds was never true for Joy or me or my troubled mother. It merely dulled the pain and fogged the memory but the scars will never heal. Yet, to me, Joy stood like a beautiful beacon of light. For 48 years she had kept the flame of hope alight for the little 'orphan' boy who lived inside her heart. She and I continued to write to each other every month until her death in 2005. She signed off her long letters with 'Fondest love, Mum Joy'.

The British child migration scheme has now passed into history. It was an era of incredible ignorance, cruelty and inhumanity. Too many children lost their country, their culture and their families. Some lived and died never knowing who they really were. Too many of my friends still live without knowing their identity or their story. Some of us still feel a deep sense of shame and humiliation at having being used and exploited by our government and the churches. Child migration was set for failure when lawful checks and balances became the first casualty in the mad scramble for children. The Australian government's insistence on institutionalised childcare – a system that was rapidly becoming discredited in countries such as Canada, North America and the UK – created enormous disadvantage for the children who ended up in the orphanages.

When I look back and weigh up all the things that happened to me, the good and bad, I have to agree with Joy that it was indeed fortuitous that they sent me to Australia. It could have been some other corner of the Empire where Britain dumped its unwanted children – a corner in which the pursuit of truth and justice for child migrants would never be allowed.

My life has been incredibly full. It is a journey of discovery for both me and my family. I have been blessed with a beautiful Australian family and a strong and supportive family in England, from Liverpool in the north to Chichester in the south. My two daughters, who have travelled with me for part of my life's journey, have gained from the generosity of my English family and have a strong connection to England. They have also benefited from my experience as a child migrant – one who was determined to never repeat the mistakes of the past.

Today I admire and respect the charitable works of the Christian Brothers in Australia, who have gone back to their roots, educating and supporting the communities in which they work, as well as the Sisters of Nazareth in England, who continue to care for the sick and the elderly, as they have done in the last 150 years. I acknowledge and appreciate these organisations' genuine efforts towards reconciliation and reparation for their victims. They cannot be solely blamed for what happened.

I have no regrets about my life or any animosity towards those who sent me to Australia. I see clearly that they were misguided and believed the government spin of the time. I believe they were captivated by self-interest to serve a higher goal in the service of God. I realise, too, that they genuinely thought, for the most part, that they were helping British orphans who needed the Christian charity offered freely by Australia.

From Tommy I learnt to appreciate the real meaning of freedom of expression. It was he who gave me the strength and confidence to challenge and question and, in effect, gave me back my life. It was in his classroom that I realised that we are each dealt a hand from life's deck of cards. Some throw their bad deal back onto the table; some play their hand and hope for luck. Others choose to make their own luck. Tommy once said that the human spirit is real and resilient and can lead us out from the worst of life's disappointments.

Australia has been good to me. It has rewarded my endeavour and hard work and enabled me to grow and prosper. It allowed me freedom of expression and tolerated my protests without locking me up – even when I pushed the envelope a bit too far at times in the search for a fair go.

All my Tardun friends, except some of the Maltese migrants, had lost their families, but we stuck together through it all, sharing the best and the worst, and enduring a tough and unsympathetic world. We supported each other through our strange journey and we developed rich bonds of friendship. We attended to each other's pain and were there at parties, weddings and funerals. Today, we gather together twice a year with our Australian wives, girlfriends and children to share our achievements, and to reminisce and have fun. We rarely speak of our past in negative terms and we make light of some of our worst moments. We respect each other – a respect that we earned from our shared experience.

We are like Shakespeare's band of brothers, described in Henry V before battle

We few, we happy few, we band of brothers;
For he to-day that sheds his blood with me
Shall be my brother.

1   I have seen a photo of the nuns and dozens of children, including me, around a football-sized Easter egg. I believe that this was Joy's Easter egg present to me, although I didn't know it at the time.

2   In my anger I wrote to the Sisters of Nazareth suggesting as compensation they set up a small education fund, which would be of benefit to my grandchildren so they would know why they were receiving this extra help. The Sisters didn't answer, and I regretted asking as I know from experience it takes a cool head to achieve a successful outcome in any negotiations. I decided to turn the case over to Towards Healing, a national Catholic organisation who are experts in achieving reconciliation. They too had no success and after about a year the matter was dropped.

PART

II

A SHORT HISTORY OF CHILD MIGRATION TO AUSTRALIA

Introduction

The first child migrants to come to Australia arrived with the First Fleet, probably in chains as child convicts. However, the mass child migration scheme from Britain to Australia effectively began in 1947 and ended in 1956, although small numbers of older children were sent to Australia in the pre–World War II period for rural farm training for boys and domestic skills training for girls, and a small number of child migrants continued to arrive from both Britain and Malta into the 1960s. The end of the scheme to Australia brought to a close a dubious time in British history. It was as if a chapter in a long-running saga had ended and, as nobody remembered the story's beginning, the book was just closed.

The British government had taken a 'creative' approach across the centuries to their social problems. The street kids of the early sixteenth century – the abandoned and destitute sons and daughters of prostitutes and the poor who were running wild on the streets of London – were sent to the new colony in Virginia where they could be of use to the new settlers. The colony would supposedly benefit and so would the children. It soon became clear this was a good way to help populate a new colony and relieve social pressures at the same time. The children could be put to work at once, turning a social problem to economic advantage.

Prominent clergymen in the United Kingdom lent their support to child migration. Reflecting an older attitude, in 1911 Father Waugh, director of the Archdiocese of Westminster Crusade of Rescue, declared:

> *A double service is rendered to religion, humanity and civilization, in carrying off the children of distress to the lands beyond the sea, to live in the open, to work with nature, to wrestle with forest, field and stream, to forget fetid city slums, to seek and strive and pray in the open, to grow strong and self reliant, and to be the guardians of the outposts of civilization, religion and new endeavour, every child a pioneer of the Empire.*[1]

This ideology continued into modern times, although euphemistic terms were used to describe the twentieth-century children sent overseas: 'home children' in Canada and 'child migrants' in Australia. Like their predecessors, these children were transported for life and were at risk of exploitation. While some older children left voluntarily, the very young were denied a choice and were sent away against their wishes or without an understanding of their fate. Stories of the children who had fared well in their new country gave a legitimacy to the schemes and, unfortunately, modern British law continued to fail these abandoned and orphaned children. Like the children of the sixteenth century, the children of the twentieth century would be told that migration was for their own good.

A common misconception in the child migration story in the twentieth century is that genuine but misguided authorities in Britain and Australia were driven by benevolence and goodwill to give abandoned and orphaned children a 'fresh start in life'. Altruistic fervour, even euphoria, soon spread to the orphanages and homes in Australia that were preparing to receive thousands of British children. Few, if any, who worked in the industry could have known that there was a much bigger agenda at a much higher level behind child migration.

Perhaps if the full story had been known, and honest, intelligent people had asked questions, no-one with a clear conscience could have continued to work in the orphanage system. In this sense, child migrants were not the only victims. Many genuine people who worked at the 'coalface' would later discover that the child migration scheme was based on deception and that institutionalisation had devastating effects on many of the children. In contrast, New Zealand, which accepted 549 British children, was mostly able to avoid the negative impacts on child migrants by assimilating them into homes across the country under the watchful eye of welfare authorities.

It took the British Home Office six years from the start of the postwar child migration program to send a delegation to check on welfare conditions in Australia. In that time several thousand children had been sent. This sent a message that Britain held little regard for the welfare of its children and any concerns expressed by the Home Office were little more then posturing that could be ignored by those in the child migration industry.

Most of the children were sent to Australia without any official identity records or travel documentation. As adults applying for Australian citizenship years later, some former child migrants had to rely on ship passenger lists as the only record of their names.

I set out to write my life story in late 2003 after being contacted by my English foster mother the year before. At first I thought the task would require a minimum of research. As I delved deeper into a mountain of material about child migration, much of which had already been researched and published, including the results of three parliamentary inquiries, I felt something fundamental was hidden or missing. I could find little evidence to support the accepted wisdom that child migration was an act of misguided benevolence. The British and Australian parliamentary inquiries exonerated the governments of the time from wrongdoing and pointed the finger at the religious and secular organisations that ran the institutions. That there was more to the whole story was confirmed after I tracked down a 'missing' Australian government document held at the Department for Community Development[2] in Perth. This document, which for years was rumoured to exist but was difficult to find, was the minutes of the special premiers' conference of January 1946 that records Australia's ambitious plans to import up to 50 000 European children a year and to house them in military-style barracks. I thought this document might provide a clue to the mindset of the policy makers of the day and what influenced this policy: perhaps it was the war and the resulting poverty or perhaps many of the policy makers had been influenced by their own harsh childhoods during the Great Depression of the 1930s. Thankfully the department handed over all their files.

Early child migration from Britain

Over a period stretching back to 1618, an estimated 150 000 children from all parts of the British Isles and Ireland were sent to the colonies, most never to be seen or heard from again. The first 100 children were rounded up on the streets of London and sent to Jamestown, Virginia, in 1618, barely eleven years after the establishment of the first colony in North America. Four years later, 350 settlers, including migrant children, were massacred by native Americans. Soon after, another 100 children were dispatched to reinforce the colony. A British parliamentary survey at the time into the fate of the first 100 children revealed only 10 had survived the first 10 years. The high mortality rate was due mainly to disease, hunger and attacks by native Americans.

These early child migrants were forced to make their own way in foreign and often harsh environments, taking their chances with disease, hunger and the tough and unsympathetic people to whom they were indentured. They were often little more than child slaves, sent to work on plantations and farms. Abandoned by parents, church and government, and reduced to mere chattels devoid of any protection, love or compassion, many children suffered physical and sexual abuse. They suffered the most miserable existence imaginable, yet many survived into adulthood and made their mark in the new colony.

The early settlers began to demand more child labour. In 1628 the child migrants were joined for the first time by Negroes after a Dutch slave ship on its way to the West Indies sailed into Jamestown Harbor for repairs. Both the Negroes and the child migrants were sold in open slave markets, officials being careful to describe white children as indentured labourers who would be released on reaching majority. To meet demand, kidnapping of children flourished, especially during the English Civil War of the 1640s. So lucrative was the trade that 500 children were kidnapped in and around Aberdeen in the 1740s. Smaller scale kidnapping or 'spiriting' was a feature of child migration for the first 130 years of its operation.

Until the War of Independence in 1812, North America continued to become home to tens of thousands of British children, after which the children were sent to Canada.[3] Then, in 1926, the Canadian government legislated that no child under the age of fourteen could be taken from Britain, believing that at this age a child could make a choice about their destiny. This, along with frequent reports of abuse, was the catalyst that ended child migration to that country in 1933. Home Canada claimed that 67 per cent of the home children had been physically or sexually abused.

Over hundreds of years, Britain had exported children to every corner of their Empire: to North America, Canada, India, South Africa, Rhodesia, Australia and New Zealand. Even though Canada had banned child migration, by 1937 it appeared that Britain was proposing to send children to Australia without the proper safeguards to prevent the Canadian disaster from being repeated.

Children and young people migrated to Australia before World War II under a number of different schemes, many of which were targeted to older children, usually between the ages of fourteen and sixteen, and centred on the farm school model, such as that pioneered by the Child Emigration Society and Kingsley Fairbridge, who set up his farm school in Pinjarra in Western Australia in 1913. Fairbridge boys were to be taught all aspects of agriculture in the hope that they would become successful farmers. Fairbridge girls would be trained in domestic skills – with the view that they would become suitable wives to the farmers. By 1933 over 300 British girls and boys had been raised on the property at Pinjarra, housed in small cottages with a house mother looking after eighteen to twenty children. Each house had bedrooms, a bathroom, a kitchen and a common room. In effect, the house mother took on the role of parent, providing as homely an atmosphere as possible. Yet, as with the postwar child migration scheme, the experiences of the farm school children varied enormously.

Postwar migration

In the dark days of 1941, the Australian Deputy Prime Minister, Francis Forde, underscored his government's fear and expressed the attitude towards migration that, after the war, drove social policy:

> The war has shown us more vividly that if we are to hold this country down the years, we must increase our present population by several millions at least over the next 30 years. Of all immigrants, children are the most readily made into good Australians. They have no preconceived ideas. They will need careful nursing after the war. Australian food and sunshine will do the rest. In the demobilised period the child migrants will not compete for jobs, they will not need family housing.[4]

In Australia, the war-drained Chifley government began to express fear of the 'yellow menace' to the north and were anxious to boost Australia's white population. The recently formed Department of Immigration, under the leadership of Arthur Calwell, began an active drive to 'populate or perish', and British migrants, including children, were targeted. A new spin on the child migration scheme emphasised that the giving of the 'fresh start' to these children would be carried out by benevolent charities that held the best interests of the migrants at heart.

This would generate public support for continued child migration.

After World War II, a financially devastated Britain needed to rebuild its economy and infrastructure and into the 1950s there was no shortage of work; indeed, Britain had to rely on imported labour. It is hard to imagine in this postwar boom any justification for sending child migrants away on economic grounds. Yet the attitude in Britain was that Australia had been a faithful wartime ally and should be rewarded and so it agreed to Australia's demands for child migrants.

Institutional care was still the preferred model of childcare for orphaned and abandoned children in Australia, even though Britain had begun to move away from this approach, recognising that fostering and adoption was more humane and gave children a better chance of a good life.

Most of the religious organisations, including the Salvation Army, the Methodist Church, the Presbyterian Church, the Church of England and the Catholic Church, had established children's homes, some dating back to the 1920s, and, together with the secular agencies, including Dr Barnardo's Homes, Fairbridge Farm Schools, Lady Northcote Farm Schools and various smaller organisations, were aware of the thousands of displaced children in Britain and were expecting most, if not all, to be sent to Australia, especially since Canada had banned child migration. Without questioning why child migration to Canada had been banned, most organisations anticipated significant amounts of financial support from the British government.

Dealing in children

In December 1944 the federal government staggered the state premiers with its incredible proposal for the migration of 50 000 children a year from Europe. The government asked the premiers for their cooperation as it was vital to the success of the program. Western European children aged between six and twelve were to be sent to converted military bases and airforce camps to be prepared for assimilation into the Australian community. Later the children would be sent to country towns across the nation and housed in purpose-built hostel accommodation. The local town authorities would bear a major responsibility in raising the children and assisting with education, training and eventual employment. Mr Forde, then acting Prime Minister, told the premiers:

There are special and urgent reasons why a major effort should be made immediately in the field of child migration. The peculiar circumstances of war have created in Europe a greater number of orphans, stray children, 'war babies etc., than ever before. This makes the present time a potentially unparalleled opportunity for Australia to build up the population with child migrants who, on account of their easier assimilation, adaptability, long working life ahead and easier housing, constitute a particularly attractive category of migrants for the first post war years.

Moreover, they will create, rather than compete for work in the period of adjustment to a peacetime economy. The opportunity must be seized immediately and exploited for two or three years ahead, or lost forever.[5]

The government was determined that the stigma associated with providing 'charity' associated with the church-run institutions should be avoided at all costs.

Above all, there should be no suggestion of charity about any aspect of the scheme such as has occasionally marred some existing non-official schemes.

Fostering and adoption were not to be encouraged.

Some State Child Welfare Authorities are understood to be vigorously opposed to private adoptions of child migrants. Experience of even the 1940 British child evacuees has led Commonwealth administrative authorities to the same conclusion. Results in the cases of alien children might be even less fortunate. In the case of British orphans there are substantial legal obstacles at the British end to private adoption here, and in any case pronouncements by the British Minister of Pensions make it doubtful whether British orphans of this war would be available for adoption in Australia.[6]

The government held a preliminary conference of state and Commonwealth officials in January 1945 to discuss the plan. The Victorian delegate immediately declared that children should be placed into private homes. The Tasmanian delegate offered an 'experimental station' to be set up on the island for the first trial group. The South

Australian delegate agreed in principle to the scheme but suggested that children should be placed into private homes. The Western Australian delegate also suggested that children be placed with families. The New South Wales delegate was in favour of a 'cottage homes' approach, but mentioned that 500 families had already registered to adopt British children, to which the South Australian and Victorian delegates added 200 and 400 families respectively. The chairman reminded the meeting that adoptions and fostering would not be allowed.

It was agreed at the conference that each state should furnish particulars, including estimates of costs where new buildings were necessary and their probable requirements in the way of reception depots, cottage homes, hostels and schools. The estimate was to also include the cost of services and equipment, information about where it was proposed to establish the buildings and details about the numbers of staff required for all purposes including teaching.

The Victorian delegate asked whether denominational schools were to be considered, suggesting that 'A proportion of the migrant children will be of Roman Catholic faith. It may be suggested that they be educated at convent schools.'

The chairman replied that this aspect had not been considered and pointed out that there would also be Jewish children.

The issue of legal guardianship of the children was raised.

The Minister [Minister for the Interior] shall be guardian of the person of the child, to the exclusion of the father and mother and every other guardian of the child, until the child reaches the age of 21 years or leaves Australia or until the Governor General, by order, directs that the provisions of these regulations shall cease to apply to and in relation to the child, whichever first happens.[7]

The delegate from Western Australia thought some exception could be made where brothers and sisters from the same family migrated together, proposing that 'It might be desirable in such a case to keep them all together'.

The Commonwealth estimated the cost over eight years at 26.3 million pounds, to be shared by the state and Commonwealth governments. The proposed plans created excitement in country towns and caused the Merredin Road Board to write to the Premier of Western Australia:

No doubt it will be the desire of the Governments of Australia to place these children preferably in rural areas and in particular in such progressive centres as Merredin. We would welcome the opportunity to assist these children to find a congenial home in our centre, and would do all we could to see that they get the best possible education, reasonable amenities (swimming pool and community centre to be established here later) and every opportunity to become very good citizens.[8]

A policy of institutionalisation

Hansard transcripts of the Australian parliament reveal that the government was aware of growing reluctance on the part of the British to send child migrants as early as 1946, yet the Australian government policy of supporting the institutionalisation of children would ultimately give the British government the perfect excuse to step back from the child migration scheme.

The Australian Immigration (Guardianship of Children) Act 1946 reflected the Commonwealth government's strong support for institutionalisation. During the debate on the Act, Dame Enid Lyons, the member for Darwin in Tasmania, expressed concern that there was no provision for the adoption of children into private families and that the Act would lead to the mass institutionalisation of children, which she and her supporters believed would do irreparable harm to the children. She told the Australian parliament that as 5000 Australian families had registered to foster or adopt English children, there was no need to institutionalise the children. Her argument had support from both sides of the House, including from the former Prime Minister, John Curtin. The Minister for Immigration, Arthur Calwell, dismissed the offers made by the adoption societies represented by Dame Lyons, as he vigorously supported institutionalisation and opposed fostering and adoption. He insisted that legal guardianship of child migrants was a Commonwealth responsibility until they were 21 years old. In the second reading of the Bill, Calwell reiterated his views.

The overriding responsibility of the Commonwealth in respect of all migrants, including the application of its social service legislation, applies in greater force perhaps to children.

It is believed that the Commonwealth government, in encouraging and financially assisting child migration by way of contributions towards passage money and payment of child endowment to organisations caring for the children accepts a responsibility which does not end with the children's arrival in Australia.

It is therefore incumbent on the Commonwealth to see that child migrants are properly accommodated and cared for until they reach 21 years of age.

The only way in which this can be achieved is by vesting in the Minister for Immigration an overriding legal guardianship in respect of all such children.[9]

The Minister's arguments were persuasive and he refused to give ground, convincing both sides of his genuine concern for the child migrants: 'We certainly require more safeguards in respect of them then we do for our own children.'

And it didn't help that the British Secretary of State made it clear that the British government would cease subsidy payments to any child removed from the legal guardianship of the Minister for Immigration.

Yet despite the commitments made in parliament, and the expressions of concerns from supporters of institutionalisation, the Commonwealth and state governments would ultimately renege on their responsibility to care for the child migrants until they were 21 years of age. Subsidy payments ceased on a child's sixteenth birthday, after which the child was left to the mercy of their carers or forced out into the world without support. The responsibility of the institutions ended once they had secured a job for the child, often as a farm labourer if a boy and a domestic servant if a girl, although some institutions did go to great lengths to secure better employment for the children.

In 1948 the Commonwealth government had a change of heart on the issue of adoption. Adoptions would be allowed subject to certain criteria:

1 The Minister's delegate in the State was satisfied that the foster parents were in every respect suitable to adopt the child and that adoption would be in the child's best interests.

2 The parents or next of kin in the United Kingdom, or where no next of kin, the organisation which had care of the child, had signified in writing that they were agreeable to the child being adopted.

In effect, this put the final decision into the hands of the institutions, yet the Commonwealth government was fully aware of the financial incentive for the institutions to not adopt out their charges. The supposed change of heart seemed a strategy just to divert criticism.

In Western Australia in 1955 the total subsidy for a child per week was:

- twelve shillings and sixpence from the British government

- ten shillings from the WA Lotteries Commission

- ten shillings from the Commonwealth government

- twenty-three shillings and three pence from the WA Child Welfare Department.

This totalled 55 shillings and ninepence per week for each child in care – funds that were needed for the continued operation and expansion of the institutions. In addition, the Commonwealth of Australia paid five pounds per child 'equipment fee' to the sending agent in the United Kingdom, a sizeable sum of money in those times. These financial incentives went some way to driving the institutionalisation mentality of the voluntary organistions.

A vastly reduced pool

Soon after the special premiers' conference in 1946, the federal government dispatched immigration officials on a recruitment drive to Europe. They discovered to their disappointment a great reluctance by local welfare officials to place abandoned children in the scheme. They also discovered that the so-called 'vast pool' of children in postwar Europe looking for a new home was non-existent. Raising these children was regarded as the responsibility of the country in which the children had been born.

Australian churches and secular organisations had to lobby vigorously for their share of the vastly reduced pool of British children who, the Minister for Immigration warned at the time, 'numbered only in dozens or scores'. While not quite the desired 50 000 children, the 'dozens or scores' did blow out to over 3000 children arriving in the period after the war.[10] The recruitment drive across Britain had achieved some success.

The first child migrants to arrive in Australia after the war were older children, aged twelve to fourteen years, who volunteered to leave Britain after being given a rosy and exaggerated spiel about life in Australia. As the scheme progressed, fewer volunteers stepped forward, so the focus began to be directed towards much younger children, who were supposedly better able to adjust to migration and institutional life. Young children had the added advantage of apparently being easier to control and train, and they would not immediately compete for jobs in postwar Australia. Their consent was not required as their legal guardians in Britain believed that they had powers to consent on these children's behalf. The Australian government supported the migration of much younger children, aged six to seven years, and set the upper age limit at twelve, yet it is known that some children as young as four years old were sent to Australia.

A number of strategies were used to maximise the potential numbers of child migrants. In some cases, sending agents from voluntary organisations in Britain manipulated a child's status to fit the official criteria for immigration that stated that children had to be entirely devoid of any family links, be small of stature and of below-average intelligence. Often malnourished and stripped of any love, these were the saddest and loneliest little children on earth. In a number of reported cases, mothers who had relinquished their children to the homes but had refused consent to their child being sent to Australia were unable to retrieve their children from the homes and so had no say over the inevitable outcome.

Such children were seen as the new foundation for postwar Australian nation-building. The public perception was that these children were being given a chance in a new country. An air of excited anticipation, even in frightened and confused children, was evident at the farewell parties and in the grand speeches of welcome when they arrived at their destination.

Child migrants were often bitterly disappointed by the conditions at the institutions in Australia, which were entirely different to the rosy picture that had been painted for them. They were often angry or despairing on arrival. Strict discipline and corporal punishment were still perceived in most institutions as being the only cure for dysfunctional behaviour, so already deeply traumatised children were made even more unhappy. With no prospect of returning home, and no sense of hope for their future, their sense of betrayal generated an 'us and them' mentality almost from the beginning.

By 1947, receiving organisations in Australia, including the Christian Brothers, had begun complaining about the large numbers of undernourished and underdeveloped children coming into their homes. The difference between British and Australian children of the same age was obvious both physically and intellectually. A 1948 Department of Immigration survey of 238 institutionalised British Catholic children described 6 per cent as being feebleminded and 23 per cent as on the border of being mentally defective. Some official estimates put British children's physiques two years behind that of their Australian counterparts. Fairbridge Farm School made a common complaint when the Director, AF Stowe, wrote to the Dominion office, 'Despite mental and other examinations, backward, stunted, unhealthy and otherwise poor quality children have arrived, and as shown by the records, quite a number of children older than we wish for have been brought out'.

This was of great concern to the Christian Brothers, who complained to the Minister for Immigration and to the state child welfare authorities. The British children were apparently also hard to control. This was all bad news because the Minister was a friend of the Brothers and was in the process of building an entire postwar immigration program on the basis that thousands of healthy, strong and bright child migrants were being sent to Australia.

Arthur Calwell was aware of the general conditions at Australian institutions and kept in touch with most of the key players, including Brigadier W. Winton, a friend from the Salvation Army's Sydney office. The Salvation Army had applied for their Riverview Training

Farm in Ipswich in Queensland to be an approved home for migrant children. In a letter to Winton on 9 September 1948, Calwell wrote: 'You will appreciate that any scheme of child migration by voluntary organisations must be controlled closely because of the possibility of the exploitation of the children.'

The Secretary of the British High Commission had insisted that the tough 'juvenile delinquents' and the 'intellectually handicapped' currently held at Riverview were to be removed before British children would be sent. This prompted the Secretary of the Queensland Welfare Department to reply that Queensland 'delinquents' compared favourably with British children in character and intelligence.

Some institutions began to develop the view that Britain was sending its 'trash' and that the children needed 'straightening out'. This suited the tough disciplinarians who had entered the childcare system without appropriate checks being made about their suitability for the job, some of whom went on to harm the children in their care. Police were given powers to apprehend absconded children and return them to the institutions. These runaways, often very young children, were severely punished and made an example of.

The role of the Catholic Church

The Catholic Church became a more significant player in the child migration scheme after World War II, sending children from Britain and later from Malta, although Catholic leaders had been keen to establish a scheme as early as the 1920s. In 1945, Archbishop Prendiville of Perth wrote to Cardinal Griffin in England, making the exaggerated claim that:

> At the present time the available accommodation would make it possible for us to receive 500 children over a period of six months. With three months notice, provisions can be made for an additional 500, and a similar number three months later. During the ensuing 12 months we shall be able to accommodate an additional 1000 children, including if necessary 50% girls, so that over a period of 18 months from the first sailing, we should find it possible to absorb 2500 children.[11]

At the time there was accommodation for only a fraction of this number of children as neither the Commonwealth nor state governments had yet committed funding to the scheme. Yet both governments were keen and had promised subsidies.

Brother PA Conlon, deputy chief of the Christian Brothers in Australia, had been appointed representative of the Catholic Church and the Australian government in 1938 to begin negotiations with Catholic sending agents in Britain. Conlon was confident of success, as the year before, the Australian Prime Minister, Joseph Lyons, had met with the English Cardinal, Arthur Hinsley, and his advisors to discuss the possibility of sending children to Australia. In July 1937, Archbishop Prendiville wrote to Brother Conlon:

> I have just been speaking to the Prime Minister over the telephone with regard to the immigration of children, and he is of the opinion that everything is now in order. He has spoken to the Premier Mr Wilcock, who is favourably disposed towards a subsidy similar to that granted to Fairbridge.
>
> He himself [Mr Lyons] can speak for the Federal government. They will be prepared to subsidise on a similar basis also. And he says that the Home authorities are becoming more enthusiastic. The next move he suggested should come from us. I would be grateful to have your opinion and your advice.[12]

Catholic child migration began the following year, but only in a small way, as the war interrupted its progress for the next eight years. After the war, Brother Conlon was soon off to London again in 1946. The Australian Minister for Immigration, Arthur Calwell, was an admirer and supporter of the Christian Brothers. As a devout Catholic he fully supported the plan to bring Catholic children to Australia, but he had even bigger plans. Australia then was a vast continent populated by barely seven million people. In his book *How Many Australians Tomorrow?*, published in 1945, Calwell wrote:

> One of the advantages of the Commonwealth Government's child migration plans which were announced at the end of 1944 by the then Acting Prime Minister, Mr Forde, is that these children will not immediately be competitors in the employment field. Moreover, children are more adaptable than adults.

When we bring alien children here they can be more readily assimilated, will learn English and will absorb the Australian point of view more quickly than adults.

The plan is to bring at least 17,000 children a year and I hope the number will be increased to 50,000 a year. It is gratifying to read that the London Daily Sketch *has hailed Australia as the coming 'greatest foster-father of children the world has known'; but the* Sketch *also warns us 'there is no vast pool of children: child welfare groups interested in emigration number their children in dozens or scores, while Australia is to deal in thousands'.*

This plan is but a first instalment of a broad immigration policy now being formulated by Cabinet and its advisers.

We must be realistic. Let us try to entice all the immigrants we can absorb; we need all the people we can gain this way.[13]

Calwell arranged priority passage for Conlon, as well as providing a letter of credit for 1000 English pounds and a letter of introduction to the Australian High Commissioner in London.

While the Australian Catholic bishops had little to do with the running of institutions, they held a genuine belief in the goodness of this work. In his book about St Mary's Tardun Farm School, author David Plowman wrote how:

Archbishop Simmonds joined Conlon in London in May 1946 and together they prepared 'The Bishops Plan' for the accommodation and training of migrant boys. In summary this provided that boys would be placed in institutions conducted by the Religious Brothers. They would receive primary education to school leaving age and in addition, training in gardening, dairying, and poultry-raising, fruit growing and general farming.[14]

In the trade schools, the child migrants were to be taught bricklaying, carpentry, plumbing, plastering and other construction-related trades, as well as truck and tractor driving, horse teamwork and sheep- and horse-raising. Boys of outstanding ability and good character would be given a full secondary education if they so desired. In a few farm schools, those with special aptitude for farm work would be given the opportunity to become owners of farms. The plan noted that the Bishops 'favour the admission of migrant boys into private families'. Plowman points out that the 'Commonwealth government agreed to this plan – except for the final point. It did not want child migrants placed into private families.'[15]

Brother Conlon was an able negotiator and convinced high-ranking church officials in England to support his plan, as well as finding political and practical support at the highest levels in the Australian government. He was directly involved with the immigration of the first 50 Catholic girls to Australia in 1939. Church authorities in England had asked Conlon whether there were any prospect for a farm scheme for girls being established. What eventuated was enthusiastic correspondence from the Reverend Canon Craven, Administrator of the Crusade of Rescue, to the Right Reverend Griffen seeking his support. The plan was that the Bishop of Geraldton and the Sisters of Nazareth would erect an institution in Geraldton to train girls in 'domestic science, general household duties, gardening … looking after their own dairy'. The Sisters of Nazareth were key players in both the sending and receiving of child migrants. They operated 26 homes across the United Kingdom and were the source of approximately 700 Catholic child migrants after World War II.

Craven suggested to Griffen that he write to Brother Conlon informing him that the church would agree to send the first 50 girls. His letter finished with the comment:

> The scheme of Brother Conlon's now completes and rounds off very satisfactorily I think our migration plan. I should myself have been very much opposed to our girls going out simply to be trained for domestic service and I ought to tell you that the LCC were absolutely opposed to such a scheme. They are afraid like myself, that it would mean using these poor girls as drudges on farms or in towns. This we must certainly prevent.[16]

This was exactly what they couldn't prevent, despite assurances from the Catholic Church in Australia that the child migrants would be given the best education and training.

Looking further afield

Brother Conlon had negotiated with the Maltese government in 1938 to take boys from institutions and poor families to Christian Brothers' institutions in Western Australia, yet, as with the British scheme, the war interrupted his plans. In 1950 the Catholic Church began to look further afield, particularly to Malta, Britain's former colony, for prospective migrants. Some 260 boys and 50 girls were sent to Australia from 1950 to 1965 under an agreement between the Maltese government and the Catholic authorities in Australia.

A significant difference from the British scheme was that families were often involved in the migration of their children, usually agreeing to send their children due to poverty and the desire to give their child a better life. More Maltese child migrants were reunited with their families, many of whom subsequently became residents of Australia. The Maltese government also had greater oversight of the scheme and, although the government did not accept overall responsibility, it did conduct inspections of institutions at the time. However, like the British child migrants, some Maltese children suffered abuse at the hands of the Brothers and were subject to the same rules and harsh discipline, with the added pressure of having to survive institution life speaking English as a second language.

Who is to blame?

While history has singled out and harshly judged the Christian Brothers and the Sisters of Nazareth for their involvement in child migration – and rightly so – other organisations, both church and secular, were also at fault.

Though conditions in the Brothers' homes and their methods of childcare generally met the government standards of the day, the standards in some of the remote institutions were even further behind those in the city homes. The Christian Brothers, like others in the industry, were ill-prepared to deal with traumatised children. There were no training programs and little capacity to weed out of the system those who were, at best, clearly unsuited to working with children or, at worst, were abusive and destructive.

Yet, the Christian Brothers succeeded to some degree in fulfilling the aims of the farm school model. Between 1934 and 1969, at St Mary's

Tardun Farm School alone, some seventeen young men were established on their own farms nearby.

Child welfare reform in Britain

On 15 July 1944 a remarkable letter by Lady Allen, a campaigner for social reform, was published in *The Times* newspaper. She claimed that British institutions were cruel and repressive and were generations out of date, stating that 'A public inquiry with full government support is urgently needed to explore this largely uncivilised territory.'

In 1945, a young boy, Dennis O'Neil, died from cruelty and maltreatment while in foster care in England. His death caused a national scandal and resulted in a major inquiry. It prompted the introduction of new laws to protect children in foster care. Yet another equally appalling tragedy was completely ignored – this time because it happened to a child migrant out of sight of the British authorities. Anne Clifford had been given into the care of Sisters of Nazareth in Newcastle-on-Tyne, but was 'approved' for migration to Australia. At seven years of age, she had signed her own medical report after her doctor had declared her fit to travel, even though she was still suffering from the bronchial pneumonia mentioned in her documentation as having been cured. Anne died two months after arriving in Perth in 1946. Her lonely grave in Karrakatta Cemetery in Perth simply reads 'Anne Clifford. Mother unknown. Father unknown'. News of her death, and the negligence that had caused it, did not reach the public in Britain. Her death should have prompted a major inquiry such as the O'Neil case.

Why was the government failing such children? Under pressure, the government was forced to act. By 1944 the process of welfare reform in Britain was underway.

The Curtis Committee Report 1946

There were more then 450 institutions scattered around Britain and an official government inspection conducted by John Curtis and the Care of Children Committee in 1945 confirmed Lady Allen's allegations of neglect, insensitivity and harshness. Curtis was outraged at the conditions he found in the institutions and noted how they damaged the lives of children in them. He made the first priority of the new Act for children to be freed from these places and returned to their families or, if this wasn't possible, be adopted or fostered out.

Curtis defined the conventional family unit as being the most conducive to the wellbeing of a child, defining four main principles of home life:

1 Affection and personal interests – understanding of a child's defects, care for the child's future, respect for the child's personality and regard for the child's self-esteem

2 Stability – the feeling that the child can expect to remain with those who will continue to care for them till they go out into the world on their own feet

3 Opportunity of making the best of a child's ability and aptitudes, whatever they maybe, as such opportunity is made available to the child in normal home

4 A share in the common life of a small group of people in a homely environment.

The emphasis placed on the psychological and not just the physical needs of children was indicative of an important change in thinking in the child welfare industry. The resulting report from the Curtis Committee in 1946 led to an entire overhaul of the British child welfare system and the spirit of the report's recommendations were later enshrined in law – the Children Act 1948. Associated departments and local authorities were set up to administer the new Act.

Of the child migration scheme, the Curtis Committee Report noted:

It follows from this conception of the kind of care which should be given to a deprived child and the prospect of its realisation in this country is that it would be difficult to justify proposals to immigrate deprived children unless the Societies or Homes to which they go are willing and able to provide care and opportunity on the same level. The first requirement from an immigration Home or Society must be therefore, the assurance that child immigrants will have equally good care and opportunity overseas as he would have had in this country.

It was clear to Curtis that overseas institutionalisation was fundamentally incompatible with his new welfare ideals and could lead to serious legal issues for Britain. Treading a thin line, he proposed that British children sent overseas would still be considered British citizens and would therefore be subject to the protection of the law and be legally entitled to the same standard of care as those children who stayed in Britain. He believed that the child migrant's legal entitlements would be enshrined after the passing of the Children Act 1948.

Agreeing with Curtis's views, the Home Office stated that it had established a new and enlarged Children's Branch, with Children's Officers appointed to local authorities who would see to it that child migrants were not disadvantaged. Organisations in Britain involved in child migration would not be allowed to wash their hands of children they had sent away and would have to maintain links with each child. The Home Office would compel those involved to ensure that only those children who were suitable and who desired to emigrate would leave Britain. Independent social workers would attend all interviews to represent the interests of the children in Britain to protect them from exploitation. The Home Office was also to see that a liaison officer was appointed by the sending organisation to make regular visits to children in Australia.

The Home Office memoranda 1947

The British Home Office released its criteria for the proper care of child migrant children around the time that postwar migration commenced in 1947. The criteria was written in government publication number 42(2483) entitled 'Children Act 1948, Memorandum by the Home Office on the main provisions of the Act affecting voluntary homes and voluntary organisations in England and Wales'.[17]

This document (described by the Department of Immigration as 'Care of Child Migrants – Statement by the United Kingdom Home Office') spelt out the precise details of what the Home Office meant by 'suitable protection and welfare' of child migrants, so establishing the ground rules for child migration to Australia. It is almost certainly similar to or the same as the five-page memorandum entitled 'Emigration of children who have been deprived of a normal home life', sent by the Home Office to the Australian government on 18 October 1947, the same time as publication 42(2483) was circulated. This strongly worded memorandum set out the principles of what constituted acceptable childcare as had come out of the 1946 Curtis Committee Report, the fundamental point of which was that children could not be sent to conditions that were not equal to or better than those from which they came. Both memoranda were a response to the upcoming Children Act 1948 and laid out basic guides and protocols for the future care of British children in Australia.

The memorandum to the Australian government covered a broad range of provisions for the children who emigrated. They were to

- be raised together in small groups in a homely environment

- join the Boy Scouts and Girls Guides and take part in outside activities

- attend school outside the orphanage to ensure that they made friends

- be educated to an appropriate standard

- be given pocket money

- have their independence and self-esteem carefully nurtured to ensure proper development

- be given skills training and aftercare until they had successfully assimilated into Australian life

- be offered the opportunity to go to university if they were high achievers where they would be housed in nearby hostels or boarded out.

This memorandum also imposed the following condition on the orphanages: 'The Principal or those in charge should be most carefully selected by an independent panel drawn from the local community.' Sensitive to Australia's policy at the time of not fostering or adopting out child migrants, no mention was made of this in the memorandum.

Finally, the Home Office warned the Australian government that child migration could not be justified unless it adhered to these new guidelines. The memorandum was to be circulated to the child welfare department in each state and, as well, the homes and orphanages in Britain were sent copies. However, in one simple statement, the integrity of the Home Office was seriously undermined. The British High Commissioner in Canberra told the Australian government in letter attached to the memorandum: 'This is a departmental expression of views only and is not to be taken as a statement of the views of the United Kingdom Government.'

This statement, casually buried in the text of his letter, seemingly invited the Australian government to ignore the recommendations of the Curtis Committee Report and the provisions of the new Children Act that was to be enacted the following year. If the British government had been prepared to enforce the Curtis Committee guidelines and the Act, child migration to Australia could not have happened. But, under pressure from its wartime ally and the voluntary organisations involved in child migration, the British government instead allowed the migration of so-called 'problem' children without any meaningful constraints being imposed on the sending and receiving organisations. In effect, child migrants would be forced to endure welfare practices and conditions that, after the passing of the Children Act 1948, were outlawed in Britain.

Had Curtis made an inspection of Australian institutions he would have found plenty to write home about. Primitive barrack-style accommodation was yet to be built in some cases and, in others, was yet to be completed. Basic infrastructure was often barely adequate and the quality of food, clothing and education was often substandard. The staff were mostly untrained and, contrary to the Home Office's instructions, children usually did not attend outside schools. In fact, some children were receiving little or no education. Brutal punishment was sometimes meted out for minor indiscretions. Mail coming in and out of the institutions was censored. Runaways were rounded up by the police and often brutally dealt with. Children in bare feet were used as forced labour to build some of the institutions. This wasn't the homely environment required by the Home Office or by Curtis.

Furthermore, contrary to the Home Office instructions, there were no *independent* social workers representing prospective child migrants' interests. According to the Home Office, these social workers were to have detailed information about a child's psychological make up and background, have an intimate knowledge of the conditions at the institution in Australia to which they would be sent and be fully convinced of each child's desire to emigrate. Yet prospective migrants were typically screened by Australian social workers, who had little capacity in Britain to fulfil the Home Office requirements and who were being influenced by the Department for Immigration.

The Australian government shelved the 1947 memorandum to gather dust, regarding it as hypocritical lecturing and interference. So too did the Australian institutions and the British sending agents who knew about it. And during the nine years of postwar child migration, the Home Office seemingly refused to police its own welfare standards in the homes run by the voluntary organisations in both Britain and Australia. It was content to just lecture and complain to the Australian government about the conditions in their institutions until 1956 when it was finally forced to act – but, by then, for many children, it was too late.

Responsibility for child migrants

On 1 August 1947, the British Secretary of State signed a four-page contract with a private Australian organisation, the Catholic Council for British Overseas Settlement, that effectively gave them unconditional access to child migrants. The contract was limited to 350 children and ran from 1 August 1947 to 31 July 1949. The British government agreed to pay the Council 11 shillings a week per child until the child reached sixteen years of age. The responsibilities of the Council were loosely worded in the contract:

> *The Council undertake that the training of children at the institutions shall be of the kind that shall fit them for life in Australia. The Council also undertake to use their best endeavours to find suitable occupations for children when they leave the institutions.*

A poorly written Section 3 reads:

> *The council undertake to furnish the Secretary of State with particulars of parties of children who they propose from time to time to send out to the Institutions with a view to the elimination of such children as he may deem to be ineligible for assistance under this agreement.*[18]

The funding arrangements in Australia were generous so as to avoid the stigma associated with charity-based childcare and to maintain a steady flow of British children to the voluntary institutions. The state and Commonwealth governments had agreed at a premiers' conference in 1946 that, along with the institution, they would pay one third each for the cost of the buildings for the children and the accommodation for staff, as well as the furniture, fittings and equipment 'necessary to place an establishment in working order'. The voluntary organisations were to also receive a subsidy for each child from the Commonwealth, state and British governments, as well as the Lotteries Commission.

The Australian government believed that this combination of assistance was adequate to avoid the stigma of charity attached to government-funded childcare. However, the institutions played the charity card regularly, as they relied on public donations for extra support. With some justification, they regarded the assistance package as totally inadequate, especially once the costs of building maintenance and of expanding the infrastructure were taken into account. Subsequently they ran media awareness programs and conducted fundraising through annual fairs, raffles, and importantly, the Lotteries.

No mention was made in the contract of the standards of childcare raised in the Curtis Committee Report and set out in the Home Office memorandum. In signing this contract and paying subsidies the British government had seemingly by committed itself to being legally responsible for the welfare of these children. But who was ultimately responsible? The Children Act promulgated the year later attempted to answer this question.

The Children Act 1948

The new Children Act 1948 (United Kingdom) was a radical departure from previous social policy and heralded greatly needed and long overdue changes to child welfare. It took the interests of children more seriously, and unambiguously demanded the local authorities now in charge of children to carry out their responsibilities in a humane manner. Section 12 read, in part, 'Where a child is in the care of the Local Authority, it shall be the duty of that authority to exercise their powers with respect to him so as to further his best interests and to afford him opportunity for the proper development of his character and abilities'.

The Act ostensibly tightened official government oversight of the child migration scheme by granting regulatory power to the British Secretary of State to oversee the immigration arrangements made by the local authorities and volunteer organisations for child migrants and to act as legal guardian to the children involved. Under previous welfare policy, the volunteer organisations had an implied right to act as guardians of so-called 'lost or abandoned' children. The loose wording of the Children Act left the door open for these organisations to continue in this role.

Despite assurances in the British parliament during the debate over the Children Act that children would not be sent to Australia unless proper arrangements had been made for their care, the Act, in Section 33, seemingly introduced a potential loophole: 'The Secretary of State *may* by regulations control the making and carrying out by voluntary organisations of arrangements for the emigration of children.' In contrast, Section 17 of the Act was precise and clear: it provided that a local authority or voluntary organisation could, with the consent of the Secretary of State, procure the immigration of any child in their care, and that the Secretary of State should not give his consent unless he was satisfied that immigration was in the best interests of the child and that suitable arrangements were made or would be made for the child's 'reception and welfare' in the receiving country. The Act also required the parents or guardians of the child to have been consulted or, in the case that this was not possible, that the child gave consent.

However, in the period of postwar child migration to Australia, the Secretary of State did not promulgate a single regulation under the auspices of the Children Act that would have more actively protected the rights of child migrants or parents, where they were involved. The word 'may' in Section 33, seeming out of context, provided the perfect loophole. While the Secretary of State chose to remain uninvolved, those wishing to exploit the ambiguous nature of the wording of the Act could argue that the legal authority for child migration had effectively been handed back to the secular and religious sending and receiving organizations – as had been the case in the past. Moreover, the Act had put an onerous, almost impossible, responsibility on the local authorities, the Secretary of State and the Home Office to know the conditions of the Australian orphanages and to assess the maturity and willingness of the children involved. The Act seemed doomed to fail from the outset.

Their 1947 memorandum proves that the Home Office was painfully aware that 'suitable arrangements' for the children's 'reception and welfare' had not been made in Australia and that the British government felt compelled to warn Australia to provide it. This raises some obvious questions: How was the Secretary of State able to consent to a child's migration to an Australian institution, claiming that this was in the child's best interest, knowing that the processes and institutions were substandard? How could he claim that the Australian institutions were suitable, when under the Children Act in Britain this entire model of care was being dismantled? How were the voluntary organisations protected under British law when their overseas institutions failed to meet the standards of childcare demanded in the Act?

At no point did the Secretary of State or any local authority seek to officially obtain knowledge of conditions in overseas orphanages, yet, it is clear from the 1947 memorandum that the Home Office and the Secretary of State were fully aware that, without a vast improvement in Australian childcare practices, child migration would almost certainly damage child migrants, as was predicted by the Curtis Report.

The Act conferred a powerful and pivotal role on the local authorities, but again one that it was difficult for them to fulfil. It was rarely possible to consult with the parents of the children, as they often couldn't be found, and the voluntary organisations, the self-appointed guardians, at best did not always act professionally and at worst were influenced by vested interest. They were able to dodge the local authorities and deal directly with the social workers at Australia House. So close was their relationship that in one month, in 1953, 114 Catholic children were sent overseas against their will by the religious volunteer organisations involved and Australia House, without the knowledge of the relevant local authority, the English Catholic Church or their official guardian, the Secretary of State. Initially, this scandal was kept from the public: no demands were made for the immediate return of the children and the Secretary of State did not consider it necessary to conduct an inquiry or promulgate regulations to stop this from happening again.

A new life of drudgery

The first negative newspaper reports in Australia about the child migration scheme appeared on the 5 April 1948 and plunged the Department of Information in Canberra into damage control. In a letter to HE Smith, Immigration Branch, Department of Lands and Surveys Perth, Mr H Murphy, the Publicity Officer, writes, 'On April 5th the Melbourne *Herald* carried a story cabled from London suggesting that child immigrants might be finding a new life of drudgery in the Dominions'. The story read:

DISTURBING REPORTS ON UNITED KINGDOM CHILD MIGRANTS

London, Monday. British welfare associations are pressing the government to investigate disturbing reports about 300 child migrants who have gone to the Dominions in the past 18 months.

Aged from 7 to 14, these migrants were orphaned, abandoned, or illegitimate children.

An official of one welfare society told the *Daily Mirror*,

'Our members have heard disturbing reports about child migrants. We have also heard from our liaison officers in the Dominions that the change, which should have done much for the children, has been for the worse in some cases.'

Some of the children are in institutions much less efficiently run than those in Britain. We are told that some will get nothing better than elementary education with little chance of rising above domestic servants and agricultural labourers.

Our greatest fear is that the Dominion's population needs are being put before the children's welfare.

We want a government inquiry to clear up these reports.'[19]

As child migration was part of a major postwar immigration policy, the Department of Information went into overdrive to counter the negative story. It asked organisations such as Fairbridge Farm School and Dr Barnardo's to provide success stories about British child migrants to be circulated in the British press.

The newspaper stories were most likely an attack on the operations of the Catholic Church in Western Australia and they were asked to explain. A month later, church authorities responded in a three-page letter, which began:

> *Regarding the 334 migrant children placed in Catholic institutions in this state, I feel very happy to be able to refute the 'disturbing' reports published in England.*
>
> *In the first instance they were placed according to age groups, keeping boys of the same age at different institutions, but that placing is now being revised. It was always intended to be subject of revision, once the Superiors of the institutions had been given a reasonable chance to study the children. The new allotment will be as follows.*
>
> *(a) The very young boys are to be placed at Castledare Boys Home where they will receive their elementary training and education.*
>
> *(b) The boys who are of an academic turn of mind will be lodged at Clontarf Orphanage, where the emphasis will be on their scholastic development.*
>
> *(c) Boys who are interested in trades will be placed at Boys Town Bindoon, which is to specialise in teaching boys trades.*
>
> *(d) Boys who are interested in farming and agriculture are to be lodged at St Mary's Farm School, Tardun, which is a modern farm school. The scheme is that when the lads are properly trained they will be given their own block, with accommodation, and assistance until such time as they are established.*
>
> *The block, with accommodation and assistance, will be given gratis and they are not expected to make any return to the institution. Tardun is a property of some 32,000 acres, and it is intended to use it all for the migrant boys who wish to take up farming.*[20]

The letter went on to explain that the relevant minister, as legal guardian, had approved the establishments and the children had been examined by doctors and dentists and had happily settled their new environment. Aftercare service would be provided once the child left the institution. It ended, 'Thanking you for the opportunity of stating the facts'.

The following year, relations between the Catholic Church, the Child Welfare Department and the Department of Lands and Surveys in Western Australia, who had been delegated legal guardians for child migrants by the Minister for Immigration, sank to new lows. Complaints had been made to both departments before and during the war about exploitation of children at Bindoon and the departmental chiefs were determined that there would be no repeat of this.

In a letter to the Premier of Western Australia in June 1946, the Secretary for the Child Welfare Department explained how he had complained directly to a principal of an institution in Australia (Brother Keaney, principal of Bindoon) and the deputy principal of an institution in Ireland (Keaney's superiors).

It has been pointed out to these reverend gentlemen that the interests of the boys who came to Western Australia in 1938 and 1939 were not safeguarded, that instead of them being placed out in employment they have been retained in connection with building operations for which, in the main, no wages have been paid to them, or if placed out they have rarely received full wages, and worse still, these lads have had no bank account when they have reached the age when they have more or less finished with the Christian Brothers.[21]

However, the Director of Bindoon, Brother Paul Keaney, had a degree of power and popularity in Australia – he was revered in political circles and was universally known as 'the orphan's friend'. Using his natural charm and energy, he had been able to raise funds, even during the shortages of the war years, for his building project at Bindoon, a large landholding north of Perth that had been donated to the Brothers to be used to help orphaned children become farmers. The Premier, also the Minister for Child Welfare at the time, was a friend and admirer of Brother Keaney. Some of the children at Bindoon, part of the first wave of postwar immigrants, were approaching sixteen and would soon be eligible to leave. Church representatives had spoken directly to the Premier, claiming that sixteen was too young an age for the child migrants to go out into the world and that they should stay until they were eighteen. They asked the Premier for a two-year stay, suggesting that, otherwise, Bindoon would have to close its doors. They also insisted that when the legislation was changed, the release of eighteen year olds would be conditional upon the young man being boarded with suitable Catholic families. The Premier agreed to look into their request.

The Child Welfare Department was convinced that the child migration scheme was a ploy to exploit cheap labour on the massive building site at Bindoon and had nothing to do with the welfare of children. They did not believe the claims that time spent on construction would be credited to the child migrants when they took up an apprenticeship upon leaving the institution. They were also aware that children were not being paid for their work. The Department had already warned Brother Keaney on a number of occasions about his poor treatment of the child migrants, but because of Keaney's status in the community and with people in high places, it took a long time for their complaints to take hold. In all, a ten-page summary from the two departments of inspectors' reports, complaints and recommendations was given to the Premier. He was reminded that it was unlawful to keep a child institutionalised past the age of sixteen unless the child was medically unfit or psychologically unready to leave. The two departments urged the Premier not to make exceptions for Catholic institutions.

A report from the Department of Lands and Surveys read, in part,

In July last I visited Bindoon in company with officers of the Child Welfare Department and also of this Department.

As the test revealed that not one boy had average ability in basic arithmetic, it is obvious that as a whole their primary education has either been missed or has been of little avail, and it is a waste of time to consider apprenticeships in any of the higher trades where mathematics are involved.

It is difficult to see that anything is to be gained by keeping them at Bindoon until 18 years of age on the pretence that they will be able to gain instruction for apprenticeship when they have the slender chance if in all of ever becoming apprenticed.[22]

The Undersecretary for Lands and Surveys reported further,

I do not think when the Roman Catholic Authorities got approval to bring migrant children to this State that they were fully aware of the Commonwealth Guardianship of Children Act. Or for that matter did not think it would be enforced or, further, that an officer of the State Government would be appointed the Guardian of the children.[23]

The tide turns

After the fiasco of the Home Office 1947 memorandum, which the British government had disowned, there were effectively no guidelines for housing, education or care of British child migrants in Australia. This frustrated the Department of Immigration in Australia, who wrote to the Home Office in November 1950 demanding official British guidelines: 'During the past year or so we have experienced great difficulty in obtaining replies within a reasonable time from the United Kingdom authorities. The reply usually takes the form of a lengthy memorandum and in many instances asking a number of questions or information which is irrelevant.' This prompted the Home Office to draw up a pro forma comprising fourteen questions in 1950 entitled 'Points on Which Information is Desired by the United Kingdom Authorities in Relation to Proposals for Immigration of Children to Australia'. The pro forma required the Australian government authorities to answer questions about what kind of childcare facilities the orphanages were prepared to provide. For example, question 1 asked about the number of staff, including teaching staff if any, engaged in the direct care of the children; question 2 about the number of staff who had received training in childcare; and question 3 about the number, sex and age range of the children accommodated or intended to be accommodated and whether the home accommodated also any children who were educationally 'subnormal' or physically handicapped, or who were delinquents, or any persons above the age of eighteen (other than the staff).[24]

The Home Office pro forma made no suggestions to or demands of the Australian government about how to meet British standards of child welfare. This was extraordinary. Despite the assurances made to parliament during the debate over the 1948 Children Act, the Secretary of State, as legal guardian, had for the previous three years been approving the migration of hundreds of children to institutions, knowing that the institutions were not working within British government standards. Worse, he was seemingly unaware that as early as 1939 the child migration scheme had already been in deep trouble. A letter sent to the Minister for Social Services from the Secretary for Lands and Immigration in Perth in 1946 explains why: 'The 1938–39 scheme in many ways was disastrous. Children brought out under the scheme became anti-social, anti-Australian, and Anti Christ, and some of them unfortunately have returned to the Old Country not at all satisfied with the treatment they received at the hands of the authorities here'.[25] Even in the early stages of the scheme it was evident that British authorities were not prepared to set proper standards or regulate to protect their children.

By 1952, however, some 2000 children had been sent to Australia and the British government came under pressure from Children's Officers to investigate conditions and to determine how the child migrants were faring.

The Moss Report 1953

So tough were their reputations that three of the institutions receiving child migrants in Western Australia were being used as part-time correctional facilities by the state government. In 1951 seventeen delinquents charged in the Children's Court on indictable offences were serving time at the Christian Brothers' homes Clontarf and Bindoon, and the Anglican Swan Boys' Homes. These homes were inspected by John Moss – a retired civil servant, who was chosen by the Home Office to go to Australia in 1951–52 to visit institutions and assess the quality of care available there – and met with his approval. His appointment to the investigation was criticised, as many of his peers believed he was out of touch with modern childcare practice.

Predictably, Moss criticised the barrack-style accommodation and the single-sex institutions, recommending a model of cottage homes, boarding out or adoption. He expressed concern about the lack of trained staff and the isolation, encouraging integration of child migrants with the wider community. However, overall he favoured child migration as an alternative welfare strategy – an opinion that angered most of his peers, who believed that Moss was unable to scratch beneath the surface to find out the truth.

The Moss Report of 1953 temporarily diminished the pressure on the Home Office to conduct a more thorough investigation. However, Moss's investigations did reveal that that the British government was effectively failing to meet its obligations – as set out in the Curtis Report and the Children Act 1948 – to provide the child migrants the same quality care that children in Britain would receive.

A change of tack

In 1954 Catholic immigration officials in Perth proposed to the Commonwealth government that the minimum age of child migrants be reduced from six to three years, as a major Catholic voluntary organisation in Britain was keen to extend the program to children of a much younger age. The Department of Immigration in Canberra was sympathetic and asked the Child Welfare Department in Perth for its opinion. A favourable opinion seemed out of the question, given the history of hostility of the two departments towards institutionalisation and the perception in child welfare circles that the Catholic Church had acquired an 'institution mentality'. The Assistant Secretary of the Child Welfare Department wrote:

> My main objection to the proposal is that it is very difficult, from all accounts, to test satisfactorily a child of three years in respect of its mental capabilities and secondly, I am opposed to the idea of children of such tender years being brought to this State for the purpose of entering institutions.
>
> As the suggestion comes from the Catholic Authorities, the children would be domiciled in St Vincent's Foundling Home, which is a very well conducted Home for young children, but which is always crowded.[26]

The Assistant Secretary for Lands and Surveys suggested that if the Commonwealth supported the idea then, at the very least, the Catholic Authorities should be compelled to put the child with Catholic foster parents: 'It is readily acknowledged that children are better catered for in a private home than in the best of institutions.'

He continued that, if this were to occur, then in all probability the child would be adopted by the family. There appears to be no further communication about the age issue and the matter was dropped;

however, it seemed to reinforce the Child Welfare Department's view that the Catholic Church was obsessed with institutionalisation.

The failed recruitment drive 1955

Most of the children sent to Australia after the war were dispatched in a steady stream from mainly religious voluntary organisations. However, the Australian government was convinced that the local council areas and municipalities of the United Kingdom were a vast untapped source of thousands of children. In April 1955 the Chief Immigration Officer and two experienced field officers from Australia met with the County Council Association as a first step in a major recruitment drive across Britain.

British welfare officers were aware of the obvious distortion in the raw numbers of available children. They didn't trust the voluntary organisations, who they saw as being only interested in running child migration programs and, moreover, high numbers of vulnerable children appeared to be quarantined by just a handful of religious voluntary organisations. In contrast, the British Children's Officers had collected personal information for thousands of children in the care of local authorities, who were busy fostering them or attempting to reunite them with their families. It was pointed out that employment opportunities in Britain were very favourable and there was little sense in encouraging child migration. Most importantly, British welfare authorities were not convinced that all was well in Australia institutions.

The County Council Association told the Australian delegates that institutional care, since the passing of the Children Act of 1948, was considered outmoded, and that abandoned and orphaned children were placed in charge of local authorities rather than being diverted to orphanages, convents and institutions. Where possible, children were being placed into foster care. There were few children available for the child migration scheme. Believing that the child migrants in Australia were attending schools outside the orphanage system, the Association asked the Australian delegates what was being done to avoid the children being stigmatised as orphans. Putting a rosy spin on the Australian conditions, the immigration officials assured the Association:

That every endeavour was made by the Voluntary Organisations, the Church Authorities, Boy Scouts Association, and other community bodies in the towns where Homes were established, to encourage friendship between the local children and the child migrants who were often invited to private homes for parties, holidays, etc. The Aunts and Uncles scheme by local townsfolk to extend hospitality and kindness to children in such Homes was a common gesture fostered by influential Church Civic and Voluntary Organisation officials.[27]

This answer was received with a large dose of scepticism. It prompted the chairman to suggest that the Association prepare a questionnaire to which the voluntary organisations could reply directly to allay concerns raised by the Association. Later the Australian delegation met with the Association of Municipal Corporations. Again the Australians were told there were few children, if any, available; the Association clearly explaining why:

The Town Clerk agreed that since the passing of United Kingdom Children Act 1948 the situation had developed more and more where children in care had been placed in charge of local authorities to a far greater extent than ever before in preference to diverting them into orphanages, convents, and other institutions conducted by the voluntary organizations.[28]

One member stated that, 'Sentiment in United Kingdom was at present generally against child immigration to Australia and elsewhere abroad'. He told the meeting that the London County Council, a separate entity, was also against sending its children away. The chairman then suggested it would be a wise tactical move to approach the Children's Committees of large cities such as Birmingham and Manchester. The Australian immigration officers visited Manchester on 16 May 1955 and held discussions at the town hall with the town clerk and a Children's Officer. The Manchester authorities told the Australians some 1700 local children were in care, but once again the message was the same.

The long-term object was to return if at all possible the children concerned to their mothers and fathers. The problem facing the Manchester authorities would be to induce the Children's Committee to do other then endeavour to affect the return of the children 'in care' to their proper parents, and this action would be attempted even in preference to placing the children with foster parents.

Moreover in most cases it is considered that the consent of any living parent would be unlikely for migration of children to a Voluntary Organisation in Australia.[29]

The town clerk expressed his concern that children in Australian institutions had no-one in whom to confide 'their innermost thoughts, perplexity and troubles'. The Australians assured him that cottage mothers and staff in Australian institutions were readily available to assist the children but the town clerk refused to believe this explanation.

Four days later, the Australian delegation held discussions with the Children's Officers and the town clerk at Council House in Birmingham. As at the other meetings, the Australians handed out brochures and information on Australian institutions with assurances that all were well run. The Birmingham Council at the time had 1300 children in care. It was pointed out only three children and not the 3 per cent thought by the Australians to be available for child migration were actually available. The town clerk stated that even if a child's parents were bad parents, the Children's Committee were most averse to sending children 12 000 miles across the other side of the world to Australia. At best children should be old enough (thirteen or fourteen years old) to make up their own minds. This put any potential migrants from Birmingham outside the age limit of twelve set by the Australian government, and definitely outside the group the Australians were most interested in – six- to seven-year-old children.

A Children's Officer declared that the local authorities were not their own masters since Section 17 of the Children Act required the authority of the Home Office to be obtained before children 'in care' are permitted to migrate. His comment revealed the few people, if any, had realised that the Home Office and the Secretary of State had unofficially relinquished their responsibility to control child migration and were therefore failing in their duty of care.

The Birmingham Council supplied the names of three children who had been sent to Australia by a local voluntary organisation between 1950 and 1952, insisting that the Australian government produce a comprehensive progress report on how the children were progressing, their future prospects and any other useful information. If, in the opinion of the Council, these reports were favourable, consideration might be given in support of child migration. There is no evidence to suggest that these reports were ever made.

Finally the Children's Officer in Lancashire told the delegates, 'Children's Officers generally in United Kingdom are not altogether satisfied that Australian methods of child care were comparable with those practised in Britain'.

The recruitment drive in 1955 failed because the Australian immigration officials failed to find a single local authority in Britain that agreed with child migration. They were reminded everywhere that since the new Act, fostering and adoption and reuniting children with their families were the new priority. But the illegal removal of the children in 1953, coupled with the memorandum outlined below, revealed that the cooperation of the local authorities was not necessary. Australian organisations had virtually assumed the local authorities' role while the English churches, the Home Office and the Secretary of State turned a blind eye.

In 1953 Australia House sent a memorandum about child selection criteria to the Department of Immigration that reveals the attitude that the Australian and British authorities held towards the Children Act. The power given to the voluntary organisations and the Australia representatives to 'select' prospective child migrants should have been impossible under the Act. Describing the selection criteria, the memo stated:

1   The children are pre-selected by the Voluntary Organisation concerned, in some instances by Australian representatives of the institution.

2   Application forms and whatever relevant documents are available (school, history etc.) are submitted by the Voluntary Organisation to Australia House. These are examined closely by a specially

qualified Children's Officer who is an Australian, and a trained social worker. The papers are not made available for interviewing purposes until she is satisfied that the child concerned appears suitable.

3   Before interviews are arranged, a special check is made to see whether the children in question have ever been previously put forward for selection.

4   Children approved at this stage are then interviewed by a Selection Officer who is specially briefed and instructed to pay particular attention to intelligence. Selection Officers invariably conduct a conversation with each child individually.

5   Medical examination of children considered suitable is carried out by an approved Doctor and subsequently when reports are returned to Australia House, the files are made available to the Chief Medical Officer for final decision. The social worker is available for consultation when necessary.

6   Where there is any doubt whatsoever regarding a child's mental capacity, the Chief Migration Officer, London, has been authorised to obtain psychological assessments including an IQ test at our expense.[30]

No mention is made of a child's right to refuse to be sent to Australia or the legal requirement to consult with parents, the local authority or the British government. In fact, the only authority recognised is that of the volunteer organisations and the Australian authorities. It is also clear that the British Children's Officers – most of whom, by this time, were opposed to child migration – were to be bypassed.

It is reasonable to conclude that without the official involvement of the local authorities, and by definition the Secretary of State, and in the absence of proof of suitable welfare provisions in Australia, many hundreds of children were removed from Britain in breach of the provisions of Section 17 of the Children Act.

Yet some of Britain's child welfare organisations, such as Dr Barnardo's Homes, complied with the spirit of the Act and did not send children overseas without consulting with the local authority and the parents or without the child's consent. In the case of Dr Barnado's Homes, this meant that it did not sustain its pre-war status as a major sending agency, particularly to Canada where it sent thousands of children, as the numbers of children it sent overseas in the postwar period diminished to just a few.

The widening divide

The contrast in thinking about childcare practices was obvious: Australian welfare authorities still believed in institutionalised care but, apart from a handful of religious organisations, the rest of British welfare had moved on. As the demand for child migrants was not lessening in Australia, this divide could only widen – and a group of abandoned children would bear the brunt of this.

It began with the questionnaire. The Department of Immigration in Canberra circulated the County Council Association's questionnaire to the authorities receiving British children in Australia. The questions were loaded and designed to incriminate. Warning the institutions, the Department of Immigration sent each receiving organisation three pages of instructions on the best way to handle the questionnaire, noting that:

> Whilst at first glance it seems the questionnaire attached is purely a matter between the Council of Voluntary Organisation and the Children and Welfare Committee of the County Council Association, there could be serious repercussions from the possible conclusions reached by the Committee.

> Suppose for instance, the Committee regarded their inquiries as substantiating the opinion already expressed that in Australia we are totally outmoded and behind the times compared with current thoughts and practice in United Kingdom.

> This conclusion would no doubt be advanced in influential circles in Great Britain. Local Authority Officers are in touch with the Home Office. This could easily lead to a hardening of the government's attitude towards child migration and the insertion of restrictive provisions in their regulations governing the departure of children.

> In other words what began as a limited inquiry into conditions and practices in Australian Homes receiving migrant children could become a sort of unofficial but accredited report on standards of child care here.

For this reason it is desired that Commonwealth and State views be presented officially to the Children and Welfare Committee.[31]

Anglican Homes, Fairbridge and the Catholic Episcopal Migration and Welfare Association in Perth were sent the questionnaire, marked for urgent attention. The task for these organisations was not helped by a failure of disclosure and wildly exaggerated descriptions by Immigration Officers in London during the failed recruitment drive of 1955.

While Fairbridge and Anglican Homes struggled with the loaded questions, the Catholic Episcopal Migration and Welfare Association, inspired by helpful hints from the Department of Immigration, was inventive to say the least. In their answers to the first part of the questionnaire, the Association claimed that young children were better suited to child migration and settled in well in their new environment. It also claimed that it provided boarding-out facilities and adoption opportunities. In the second part of the questionnaire, the Catholic Association claimed that no more than 50 per cent of the institutionalised children in their homes were child migrants, and often this figure was much less. Three of its homes were supposedly mixed sex and that children joined outside groups such as Boy Scouts, Girl Guides and Cadets. Anglican Homes, more honestly, claimed that boarding out was the Child Welfare Department's responsibility and that it ran no programs as its homes were located in a semi-rural area.

The reality was quite different. The Catholic Church in Western Australia ran five homes: four were all boys homes and one was an all girls home and probably 80 per cent or more of the occupants were child migrants. It had no mixed-sex homes. It claimed that the ratio of staff to children was one to ten; whereas, Anglican Homes more honestly claimed one to nineteen. Castledare Home at the time had, in reality, a ratio of one staff member to twenty-five or more. The Catholic Association claimed that annual reports were made on each child covering their progress in health, Australian contacts and English contacts. This, too, was not true.

In the third part of the questionnaire, the Catholics claimed that 20 per cent of the children were boarded out, leading to fostering and adoption. Social workers visited these children once every four months.

To question (f) 'If boarding out is considered to be impractical by your organisation, please give reasons for this opinion', the Catholic Association replied, 'We are in favour of boarding out. We also think it is essential that a child should have a family home. Our principal is – immigration to a Home for a home'.

Again, the reality could not have been more different. The Catholic Church had a well-entrenched institution mentality and opposed fostering and adoption. Few if any British children in the care of the Catholic Church in Western Australia were ever boarded out to foster families – a fact about which the Child Welfare Department commonly complained.

In the final part of the questionnaire, the Catholic Association claimed that it ran vocational classes in conjunction with the Child Welfare Department. It employed social workers with appropriate university qualifications to visit every four months.

The combined results of the questionnaires served to deepen suspicions in the United Kingdom – the results were just too good to be true. The County Council Association won the first round and a dejected Secretary for the Department of Immigration in Australia wrote to the organisations

> *You will note there is little prospect of the Chief Migration Officer recruiting children in care of Local Authorities in Britain. The flow of children to approved institutions in Australia will therefore continue to depend on the efforts of the 'Voluntary Organizations'.*[32]

The Home Office was aware that some voluntary organisations were creating a pool of severely disadvantaged children, either deliberately or inadvertently, by failing to register details of their parents or their family history. Importantly, Children's Officers from local authorities were not given access to these children. Their involvement was not welcomed. If they had gained access to the sending institutions, child migration would have been reduced to a trickle. The British government was turning a blind eye to the behaviour of the voluntary organisations who had inherited the unofficial right to run and control child migration since 1937. Consent to their activities was implied through the government's silence.

Supporters of voluntary organisations in the House of Commons continued to urge the British government to put pressure on *'sticky fingered*

Children's Officers' who were reluctant to send children to Australia.

But by 1955 the mood in Britain had changed. There were far too many professionals who believed child migration couldn't be supported on any grounds and that the program could only be exploitative. Children's Officers from the ground up were demanding action from the Home Office. Moreover, looming on the horizon were possible legal implications.

The Western Australian inquiry 1953

In 1953, RH Hicks, Director of the New South Wales Child Welfare Department, was commissioned by the Western Australian Premier, Albert Hawke, to report on welfare matters following criticisms from local childcare experts. Hicks was scathing about the backward childcare practices in Western Australian institutions. Like John Curtis, he detested institutions, believing that they damaged the lives of children. His report contained 59 recommendations ranging from major changes to the operation of the Children's Court, to the establishment of a training school for 'delinquents' and to the immediate fostering out of all wards of the state, including the English child migrants.

His report was a political bombshell. It was personally delivered to the Premier, who still held the portfolio of Minister for Child Welfare. Determined to keep the report from public scrutiny, the Minister quarantined the document to the eyes of cabinet only and a handful of people whose opinion he could trust.[33] The reaction was as expected. In 1954, TL Robertson, the Director-General of Education in Western Australia, wrote to the Minister for Education:

Although comment on the Hicks report is not required by me, it should be remembered that the report is written by a New South Wales public servant who repeatedly in the report shows that he considers the organisation of child welfare in that State the perfect and only solution to the problem.

He continues: 'I feel, too, that some of his judgements are hasty and superficial and made without a close knowledge of Western Australian conditions.'

On Hicks's recommendation for a training school for delinquents he writes,

The economical solution now would be for the Government to purchase Seaforth and gradually replace existing buildings. The boys themselves could do much of the work involved as part of their training under Education Department instructors in somewhat similar fashion to the Bindoon scheme. [British children were used as forced labour on building sites at Bindoon, a Christian Brothers' home in Western Australia.]

Roy Peterkin, Director of Anglican Homes in Western Australia, also responded to the Hicks report. Premier Hawke held high regard for Peterkin's knowledge and experience in childcare. Peterkin was largely in favour of Hicks's findings and joined in his criticisms of the government's 'disinterested and niggardly' attitude to childcare and the lack of resources and financial support. Yet, like so many experts of his day, he was a supporter of institutionalised care. Alarmed at Hicks's attack on institutions, Peterkin produced a five-page addendum to Hicks's report. He espoused the great advantages of raising children in institutions over placing them in foster care. Peterkin also believed that children from broken homes were better off without their parents.

In April 1954, JA McCall, Director of Child Welfare in Western Australia, wrote to Premier Hawke, concerned over reports in the newspaper that the Premier might make the Hicks report public. Worried that its publication could affect morale, he requested,

That its publication be accompanied by a statement from yourself in support of the quality of the staff and their work. Frequent public criticism of them, the period of review by Mr Hicks, together with recent adverse newspaper comment has made them fear that they may no longer enjoy your confidence.

By 1957, McCall reported that most of Hicks's recommendations had been implemented:

There are now more wards in foster homes than in institutions. The Department now has a long list of foster mothers awaiting the placement of wards in their families. Those wards still in institutions are not generally suitable for foster placement for one or another reason.

In the last sentence he was referring to the child migrants. There was always confusion over the status of the British children and whether they could be classified as wards of the state while their legal guardian continued to be the Minister for Immigration.

As late as June 1964, McCall wrote to his counterpart in Brisbane that:

Our experience with Fairbridge has generally been very satisfactory. The type of child that they sponsor from Great Britain is generally superior to the children sponsored under the child migration scheme by the Roman Catholic and Anglican Churches.[34]

It was a stunning conclusion to draw, even at that point. The 'quality' of the child migrants had little to do with the success of various schemes. Surely it would have been obvious that the model of care used at Fairbridge and the voluntary nature of its scheme came closest to the childcare model demanded of the Australian institutions by the Home Office in 1947 and that, as a result, fewer children were damaged by their experience.

With the spotlight on the institutions, the Child Welfare Department was sometimes forced to remove a child from an institution. The first reported case of psychological damage to a child was referred to the Department in November 1955. An English boy had been sent to Swan Homes, which was run by the Anglican Church. Like many children before and after him, he had been given glowing reports of life in Australia. After his arrival, he became seriously ill and was sent for a psychological assessment. His report read in part:

... this boy is suffering from a severe emotional disturbance which is having an adverse affect on his behaviour, stability and psychological development. He states that his parents told him that he would not be sent to an institution, but would go to an uncle in Queensland and that, because of this promise, he was quite happy to be sent to Australia.

He now feels let down and rejected, seldom hearing from home, and seeing no future beyond institutional control. His emotional reaction is serious and will not be modified while he continues to suffer from these feelings of rejection and insecurity.

If these statements are correct it would be appear to be a matter to refer to the Commonwealth migration scheme as migrants bought out under such circumstances will merely become psychiatric casualties and social liabilities.[35]

The Department placed him with understanding foster parents and the child recovered.

In 1956, alarm bells were ringing once more. Australian institutions were about to be scrutinised yet again in another inquiry, one that eventually brought matters to a head.

The Ross Report 1956

Finally forced to act, the Home Office sent John Ross, the Assistant Under-Secretary, and his team on an official fact-finding mission in 1956 to investigate conditions in Australian institutions. The Ross Report condemned the very principle of child migration – that deprived children would benefit from a 'fresh start' – as being flawed and that such children, already rejected and insecure, would struggle to cope with the added strain caused by migration. Child migration was seen at best to be unnecessary. The mission recognised that unless the Curtis Committee caveat that required British children in care in Australia to receive at least the same quality care as they received in Britain was fulfilled, that child migration was potentially damaging.

As with the earlier Moss Report, this report criticised the institutional-style accommodation in which most child migrants in Australia were accommodated. Of the 26 institutions visited by the Committee, eleven were barrack-style, eight were cottage-style homes and seven were individual houses or groups of houses. The larger institutions were criticised for the lack of 'homely' atmosphere and too little privacy. The evidence of the separation of siblings, in the eyes of the Committee, indicated that the Australian institutions had not grasped the importance of family-focused childcare. The Ross Report also commented on the lack of staff training and the poor knowledge of appropriate childcare methods, the lack of educational and employment opportunities for children, the isolation of some of the institutions, the lack of contact between the children and the local communities and that some of the children were being exploited for cheap labour. The report condemned various religious organisations involved in children migration but singled out five institutions for particular criticism: the Presbyterian Dhurringle Rural Training Farm in Victoria, the Christian Brothers' St Joseph's Farm School at Bindoon in Western Australia, the Salesians' St John Bosco Boys' Town in Tasmania, the Methodist Children's Home at Magill in South Australia and the Salvation Army Riverview Training Farm in Queensland. It was privately noted by John Ross that other institutions could easily have been added to the 'condemned' list, but 'considerations of practical politics' prevented this.

The report left no doubt that unless existing practices in Australian institutions were improved, there would be no further funding from the British government.

The Australian government reacted angrily to the contents of the Ross Report and would not agree to its publication until it carried out its own investigation. The Prime Minister's Department conducted a brief investigation and found minor issues at only two institutions: Bindoon and Dhurringle. The government claimed that these were quickly rectified and told the British government that there was no justification for 'even the temporary deferment of child migration to Australia'. Yet in the eyes of one senior Home Office official, the report from Australia was seen to confirm that thinking about childcare practices in the United Kingdom and Australia was 'poles apart'.

Soon after the Ross Report, the remaining children in homes and institutions in Britain were removed from the care of volunteer organisations and placed with foster families, adopted out or reunited with their families. The report also put an end to unrestricted child migration to Australia – and a scandalous period of British history finally came to an end.

The British parliament inquiry 1997

Following sustained pressure and criticism over many years the British government launched a parliamentary inquiry in 1997. The Select Committee on Health, made up of parliamentarians from both sides of the House of Commons, followed a narrow investigative line, generally avoiding questions of British government negligence or wrongdoing and focused on practical considerations to assist surviving child migrants to establish their identity and be reunited with family. The inquiry concluded that its predecessors in government did not break any law or breach any act, but conceded that there were some 'irregularities and indiscretions'. Avoiding legal and moral questions, it put the blame squarely on the institutions.

In the First Report of the Select Committee submitted to the House of Commons the Committee was critical about the lack of records for child migrants and estimated that thousands of letters personally signed by the Secretary of State at the time may have been destroyed. The report went further, claiming that no files on child migration existed from about the mid 1950s when child migration effectively ended, saying that 'the records had dried up'. In addition, there were no financial records between the British government and the Australian institutions. The report demanded an investigation into who destroyed or removed the files from the Public Records Office, yet the missing files were never located. Despite not having access to these missing records, the parliamentary inquiry was allowed to continue.

The Committee received hundreds of letters describing abuses in Australian institutions but, predictably, the investigation centred on the involvement of secular and religious receiving and sending agents and the institutions. The Committee claimed, 'It was the charitable and religious organisations who maintained the child migration policy, often apparently motivated by the need to keep the institutions overseas financially viable', yet failed to comment on the social policy of the government that allowed child migration to take place or the lack of protection given by relevant ministers and departments to child migrants.

In a submission to the inquiry, the British government claimed that its predecessors had operated legally under the Empire Settlement Act 1937 and the Poor Law Act 1930. Yet the new Children Act 1948 replaced all of the old Acts but the inquiry avoided investigating whether the government of the time had failed to meet its responsibilities under the Act. The British government concluded:

> *These policies were at various times the subject of debate and controversy, including debate in United Kingdom Parliament and the legislature of the receiving countries, but they were conducted within the relevant laws then current in United Kingdom and in the receiving countries.*

The Committee investigated any potential legal liability and sought the legal advice of British lawyer Francis Swain, who reported:

> *Formal British government approval for the migration of children without their families was given a fillip by the Empire Settlements Acts of 1922 and 1937 in which a per capita sum of 10 shillings per week was promised to the institution responsible for caring for the child until they reached 16. Such remuneration was to follow the signing of a contract between the Government and institution, by which it could be argued that the government impliedly accepted the institution as one fit to be part of the scheme. We received a copy of such contracts. It sets out in great detail the respective responsibilities of the British Government and institution. This clearly shows that the British Government had not only a moral responsibility but also a contractual responsibility for the welfare of these children.*[36]

However, the Committee was unable to find proof of any such payments that would give a sound legal base to the validity of the contracts. The Ross Report had previously noted that Britain was spending 40 000 pounds per year in support of children in Australia, yet the Health Department told the Committee, 'We guess that there must be some other files that contain details of such expenditure but we don't know where they are'.

Tossing in a red herring, the British government told the Committee:

> *Many children living in some overseas countries have for a variety of reasons been abandoned or relinquished for adoption by their birth parents. Their chances of being adopted or otherwise cared for by substitute families in their own country are often remote. The realistic alternative for the vast majority of these children is a childhood spent in institutional care.*

That institutional care was the only alternative for the child migrants has been proven to be untrue, but, at the time, the British government tacitly supported the institutionalisation policy of the Australian government, although there is no mention of this in the parliamentary inquiry. British-born children in institutions were not going to be fostered or adopted out while the British government subsidised the organisations to keep each child in the institutions. While this was happening in Australia, children left behind were being freed from institutions and adopted or fostered out with British families, as stipulated under the Children Act 1948.

No mention also was made of what caused the Home Office to turn its back on the welfare standards it demanded in its memo to the Australian government in October 1947, and likely demanded in its memo of the same year to its own authorities and voluntary organisations. There was also no mention of the children who had died in Australian institutions, whose lives both governments had failed to protect.

Even though the Home Office had condemned childcare practices in Australia in 1956, declaring the Australian institutions unfit places to raise children, the inquiry did not investigate why no children were ever brought back to the United Kingdom or why no funds were offered to Australia to upgrade and improve conditions for these children.

Importantly, the parliamentary inquiry failed to tackle some fundamental concerns about the issue of consent – were parents actively consulted by the voluntary organisations and were young children able to give their consent freely and in full knowledge of the consequences of agreeing to go to Australia?[37]

The British Parliamentary Committee recommended that there should be no compensation for former child migrants, arguing that governments and voluntary agencies could become unduly nervous of their past 'indiscretions and irregularities', which, in turn, could affect the services they were currently providing. The British government enthusiastically agreed: 'the question of compensation is inappropriate in this matter. Practical help and support to trace and unite families is a much greater significance to those involved'. The Committee recommended that a travel fund be established for the purpose of family reunion to which the government agreed, providing a million pounds over a three-year period. The funds were to be made available to child migrants to visit family (birth parents, aunts, uncles and siblings) for the first time if they met a means test and could prove that they were unable to afford the cost of travel themselves.

For many, the British parliamentary inquiry was a bitter disappointment and it seemed just another betrayal.

The Australian government inquiry 2001

Both the British and Australian inquiries into child migration were notable for their inability to deal with the big issues. The Australian Senate Community Affairs Reference Committee report, *Lost Innocents: Righting the Record – Report on Child Migration*, of August 2001 was a comprehensive but largely unsatisfying 325-page publication. The Australian inquiry in 2000 followed on from the Australian government's response to the recommendations of the earlier British inquiry, from various state and territory inquiries and from the numerous calls in the late 1990s from different groups and individuals in Australia for an independent national inquiry.

The Committee received over 250 individual submissions and heard evidence from a range of interested parties, including state government agencies, receiving organisations, child migrant groups and individual child migrants.

In evidence to the inquiry, the English Catholic Child Welfare Council (CCWC) noted that, of the 1149 Catholic children migrated to Australia after the war, only 20 per cent had done so with consent from birth parents. Of the other 80 per cent 'it was unknown if consent was given … as documentary evidence remains unfound'. As the Committee required no proof where consent had been given, and given other evidence about the issue of consent, it is likely that the figure of 20 per cent of parental consent was exaggerated. Dr Barnardo's Homes, who, unlike Catholic Church authorities, kept thorough records, had told the British government in 1954 that 'more than two-thirds of parents consulted had refused consent to emigration and as a result Barnados had only sent to Australia about 2 per cent of the potential pool of children'.

Sending children to Australia without records or consent was not unique to Catholic immigration authorities; however, the inquiry found that some organisations seemed to play more by the rules. Dr Barnardo's Homes demanded and recorded vital family information before a child was admitted into their homes. Their records generally included a photograph of the child and the child's mother or relative, and a written document stating that the child migrant had volunteered to come to Australia.

In Chapter 2, the inquiry also addressed the issue of the illegal removal in 1953 of the children from England and Wales. The CCWC noted to the inquiry that these children had been sent without the Council's knowledge, the implication of which was that the Catholic Church in Australia, under the guidance of Brother Conlon, was receiving children without the consent of the Catholic authorities in Britain. In an angry letter to Conlon in 1953, the CCWC wrote:

> *The Catholic Child Welfare Council does not hold itself responsible for possible future inquiries concerning these children whose immigration it did not sponsor.*

So serious had been the concerns of the CCWC that the Australian Catholic Migration Committee had to agree in 1954 that all negotiations about the migration of children were to go through the CCWC.

Other issues about parental consent were raised in the inquiry. Parents may have given consent to adoption by a voluntary organisation without being made aware that this was taken as agreement to migration. Some parents signed documents that contained clauses about child migration but, as they were unable to read, were not able to fully consent and later claimed that their children had been sent to Australia without their knowledge. The institutions were known to claim that all contact had been lost with parents or that they were 'protecting' children from their past by not contacting their unmarried mothers.

Many submissions challenged the notion of child migrants giving consent on the grounds that the children were deceived into signing the paperwork by being told exaggerated stories about life in Australia. Many former child migrants asked the obvious question that how could such young children, some as young as five years of age, give informed consent to migration?

In Chapter 3 of the report the Committee noted

> *the appalling inaccuracies and discrepancies in the data on the numbers of child migrants by governments as well as the receiving and sending agencies. The committee suspects that this goes far beyond the imperfect record-keeping characteristic of the time, and at best amounts to gross incompetence.*

Not only were the numbers difficult to pin down, but also so were the identities of many child migrants. Sloppy record-keeping, deliberate or otherwise, went back as far as 1948. A letter from the head of the Department of Immigration to Australia House in 1948 complained about children arriving with no birth certificates, the wrong names and the wrong ages. The memorandum stated,

> *He referred to the fact that a number of such children had arrived for whom no copies of Birth Certificates had been forwarded from your office. In a number of cases he stated that the names and ages on Birth Certificates received did not agree with those recorded on the final roll.*[38]

The inquiry confirmed that a large number of Catholic children had been sent away without records of family history or having had their names, ages or birthdays changed. In some cases, twins were separated and, in others, full brothers would be given different surnames and be raised in the same institution never knowing their true relationship. It was as if a small army of stateless and identity-less children just landed in Australia with no family, no documentation and no return address. Most of these former child migrants were middle-aged before they would discover their true identity – some never would.

A memorandum from Australia House in London, dated 13 January 1952, to the Department of Immigration in Canberra sheds light on the attitude of the time towards the parents who relinquished their children to care. Such an attitude could have been seen to promote a certain laxity in record-keeping in the institutions. On 12 December 1951, the Chief Immigration Officer at Australia House held a conference attended by all the British voluntary organisations involved in child migration. The Department revealed the growing problem of single mothers who were using their children to 'extort' their own passage to Australia, then reclaiming their children once they had arrived. This led to confrontations between these mothers and the institutions, who were refusing to relinquish custody. At the conference, the Department proposed a harsh new policy designed to prevent mothers regaining custody of their children:

1   The parent will not come to Australia within twelve months of their child's arrival.

2   As from the date of the parent's arrival, she will be prepared to contribute to the extent of her ability to pay for the maintenance of their child in the institution.

3   The parent will recognize under that under the terms of the Immigration (Guardianship of Children) Act, the Minister for Immigration is the legal guardian of the child and the head of the institution is the child's legal custodian.

4   The parent will not attempt to obtain custody of the child without the approval of the Minister's delegate.[39]

Finally, the Department asked the voluntary organisations not to register British children whose mothers might follow them to Australia as child migrants. The conference rejected the new policy on moral grounds; however, the voluntary organisations were made aware of the Department's implied message and may have interpreted it to mean that Australian institutions only wanted children who couldn't be traced by their mothers.

Four years later, in 1955, the Council of Voluntary Organisations for Child Migration in Britain wrote to the Chief Immigration Officer at Australia House, pleading for a change of the policy of discrimination against single mothers claiming that by including them child migration could increase. The Chief Immigration Officer replied coldly, reasserting Australia's policy against single mothers: 'The situation at present is that by agreement with the State governments children are not accepted under the child migration scheme when the parents intend to follow.' This prompted an angry response from the Church of England in London:

My Council is very concerned with the suggestion that children should not be accepted for migration if the parent or the parents wish to follow. It is not the practice of this Council to encourage the breaking up of families, but rather to reunite them.[40]

The senate inquiry looked exhaustively at the operation of the sending and receiving agents in the institutions. Similar to the British inquiry, it received hundreds of letters detailing sexual, physical and psychological abuse and exploitation.

As with the British parliamentary inquiry, the Australian inquiry did not attach significant blame to the actions of the government of the time, but instead focused on the wrongdoings of the churches and organisations involved. The inquiry condemned the British voluntary organisations for their carelessness with the records of children's identities, describing it as 'criminal neglect'; however, it failed to find fault with the Immigration (Guardianship of Children) Act or the Department of Immigration.

Nothing was said of Australia's unconscionable conduct during the failed recruitment drive in 1955, which occurred at a time when Children's Officers all over Britain were actively trying to reunite children with their families or adopt or foster them out. Australian immigration officials, in contrast, were busy implementing a scheme about which there were already serious ethical concerns.

The Australian government agreed to meet most of the recommendations of the senate inquiry. Its main initiative was to set up a $3 million travel fund to continue family reunions.

Neither the British nor the Australian inquiries tried to justify child migration, although the British inquiry mentioned the 'genuine philanthropic desire to rescue children from destitution and neglect', yet neither delved too deeply into government files to investigate the role of the governments in general or certain ministers in particular. Crucial archival material still remains hidden and unexamined.

Denial and reparation

Excuses, denial and rejection were signposts along the lonely journey of child migrants and these same signposts have largely marked their attempts as adults to find out their stories. Church and welfare authorities, both in Australia and the United Kingdom, seemed ill-prepared to deal with the search by many former child migrants for their roots.

My desire to find out about my foster family in 2002 is a good example. It is doubtful the Sisters of Nazareth kept an adoption register, as they claimed in a letter to me, as adoptions from their homes were extremely rare. In this same letter they said they could not explain why I had been sent to Australia in 1954 as all their records had been destroyed during the war when the Germans bombed Southampton, yet I had emigrated well after the war.

In recent years the Canadian government has set a precedent in recognising that it failed in its duty of care towards the native peoples who were abused in church schools and homes. It has set aside millions of dollars in reparation. The Irish government has done similar. Some religious organisations have accepted the blame for the abuse suffered by child migrants and have paid millions in compensation. Yet both the Australian and British governments at the time of the child migration scheme have been exonerated by political inquiries and stopped well short of an apology for the involvement of their predecessors.

The Australian government appeared unsure that children had been damaged by their experience, but just in case it said:

The government regrets the injustices and suffering that some child migrants may have experienced as a result of past practices in relation to child migration. The government supports the Committee's emphasis on moving forward positively to concentrate on improving support and assistance to those former child migrants who may need or want such services, as noted throughout the recommendations.

Not much of an apology and small recognition for the former child migrants.

On the 17 December 2007 the state government of Western Australia joined Tasmania and Queensland as the only states in Australia to acknowledge in a meaningful way that abuse had taken place in state institutions. The Western Australian government will put aside $114 million for support services and ex gratia payments for the Stolen Generation (Aboriginal children who had been removed from their families), for child migrants and for others who were abused in foster care or as wards of the state. These payments will range from $10 000 to $80 000 for the worst cases. The state government claims that 3000 Aboriginal people and nearly the same number of child migrants were implicated, but not all of them necessarily suffered.

Providing proof and documentary evidence of abuse is difficult. There is no question that removing a child from their family and other ties, and from the country of their birth, then transplanting them on foreign shores in mostly isolated institutions will have a major impact on the child. For some of the child migrants, beatings and abuse were commonplace – just part of the 'correction' methods used in the institution. Many had little access to positive and caring family environments and were often restricted in their opportunities to join in community life. Yet there is little evidence of the psychological trauma inflicted on these children – only their word.

The lessons of history have taught us that children, above all else, need consistent nurturing and love in their lives. The authorities involved in the child migration scheme mistakenly believed that the Church and the State would be a suitable substitute for loving and well-adjusted parents and role models. They also assumed that children could be uprooted and transplanted into a foreign culture without ill-effects. If Dame Enid Lyons and John Curtin had won their argument to have young British children fostered or adopted into Australian society, then the scheme might have been more successful. It is no surprise that the orphanage system caused great social, educational and psychological disadvantage for the child migrants, yet to their great credit, they have overcome these disadvantages and have taken their place, along with their children, in Australia, making a large and valuable contribution to the richness of Australian life.

1 In Barry M. Coldrey, *Good British Stock: Child and Youth Migration to Australia*, National Archives of Australia: Canberra, 1999, p. 14.

2 The Department for Community Development in Perth decided to release to me all their files in 2004, some 950 pages of British and Australian government documents, much of which I had not seen before. Some had restricted access dating back 60 years. For this, I am grateful to the Department for Community Development as it helped me to piece together an unknown part of the story of child migration.

3 Today, one in eleven Canadians can trace their ancestry to the British child migrants.

4 In Barry M. Coldrey, *The Scheme: The Christian Brothers and Childcare in Western Australia*, Argyle-Pacific Publishing: O'Connor, WA, 1993, p. 129.

5 In Coldrey, *The Scheme*, 1993, p. 131.

6 Department for Community Development files (WA), the Chairman, Special Premiers' Conference 1946, Vol. 1 A56-39.

7 Department for Community Development files (WA), the Chairman, Special Premiers' Conference 1946, Vol. 1 A56-39.

8 Department for Community Development files (WA), Merredin Road Board to Premier of Western Australia, Vol. 1 A56-i6.

9 Commonwealth of Australia, House of Representatives, Parliamentary debate on second reading of the Immigration (Guardianship of Children Act) 1946, 1946.

10 Estimates of the numbers of child migrants sent after World War II to Australia vary considerably. The British parliamentary inquiry estimates the number to be more like 7000 to 10 000 children (Select Committee on Health (1998), 'Introduction', note 13, *The Welfare of Former British Child Migrants*, at www.publications.parliament.uk/pa/cm200001/cmselect/152/15206.htm); however, it is thought that this is excessive and others have put the official figure closer to 3000–4000.

11 In David Plowman, *Enduring Struggle: St Mary's Tardun Farm School*, Scholastic Press Australia: Broadway, WA, 2003, p. 206.

12 In Plowman, *Enduring Struggle*, 2003, p. 198.

13 Arthur A. Calwell, *How Many Australians Tomorrow?*, Reed & Harris: Melbourne, Victoria, 1945, chapter 4.

14 Plowman, *Enduring Struggle*, 2003, p. 207.

15   Plowman, *Enduring Struggle*, 2003, p. 207.

16   Western Australian Legislative Assembly, Select Committee into Child Migration, *Interim Report*, Western Australia State Publisher: Perth, November 1996, p. 33.

17   This document can be found at the London School of Economics. I was denied access to this memorandum after openly admitting I was a child migrant writing a book about my experience. It seems that the complete document cannot be publicly viewed, even today. I was offered access to only 5 per cent of the memorandum, if I had written proof from a professor of a university that I was completing a PhD and needed the document for research purposes. I suspect that other missing documents may be among these files.

18   Department for Community Development files (WA), contract between the British Secretary of State and the Catholic Council for British Overseas Settlement, Vol. 3 A56-143.

19   'Disturbing reports on United Kingdom child migrants', *Daily Mirror*, in *The Herald*, Melbourne, 5 April 1948.

20   Department for Community Development files (WA), letter from Catholic Church authorities in Western Australia, Vol. 3 A56-132.

21   Department for Community Development files (WA), letter from the Secretary of the Child Welfare Department, Perth, to the Premier of Western Australia, June 1946, Vol. 2 A56-12.

22   Department for Community Development files (WA), Department of Lands and Surveys report, Vol. 2A 56-142.

23   Department for Community Development files (WA), Undersecretary for Department of Lands and Surveys, Vol. 2A 56-142.

24   Department for Community Development files (WA), 'Points on Which Information is Desired by the United Kingdom Authorities in Relation to Proposals for Immigration of Children to Australia', British Home Office pro forma, Vol. 3 A56.

25   Department for Community Development files (WA), letter from the Secretary for Lands and Immigration, Perth, Vol. 2-17.

26   Department for Community Development files (WA), letter from the Assistant Secretary of the Child Welfare Department, Perth, Vol. 4 A56-393.

27   Department for Community Development files (WA), Vol. 4 A56-445.

28   Department for Community Development files (WA), Association of Municipal Corporations, Vol. 4 A56-448.

29	Department for Community Development files (WA), Vol. 4 A56-448.

30	Department for Community Development files (WA), Australia House memorandum to Department of Immigration, Vol. 4 A56-251.

31	Department for Community Development files (WA), Department of Immigration to voluntary agencies, Vol. 5-607 46-6.

32	Department for Community Development files (WA), Secretary for the Department of Immigration to voluntary agencies, Vol. 4 A56-457.

33	Unfortunately no record of Hicks's report exists today or perhaps it is still hidden in a secret government file.

34	Department for Community Development files (WA), JA McCall, Director of Child Welfare, Western Australia, to Director of Child Welfare, Queensland, Vol. 5 A56-35.

35	Department for Community Development files (WA), Vol. 4 A56-472.

36	Select Committee on Health, Third Report, *The Welfare of Former British Child Migrants*, House of Commons: United Kingdom, 1998, p. 25.

37	My experience of 'giving consent' is a damming one. At the age of seven, on 5 April 1954, I was coerced by Australian immigration authorities into signing a false medical declaration, which made no mention of my previous illness and consequent hospitalisation brought about by the stress I experienced as I faced migration to Australia. Despite knowing about the trauma I had suffered the year before, the Australian child psychologist ignored my terror about migrating and also overlooked the fact that I had developed a happy relationship with my foster family, the Brooms, who had applied to adopt me.

38	Department for Community Development files (WA), head of Department of Immigration to Australia House, Vol. 3 A56-117.

39	Department for Community Development files (WA), Department of Immigration proposal, Vol. A56-236.

40	Department for Community Development files (WA), Church of England, Vol. 4 A56-425-424-422.

APPENDIX:

The Benhi Karshi orphanage and the Edmund Rice Camp for Kids

In 1989 Julie and I divorced after twelve years of marriage. While divorce is never easy, we have maintained a strong friendship and have dedicated our lives to our two children. I sold my farm in 1999 and moved to the city to be close to my daughters, who had both started university in Perth. To keep busy, I began to develop property in the western suburbs of Doubleview and Innaloo. I dropped these activities in 2003 and began concentrating on research and writing this book. Today I could be best described as a self-funded retiree who causes problems for the social club!

I joined a local social club that was run and supported by the patrons at the Indian Ocean Hotel in Scarborough, a suburb of Perth. Formerly the Hastings Golf Club, in 2002 the reconstituted Indi Social Club emerged with a social conscience and I became its inaugural president. A year after the 2002 Bali bombings the committee asked me to go to Bali to find a project the club could support. I visited a number of orphanages where infrastructure conditions were much worse than anything I had experienced. Despite this, from the happy smiling faces of children it was clear they were much loved by their Balinese carers. Our club, which at times has up to 200 members, adopted Benhi Karshi, a Christian orphanage where children of mixed religion are being cared for in a remote part of Bali. Since then we have provided cows, pigs, chickens, ducks and cooking facilities, including fridges and dining-room furniture. We also drilled a bore through metres of hard volcanic rock to reach an abundance of potable water beneath. We have since equipped the orphanage's small property with a new irrigation system so that in time they can become self-sufficient, growing their own food and having clean drinking water. However, the orphanage still needs funding for a building to house the boys and girls in separate units – as well as the ongoing costs of school uniforms, education and health.

The club also supports the Edmund Rice Camp for Kids, a national organisation that provides disadvantaged Australian children a chance to spend a holiday weekend with young carers at no cost to the parents.

If you'd like to help these worthy causes, please contact:

Benih Kasih orphanage in Bali
<http://benihkasih.org>

Edmund Rice Camps for Kids WA
<www.edmundricecampswa.com.au/Content/8685>

BIBLIOGRAPHY

Barry M. Coldrey, *The Scheme: The Christian Brothers and Childcare in Western Australia*, Argyle-Pacific Publishing: O'Connor, WA, 1993.

Barry M. Coldrey, *Good British Stock: Child and Youth Migration to Australia*, National Archives of Australia: Canberra, 1999.

David Hill, *The Forgotten Children: Fairbridge Farm School and its Betrayal of Australia's Child Migrants*, Random House: North Sydney, NSW, 2007.

Colm Kiernan, *Calwell: A Personal and Political Biography*, Thomas Nelson: West Melbourne, Vic.

John Lane (1990) *Fairbridge Kid*, Fremantle Arts Centre Press: WA, 1978.

David Plowman (ed.), *Our Home in the Bush: Tales of Tardun*, Tardun Old Boys' Association: Como, WA, 1994.

David Plowman, *Enduring Struggle: St Mary's Tardun Farm School*, Scholastic Press Australia: Broadway, WA, 2003.

Select Committee on Health, *The Welfare of Former British Child Migrants*, House of Commons: UK, 1998.

Senate Community Affairs References Committee, *Lost Innocents: Righting the Record – Report on Child Migration*, Commonwealth of Australia: Canberra, 2001.

Olive Stevenson (ed.), *Child Welfare in the United Kingdom 1948–1988*, Blackwell Science: Oxford, UK, 1999.